Families of
CABARRUS COUNTY
NORTH CAROLINA
1792–1815

by
Kathleen Marler

CLEARFIELD

Printed for
Clearfield Company, Inc. by
Genealogical Publishing Co., Inc.
Baltimore, Maryland
2004

International Standard Book Number: 0-8063-5233-7

Made in the United States of America

Introduction

The information contained in this book has been taken from many different sources: the 1790 Mecklenburg census, the 1800 Cabarrus census, Cabarrus county court records, Mecklenburg county deed records, marriage records from both counties, some wills, and deaths listed in newspapers. The use of an asterisk (*) before a name indicates that a death notice appeared in the *The Catawba Journal*. Bastardy cases that appear in the court of Pleas and Quarters Sessions are listed after the introduction. It is an attempt to put families together with their neighbors so that it might be easier to see allied family connections and make the search for additional family members easier. The listing of 1790 next to a name indicates that a person was present in Mecklenburg County in 1790. The omission of a year beside the name indicates that the person did not show up until the 1800 census or later. Some individuals are listed without additional description. In these cases an individual was listed only in court records and did not appear in either census. A couple could have been married, for example, in 1793, and moved away before the 1800 census. Some couples married in Cabarrus County, but they ended up living in Mecklenburg County. For example, the brother of one of my ancestors was married in 1797 and died in 1799. The only record of his existance is in a court

dispute regarding his child's legal right to the estate of
his grandfather.

I tried to include all the information that could be
gleaned from deeds and court records on as many individuals
in Cabarrus County as I could. I wanted to put these people
together in a community and make it easier to see how and
where they lived.

Families of Cabarrus County bastardy records

Father	Mother	
John Klutts	Mary Russell	1799
Samuel Martin	Polly Fibbs	1803
Robert Ross	Polly Fibbs	1806
(Robert to take child in his care.)		
Archibald, McCurdy, Jr	Jean Spiers	1806
Abraham Hartsell	Molly Heagler	1806
John Ross	Margaret Purviance	1808
Thomas Mock	Christena Walker	1808
James Plunket	Margaret Purviance	1808
John Mitchell	Eve Crider	1819
William Brians	Rachel Long	1809
George Petrea	Susannah Fisher	1810
John Bost	Sussina Misenhimer	1810
Moses Clay	Jean Spiers	1811
Thomas Martin	Julia Kilgrow	1812
Isaac McEntire	Sarah Miller	1812
Richard Martin	Nancy Gunn	1812
George Petrea	Susannah Fisher	1812
John Propst	Betsy Cress	1812
Joseph Plunket	Jean H McNulty	1812
Long David	Elizabeth Overcash	1812
John Fleming	Molly Hoover	1813
Ransom Parham	Elizabeth Goodman	1813
John Ross,		
Spencer Underwood	no name provided	1813
Benjamin Plunket	Elizabeth Kimley	1813
John Bond	Caty Keever	1813
Jacob Cline	Rachel Blackwelder	1813
Archibald Sawyers	Leah Shinn	1813
Michael Scott	Elizabeth Murph	1814
Archibald, McCurdy, Sr	Mary Russell	1814
Archibald, McCurdy, Sr	Mary Russell	1814
Joseph Plunket	Jean McNulty	1814
Jacob Cline	Rachel Blackwelder	1814
Murrel Sugs	Catherine Nisler	1815
John Barnhart	Elizabeth Barnhart	1815
Charles Willeford	Mary Murph	1815
James Nickason	Polly Wason	1815
Jacob Cline	Rachel Blackwelder	1815
Solomon Bost	Rachel Jordon	1816
James McGraw	Eve Crisko	1816
Ransom Parham	Betsy Goodman	1816
William Hunt	Caty Shinn	1817

Alexander, Abijah
    1810: Abijah 45+, 1 female 26-44, 1 female 16-25, 1
    female 10-15, 1 male -10, and 1 female -10.
1790 - *Alexander, Abraham
    1800: Abram and wife 26-44, 1 male 10-15, 1 female
    10-15, 1 male -10, and 3 females -10. Listed next to
    Hezekiah Alexander, Moses Alexander, Moses Alexander
    (Big), James Christopher, John Cannon, and Arthur
    Donelson.
    1810: Abraham 45+, 2 females 45+, 2 males 16-25, 1
    female 16-25, 2 females 10-15, 1 male -10, and 1
    female -10.
    Abraham was born 1762, died March 11, 1829 in
    Iredell Co.
Alexander, Alphonso
    shoemaker
Alexander, Alihu
Alexander, Allen & Margaret
    Sold land in Oct 1797.
Alexander, Ambrose
    1810: Ambrose 26-44, 1 female 16-25, 1 male 16-15, 1
    male -10, and 1 female -10.
1790 - Alexander, Andrew
    1800: Andrew and another male, and wife 45+, 1
    female 26-44, 1 male 16-25, 1 male 10-15, 4 males -
    10, and 1 female -10. Listed next to Nelson Gray,
    Thomas Gray, George Alexander, Joseph Young, David
    Crawford, and William Wallace.
Alexander, Azariah & Fany Alexander
    Children: Franklin
    Married Nov 16, 1802 in Mecklenburg Co., Ephraim
    Alexander, bondsman.
    Owned land on Coddle Creek in 1805, sold to Samuel
    L. Erwin.
    Samuel Erwin also bought land from Josiah Alexander
    on Coddle Creek.
1790 - Alexander, Benjamin & Susannah
    Benjamin owned land on Back Creek and Mallard Creek
    near William and Thomas Alexander, Edward Giles,
    George Reed, John & Hannah Garrison and William
    Shields.
    1800: Benjamin and Susannah, and wife 45+, 2 males
    16-25, 2 females 16-25, and 1 female 10-15. Listed
    next to James Caragin, Samuel Kenly, John Gilmore,
    John Jones, Duncan Smith, and Hugh Pickens.
    1810: Benjamin and wife 45+, 1 male 26-44, and 1
    female 26-44.
Alexander, Benjamin & Polly Alexander
    Married in Cabarrus Co., bond dated June 27, 1808,
    bondsman, George Allen, Jr.
    Benjamin is shown in the 1860 census for Cabarrus
    Co. as 77 years old.

Alexander, Cyrus A., MD & Erixene Morrison
      Children: Julias(died at the age of 1)
      Erexene was the daughter of William and Abigail
      McEwen Morrison.
Alexander, David & Elizabeth
      Children: Ephraim, Fany, Joel, Thomas, David, James,
      Mary, Sarah, Isaac
      David's will was probated 1796.
Alexander, Eli
      1810: Eli and wife 26-44.
Alexander, George
      Children: Peggy (? Spiers), Margaret (Nathaniel
      Alexander)
      1800: George and wife 45+, 2 males 26-44, 1 female
      26-44, 1 male -10, and 3 females -10. Listed next to
      William Callon, Sr. and Jr., Ezekiel Sharpe, Thomas
      Gray, Nelson Gray, and Andrew Alexander.
      1810 George and wife 45+, and 2 males 16-25.
Alexander, Hezekiah & Patsey
      Children: Laird
      Owned land on Mallard Creek
      1800: Hezekiah and Patsey 26-44, 1 female 10-15, and
      1 male -10. Listed next to Moses Alexander, Moses
      Alexander (Big), John Reed, Abram Alexander, and
      James Christopher.
      1810: Hezekiah and Patsey, and wife 26-44, 1 male
      16-25, and 1 male 10-15.
      Son of Hezekiah and Mary Alexander
Alexander, James
      1800: James and wife 26-44, and 1 male -10. Listed
      next to John Alexander, Hugh Pickens, Duncan Smith,
      William Gray, John Robinson, and Elenor Erwin.
Alexander, John
      1800: John 26-44, his wife 16-25, and 1 female -10.
      Listed next to Hugh Pickens, Duncan Smith, John
      Jones, James Alexander, William Gray, and John
      Robinson.
1790 - Alexander, John
      Son of Abraham Alexander
Alexander, Joseph & Margaret Hope
      Married in Cabarrus County on July 13, 1796, James
      Hope, bondsman.
      1800: Joseph and Margaret, and wife 26-44, 1 male -
      10, and 2 females -10. Listed next to John
      Skilinton, Stephen Alexander, William Houston,
      Robert Andrews, Moses Andrews, and Mary Bradford.
      1810: Joseph and wife 26-44, 3 males 16-25, 1 male
      10-15, 1 female 10-15, 1 male -10, and 1 female -10.
1790 - Alexander, Josiah & Mildred
      Sold land on Coddle Creek to Samul L. Erwin in July
      1806.
Alexander, Laird & Jane Meek

Son of Hezekiah Alexander
Owned land on Mallard Creek.
Laird is listed in the 1860 Cabarrus Co. census as
67, and Jane is listed as 66 years old.
Alexander, Moses & Elizabeth Orr
Owned land on Mallard Creek.
1810: Moses 26-44, 1 female 45+, 2 females 16-25, 1
male 10-15, and 1 male -10.
Alexander, Moses (Big)
1800: Moses and wife 45+, 4 males 16-25, and 2 males
10-15. Listed next to John Reed, Josiah Wallace,
Ludwick Wallace, Moses Alexander, Hezekiah
Alexander, and Abram Alexander.
Alexander, Nathaniel & Esther Phifer
Married April 10, 1793 in Cabarrus Co., Paul Phifer,
bondsman.
Alexander, Nathaniel & Margaret Alexander
1810 Nathaniel and Margaret, and wife 26-44, 1
female 16-25, 1 male 10-15, 2 females 10-15, and 3
females -10.
Margaret was the daughter of George Alexander
Alexander, Nathaniel & Jane Harris
Children: Elam, Mary Wilson, Eliza Brisbane, Dorcas
Jane, Abraham Franklin, Charles Harris
Son of Dorcas Alexander
Alexander, Robert & Teresa (Clarissa)
1800: Robert 26-44, 2 females 16-25, and 2 females -
10. Listed next to Susanna Russel, Mary Fulham,
Catherine Flemmon, John Gilmore, Samuel Kenly, and
James Caragin.
Bought land from Stephen Alexander on Coddle Creek.
Blacksmith
Alexander, Stephen & Isabel Shelby
Married Nov 22, 1797 in Mecklenburg Co., William
Alexander, bondsman.
1810: Stephen and wife 26-44, 1 male 10-15, 2 males
-10, and 2 females -10.
Alexander, Stephen
1800: Stephen 45+, Isabel 26-44, 1 female 16-25, 1
male 10-15, 1 female 10-15, and 1 male -10. Listed
next to William Houston, Robert Allison, Arthur
McCree, John Skilinton, Joseph Alexander, and Robert
Andrews.
1810: Stephen and wife 45+, 2 males 16-25, 1 female
16-25, 1 male 10-15, 1 female 10-15, and 1 female -
10.
Stephen owned land on Coddle Creek.
1790 - Alexander, William Lee (B) & Sarah Rogers
William was a blacksmith.
1800 his family contained himself 26-44, 1 female
16-25, 1 male 16-25, 2 males 10-15, and 1 male -10.
Listed next to James Scott, James Russell, James

Plunkett, Sr., Peter Huey, Isaac Neeley, and Hector
McAharon.
1810: William 45+, 1 male 26-44, and 3 males 16-25.
Son of Hezekiah and Mary Alexander.
Alexander, William M.
    William died in Cabarrus Co. in May of 1850 at the
    age of 66 from a goiter.
Alexander, William Samuel & Sarah
    Buried in Old Rocky River Cemetery
    William born 1751, died 1826
    Son of Dorcas Alexander
*Allemong, Henry & Leah Shinn
    Henry was born 1787, died Feb 16, 1829
1790 - Allen, Alexander, Sr. & Margaret
    1800: Alexander over 45, Margaret 26-44, 1 male 16-
    25, 1 female 16-25, 3 males 10-15, 1 male -10, and 3
    females -10. Listed next to Valentine Kirkpatrick,
    Hector McAharon, Isaac Neeley, Daniel Bean, James
    Burns, and John Cromwell.
    1810: Alexander age is not shown. His household
    consisted of 1 female 26-44, 2 females 10-15, 2
    males -10, and 2 females -10.
Allen, Alexander, Jr & Eleanor McCurdy
    1810: Alexander and wife 16-25, and 1 male -10.
Allen, George & Sarah Alexander
    Married in Cabarrus Co., bond dated March 16, 1802,
    bondsman, Stephen Alexander.
    In the 1860 Cabarrus Co. census, Sarah is listed as
    77 years old.
1790 - Allen, Thomas
    1800: Thomas and wife 45+, and 1 female 16-25.
    Listed next to Randle Studevant, George Miller,
    Andrew Sides, Jesse Herrin, Jacob Buzzard, and
    Martin Harkey.
Allen, William
    1810: William and wife 26-44, and 1 male -10.
1790 - Allison, John, Esq
    On 1810: John 45+, 1 male 45+, 1 female 26-44, 2
    males 16-25, 1 female 16-25, 2 males 10-15, and 1
    female 10-15.
    John LWT was proven Jan 1815. Receipts from
    Margaret, John F, William L, Peggy, James.
1790 - Allison, Robert & Sarah
    Children: John, James
    1800: Robert 45+, his wife 26-44, 1 male 16-25, 1
    male 10-15, 1 female 10-15, 1 male -10, 2 females -
    10. Listed next to Arthur McCree, William Wiley,
    Elizabeth Posey, William Houston, Stephen Alexander,
    and John Skilinton.
    1810: Sarah 45+, 1 male 26-44, 1 male 16-25, and 1
    female 10-15.
Almon, Gideon

1800: Gideon and wife 16-25. Listed next to John
Still, Martin Slough, David Nishler, Elizabeth
Young, Delphie Lewis, and Noah Sandiford.
Owned land on Great Cold Water Creek in 1805.
Almore, Athen
1800: his and wife 26-44, and 5 females -10. Listed
next to John Neihler, Benjamin Biggs, William
Houston, Sr., Robert Martin, James Sullivan, and
James Gailor.
Anderson, John
Owned land on Three Mile Creek
1790 - Anderson, Robert
Owned land on Three Mile Creek
Andrew, Elizabeth
1810: Elizabeth 26-44, 1 female 16-25, and 1 male
10-15.
1790 - Andrews, Moses
Son of John, Sr.
1800: Moses and wife 45+, 1 female 16-25, and 1 male
10-15. He listed next to Robert Andrews, Joseph
Alexander, John Skilinton, Mary Bradford, David
Bradford, and John Brown.
1810: Moses and wife 45+, and 1 female 16-25.
Moses' LWT was proven in July 1813.
1790 - Andrews, Robert
1800: Robert and wife 45+, 1 male 26-44, 1 female
16-25, and 2 females 10-15. Listed next to Joseph
Alexander, John Skilinton, Stephen Alexander, Moses
Andrews, Mary Bradford, and David Bradford.
Andrews, William & Elizabeth Morrison
1800: William 26-44, 1 female 26-44, 1 male -10, 1
female -10. Listed next to Edward Neil, Joseph
Welsh, Alexander Scott, Francis Greer, James Snell,
and Mark Evans.
1810: William (age not given), his wife 45+, 1 male
10-15, and 1 female 10-15.
1790 - Andrew, William & Barbara Caldwell
Married April 16, 1792 in Mecklenburg Co., Robert
Caldwell, bondsman.
William was born Aug 13, 1758, died March 13, 1806
Barbara died July 1, 1800
Buried in Spears Cemetery of Rocky River Church.
Archibald, Moses
1810: Moses and another male 16-25, 1 female 26-44,
and 1 female 16-25.
Armstrong, James
Children: Mary, Ezekiel, James Smith
Armstrong, John
John was declared a lunatic in the April session of
court in 1799. His guardian was Matthew Brandon.
Ashley, James

1810: James 16-25, 1 female 45+, 1 female 16-25, and
1 female -10.

Atkinson, William
1800: William 26-44, and 1 female 16-25. Listed next
to John McGraw, Thomas Voiles, James Purviance,
George Carosine(Corzine), John Wilson, and Charles
Bane.
1810: William and wife 26-44, 1 male -10, and 1
female -10.

Awalt, Michael
1800: Michael and wife 26-44, 1 male 16-25, 3 males
10-15, 1 female 10-15, and 3 females -10. Listed
next to John Neshler, Sr., Jacob Misenheimer,
Frederick Minster, James Scott, John Conder, and
Michael Young.

Bain, ?
Children: Matthew, James

Bain, Charles & Peggy Carithers
Filed a marriage contract in court, Oct 1811.

Bain, John (Not 1800: census)

Bain, Robert & Rachel Killens ?
1800: Robert and wife, 1 male 16-25, 2 males 10-15,
and 1 female -10. Listed next to Moses and Oliver
Wiley, William Bain, and John Davis.

Bain, William
William household contains himself and 2 females 26-
44, and 1 male -10 1800. Listed next to Robert Bain,
Moses Wiley, John and Andrew Davis.

Baker, Aaron & Jean Davis
Married Feb 23, 1805 in Mecklenburg Co., Robert
Davis, bondsman.
Son of George and Rachel Baker

Baker, Benjamin & Elizabeth Holbrook
Children: Joshua (Elizabeth Weddington), John,
Annie, Nelly, Comfort
Elizabeth was the daughter of John Holbrook.
Benjamin and Elizabeth were married about 1779.

Baker, Elias & Sarah Holbrook
Sarah was the daughter of John Holbrook.
Lived within a mile of Caleb Holbrook in 1779.
Moved to Gwinett Co., GA with Sarah father and
brother, John and Caleb Holbrook.
Elias & Sarah testified on behalf of Drucilla
Holbrook, Caleb wife, in her 1841 pension
application.

1790 - Baker, John
Children: Joseph, Benjamin, Joshua, John, Mary,
Eleanor, Richmond, Griffin
1800: John and wife 45+, 2 males 16-25, 1 female 16-
25, 2 males 10-15, 1 female 10-15, 2 males -10, and
1 female -10. Listed next to John Smith, James

Cannon, David Suther, Alexander Patterson, Hugh
Carrithers, and Alexander McClary.
1810: John and wife 45+, 2 males 26-44, 1 male 16-
25, and 1 male -10.
Baker, Joshua
1810: Joshua and wife 45+, 1 male 26-44, 3 males 16-
25, and 2 females 16-25.
Baker, Joshua
1810: Joshua 26-44, 1 female 16-25, 1 male -10, and
2 females -10.
Balch, Hezekiah James
Owned land on Coddle Creek
Balch, James
Children: Amos, Hezekiah
Balch, William
Bane, Charles
1800: Charles and wife 26-44, 3 males -10, and 3
females -10. Listed next to John Wilson, George
Carosine(Corzine), William Atkinson, John McGraw,
George Overcash, John Rumple, and Josiah Bradly.
Barber, John
1810: John and wife 16-25, and 2 males -10.
1790 - Barbrick, Leonard
Children: Catharine (Samuel Shinn), Elizabeth
(Nicholas Neisler), Frederick, Polly (Isaac West).
These children need to be proven, but there were no
other Barberick in the area at this time.
1800: Leonard 45+, 1 female 26-44, 1 male 16-25, 1
male 10-15, 1 female 10-15, and 3 females -10.
Listed next to Henry Propst, Michael Pealer, Joseph
Russell, John Gallimore, John Skilhouse, and Henry
Simmons.
1810: Leonard and wife 45+, and 2 females 10-15.
Leonard bought land from David Mitchler on Cold
Water Creek in Oct 1811.
Barger, Jacob
1810: Jacob 26-44, 2 females 16-25, and 4 males -10.
Barger, Jacob
1810: Jacob and wife 16-25, and 1 male -10.
Barger, John
1800: John 45+, 1 female 26-44, 3 males -10, and 2
females -10. Listed next to Nicholas Rough, John
Cauble, Henry Melchor, Charles Clover, Jacob Hoover,
and Rinehold Overshine.
1810: John and wife 26-44, 2 males 10-15, 2 males -
10, and 1 female -10.
Barger, John
1810: John and wife 26-44, 2 males 10-15, 2 males -
10, and 1 female -10.
John sold to Samuel Barger on the west side of
Little Buffalo Creek in Oct 1812.
Barger, John

1800: John and wife 26-44, 2 males 16-25, and 1 male
-10. Listed next to Michael Isenhour, Peter
Isenhour, Christopher Beaver, Mathias Barnhart,
Jacob Berry, and Mathias Barringer.
1810: John and wife 26-44, 1 male 10-15, 1 female
10-15, 2 males -10, and 2 females -10.
Barger, Samuel
Barker, Thomas
    Thomas bought land on the east side of Rocky River
    in April 1812.
1790 - Barenhart, Charles
    Children: Adam, George
    1800: Charles and wife 45+, 2 males 16-25, 1 female
    16-25, 3 males 10-15, 1 female 10-15, and 1 female -
    10. Listed next to Daniel Boger, George Wilhelm, Eve
    Wilhelm, John Barnhart, Jacob Barnhart, and Elias
    Bost.
    1810: Charles 45+, 1 male 16-25, and 2 females 16-
    25.
Barnhart, Charles
    1810: Charles and wife 16-25, and 1 male -10.
Barnhart, Charles
    1810: Charles 45+, 2 males 16-25, 1 female 16-25, 2
    females 10-15, and 1 male -10.
1790 - Barnhart, Christian, Jr
Barnhart, Christopher
    1810: Christopher 16-25, 1 female 26-44, and 3
    females 16-25.
1790 - Barnhart, George
    1800: George and wife 26-44, 2 males -10, and 3
    females -10. Listed next to John Wisiner, George
    Tucker, Sr., William Smith, John Suther, Christian
    Barnhart, and Christian Blackwelder.
    Catherine Barnhart, an orphan, was living in George
    household in 1811.
    1810: George 45+, 1 female 26-44, 1 male 10-15, 1
    female 10-15, and 2 males -10.
Barnhart, Jacob & Rhody Cox
    1800: Jacob and Rhody, and wife 26-44, 1 male -10,
    and 2 females -10. Listed next to John Barnhart,
    Charles Barnhart, Daniel Boger, Elias Bost, Philip
    Dry, and Martin Dry.
Barnhart, Jacob
    1810: Jacob and wife 16-25, 1 male -10, and 1 female
    -10.
Barnhart, John
    1800: John 26-44, 1 female 16-25, 2 males -10, and 1
    female -10. Listed next to Charles Barnhart, Daniel
    Boger, George Wilhelm, Jacob Barnhart, Elias Bost,
    and Philip Dry.
    1810: John 45+, 1 female 26-44, 1 male 10-15, 1
    female 10-15, 2 males -10, and 1 female -10.

Barnhart, John
    1810: John 26-44, 1 female 16-25, 2 males 10-15, 1
    female 10-15, 1 male -10, and 1 female -10.
1790 - Barnhart, Mathias
    1800: Mathias' age does not appear in the
    enumeration. His household consisted of 1 female 26-
    44, 2 males 10-15, 1 male -10, and 1 female -10.
    Listed next to John Barger, Michael Isenhour, Peter
    Isenhour, Jacob Berry, Mathias Berry, and Mathias
    Barringer.
    1810: Mathias and wife 45+, 1 male 26-44, 1 male 16-
    25, 1 female 10-15, and 1 female -10.
    Mathias registered his mark for cattle and horses in
    Jan 1799.
Barnhart, Mathias
    1810: Mathias 26-44, 1 female 26-44, 2 males 16-25,
    and 1 female 10-15.
Barnhart, Nancy
    1810: Nancy 45+, 1 male 16-25, 3 females 16-25, 1
    female 10-15, and 1 female -10.
Barnhart, Paul
    1810: Paul 26-44, 2 females 10-15, and 1 male -10.
Barnhart, Philip
    1800: Philip and wife 16-25, and 1 female -10.
    Listed next to Daniel Blackwelder, Christian Morris,
    George Moyer, Godfred Lype, Andrew Sides, and George
    Miller.
    1810: Philip and wife 26-44, 2 males -10, and 2
    females -10.
    Philip owned land on Cold Water Creek in 1813.
Barnhart, Staphel
    1810: Staphel and wife 16-25, 1 male -10, and 2
    females -10.
Burnhart, Stephen
    1810: Stephen and wife 16-25, and 2 females -10.
Barrack, George
    George bought land on Coddle Creek from Josiah
    Alexander in Oct 1807.
Berringer, Elizabeth
    Children: Christina
Barringer, George
    1800: George and wife 16-25, 1 male -10, and 1
    female -10. Listed next to Mathias Barringer,
    Mathias Berry, Jacob Berry, John Barringer, John
    Culp, and John Cox.
    1810: George 26-44, 1 female 26-44, 2 males 10-15, 2
    females 10-15, 2 males -10, and 2 females -10.
Barringer, George & Elizabeth Culp
    Married in Cabarrus Co., bond dated Aug 13, 1807,
    Mathias Barringer, bondsman.
    1810: George 26-44, and 1 female 16-25.
Barringer, Jacob

1810: Jacob and wife 16-25, and 1 male -10.
Jacob owned land on Little Buffalo Creek.
Barringer, John
1800: John 26-44, 1 female 16-25, 1 male -10, and 1
female -10. Listed next to George Barringer, Mathias
Barringer, Mathias Berry, John Culp, John Cox, and
William Cox.
1810: John and wife 45+, 1 male 16-25, 1 female 16-
25, and 1 female 10-15.
1790 - Barringer, John
1800: John 45+, 1 female 26-44, 3 males 16-25, 2
females 16-25, 1 male 10-15, 1 female 16-25, and 3
females -10. Listed next to Valentine Faggot, Aaron
Curry, Sarah Neely, Solomon Davis, Jacob Bost, and
Paul Barringer.
Barringer, John, Jr. & Catherine Myer
Married in Cabarrus Co., bond dated July 5, 1800,
bondsman, George Barringer.
Bought land from Robert Lee on the east side of
Dutch Buffalo Creek in April 1807.
1810: John 26-44, 1 female 16-25, and 4 males -10.
In tha 1860 Cabarrus Co. census, Catherine is listed
as 75 years old.
1790 - Baringer, Mathias
Children: Paul, Jacob, John.
Died before 1797
Son of John Barringer who was the son or grandson of
Michael Barriger from Northampton Co., PA
Barringer, Mathias
1800: Mathias and wife 16-25, and 3 females -10.
Listed next to Mathias Berry, Jacob Berry, Mathias
Barnhart, George Barringer, John Barringer, and John
Culp.
1810: Mathias and wife 26-44, 2 females 10-15, 3
males -10, and 2 females -10.
Mathias bought land on Sugar Run Branch of Cold
Water Creek in Jan 1814.
Barringer, Matthew
1810: Matthew and wife 45+, 1 male 26-44, 1 female
26-44, 1 male 16-25, 1 female 10-15, 3 males -10,
and 2 females -10.
1790 - *Barringer, Paul & Elizabeth Peck
Children: Mary (Charles Harris), Jacob, Leah, Susan,
Richmond, Caty, George
1800: Paul and wife 45+, 3 males 16-25, 1 female 16-
25, 1 male 10-15, 1 female 10-15, 1 male -10, and 2
females -10. Listed next to Jacob Bost, Solomon
Davis, John Barringer, Martin Harkey, Nicholas
Ridenhour, and Mathias Moyer.
Owned land on Three Mile Creek
Qualified as Brig. General in 1813
Barringer, Paul

1810: Paul and wife 26-44, 3 males -10, and 1 female
-10.
Barringer, Paul
1810: Paul 26-44, 1 female 16-25, 2 males -10, and 1
female -10.
Barringer, Mathias & Susannah Bolinger
Children: Jacob
Barringer, Mathias & Barbara
Children: Paul, Jacob, John
Barbara LWT was proven in July 1797.
Barringer, Thomas
1810: Thomas 45+, 1 female 26-44, 2 males 16-25, 2
males 10-15, 2 males -10, and 1 female -10.
Bassinger, M
Children: George
Bean, Alexander & Margaret Patterson Andrew
1790 - Bean, Daniel & Sarah Ross
Married Dec 29, 1789 in Mecklenburg Co., William
Ross, bondsman.
1800: Daniel and Sarah 26-44, 1 male 10-15, 1 male -
10, and 1 female -10. Listed next to Alexander
Allin, Valentine Kirkpatrick, Hector McAharon, James
Burns, John Crumwell, and James Crumwell.
Bean, Margaret
1810: Margaret 45+, 1 male 45+, 1 male 16-25, 1
female 16-25, 1 male -10, and 1 female -10.
Bean, Mathias
1810: Mathias and wife 45+, 1 female 26-44, 1 male
16-25, 1 female 10-15, and 1 female -10.
1790 - Bean, Robert
Children: Alexander, John, James, Matthew, Nancy.
Bean, William
1810: William and wife 45+, 1 male 10-15, and 3
females -10.
Beam, Jacob
1810: Jacob and another male 16-25, 1 female 16-25,
and 1 female -10.
Beam, Mathias
1800: Mathias and wife 26-44, 1 male -10, and 1
female -10. Listed next to Michael Wiser, George
Seffred, Martin Penninger, George File, Asemus
Peninger, and Charles Seffrid.
Beaver, Christopher
1800: Christopher and wife 26-44, 1 male 10-15, 1
female 10-15, 1 male -10, and 1 female -10. Listed
next to Lewis Fouts, Martin Harkey, Jacob Buzzard,
Peter Isenhour, Michael Isenhour, and John Barger.
Christopher bought land on the north side of Big
Buffalo Creek in Jan 1812.
Beevins, Leonard
Leonard was a minor of 18 years in July 1813, and
bound to Alexander Holly.

Bell, James
        1800: James 45+, 1 female 26-44, and 2 males 16-25.
        Listed next to Walter Bell, Samuel Brown, John
        Brown, George Brackfriend, Robert Biggers, and John
        Coruthers.
Bell, James
        1810: James and wife 26-44, and 2 females -10.
        James sold to William Bell on Coddle Creek in April
        1813.
1790 - Bell, Walter
        1800: Walter and wife 26-44, and 1 male -10. Listed
        next to Samuel Brown, John Brown, David Bradford,
        James Bell, George Brackfriend, and Robert Biggers.
        1810: Walter and wife 26-44, 1 male 10-15, 1 male -
        10, and 2 females -10.
        Walter bought from James Bell, Sr. on Coddle Creek
        in April 1813.
Beninger, Arasmus
        1810: Arasmus' 45+, 1 female 26-44, 2 males 16-25, 1
        male 10-15, 1 female 10-15, and 4 females -10.
Beninger, Paul
        1810: Paul 26-44, 2 females 16-25, 2 males -10, and
        2 females -10.
Benson, Thomas
        1810: Thomas 45+, 1 female 26-44, 2 males 16-25, 1
        female 16-25, 1 male 10-15, 1 male -10, and 2
        females -10.
        Thomas was accused of a shooting disturbence in the
        courthouse in the April 1812 session, along with
        John Cress and John Weddington.
Berry, Adam
        Children: Leonard-born July 1788
 Berry, Jacob
        1800: Jacob and wife 26-44, and 1 female -10. Listed
        next to Mathias Barnhart, John Barger, Michael
        Isenhour, Mathias Berry, Mathias Barringer, and
        George Barringer.
Berry, Mathias
        1800: Mathias 16-25, 1 female 16-44, 1 female 16-25,
        4 males -10, and 1 female -10. Listed next to Jacob
        Berry, Mathias Barnhart, John Barger, Mathias
        Barringer, George Barringer, and John Barringer.
Berry, Thomas
        Sold land to William Cratton on Meadow Creek in Oct
        1805.
Best, John
        Children: Jacob(born Sept 1788), Elizabeth(born
        1792)
        John died before Jan 1798.
Beaver/Beiber, Christopher
        Children: Isaac
Bice, James

1810: James 45+.
Bice, William
        1810: William and wife 16-25, and 2 females -10.
Bigger, John
        1800: John and wife 45+, 2 males 10-15, 1 female 10-
        15, and 1 male -10. Listed next to Peter Simmons,
        George Stickleather, Michael Sides, Henry Walker,
        Henry Ludwick, and Peter Boiles.
Bigger, Johnston Newell & Jean McLarty
        Children: Jane Elvira (John M. Black), Joseph
        McKemie Wilson (Martha Robinson), Elizabeth (John
        Frazier), Robert Hale (Caroline Easley, Mary Ann
        Gilmer), Alexander McLarty (Elizabeth Morgan),
        Samuel B. (Elizabeth C. Furr), Sarah Clorinda
        (George A. Rogers), Archibald Johnston (Priscilla
        Easley), Nancy E. (died as an infant), James Harvey,
        Mary E. (William Rogers, Archibald McKnight McLarty)
        1810: Johnston 26-44, 1 female 45+, 1 female 26-44,
        1 male 16-25, 1 female 16-25, 1 male -10, and 2
        females -10.
        Johnston and Jean moved to Alabama after the death
        of their oldest daughter, Jane Black, in 1833. Later
        they moved to Mississsippi.
        Jean was the daughter of Alexander and Jenny
        Morrison McLarty.
1790 - Biggers, Joseph
        1800: Joseph and wife 45+, 1 female 26-44, 1 male
        26-44, 1 female 16-25, and 1 male 16-25. Listed next
        to John Newell, William Newell, Benjamin Cockran,
        William Johnston, Hannah McFaddon, and Francis
        Newell.
        Joseph bought lots 2 & 9 in Concord in Jan 1807.
1790 - Biggers, Robert & Catherine Thompson
        Married Jan 1, 1788 in Mecklenburg Co., Joseph
        Patton, bondsman.
        1800: Robert and wife 26-44, 1 female 16-25, 1 male
        10-15, 3 males -10, 1 female -10. Listed next to
        George Brackfriend, James Bell, Walter Bell, John
        Coruthers, Widow Caragin, and Thomas Erwin.
Biggs, Benjamin
        1800: Benjamin and wife 26-44, 1 male 16-25, 1 male
        10-15, 2 females 10-15, and 3 females -10. Listed
        next to William Houston, Sr., Thomas McCain, William
        Wallis, John Niehler, Athen Almore, and Robert
        Martin.
1790 - Black, James
        1800: James and wife 45+, and 1 female -10. Listed
        next to John White, Jr., Samuel White, Archibald
        White, John Black, Jr., Thomas Black, and Samuel
        Blair.
1790 - Black, John, Jr

Children: John, Martha (? McAuley), William,
Samuel, Elizabeth (? Robinet), Rosannah (?
Walker), Margaret (? McAuley), Esther (? Walker),
Jane (? Witherspoon), Deborah (? Bays)
1800: John and wife 26-44, 2 females 10-15, 2 males
-10, and 1 female -10. Listed next to Robert
McEchron, John Crumwell, Sr., William McAnulty,
Samuel McCurdy, Josiah Spears, and James Bradshaw,
Sr.
John's will was probated in April 1809
Black, John, Jr. & Rebecca McKinley?
Married in Cabarrus Co., bond dated June 6, 1793,
bondsman, Charles C. Black.
1800: John 26-44, 1 female 16-25, and 1 female -10.
Listed next to James Black, John White, Jr., Samuel
White, Thomas Black, Samuel Blair, and Charles
Dorton.
1810: John and Rebecca 26-44, 1 male 10-15, 1 female
10-15, 2 males -10, and 1 female -10.
Black, Samuel
1810: 1 male 45+, 1 female 26-44, 1 male 26-44, 2
males -10, and 2 females -10.
1790 - Black, Thomas
1800: Thomas and wife 26-44, 1 male 10-15, 1 male -
10, and 3 females -10. Listed next to James Black,
John White, Jr., Samuel Blair, Charles Dorton, and
Sameul Weddington.
Sold land on Rockhole Creek in July 1806 to Martin
Blackwelder.
Thomas owned land on Muddy Creek bordering David
McKinley, Joseph McClelland and John Long.
Blackwelder, Andrew & Rachel Bost
Married in Cabarrus Co., bond date unclear, about
1815, bondsman, Henry Blackwelder.
Rachel was listed as head of household in Cabarrus
Co. in 1880, shown as 84 years old.
Blackwalter, Caleb
Caleb died before July 1797.
Blackwelder, Caleb
1810: Caleb and wife 16-25, and 1 female -10.
Blackwelder, Charles
1810: Charles and wife 45+, 3 males 16-25, 2 females
16-25, 1 male 10-15, 1 male -10, and 3 females -10.
Blackwelder, Christian
1800: Christian and wife 26-44, 1 female 16-25, 1
male 10-15, 2 females 10-15, 2 males -10, and 1
female -10. Listed next to Christian Barnhart, John
Suther, George Barnhart, Adam Bowers, Sr., Adam
Bowers, Jr., and John Chamerlin.
Blackwelder, Daniel & Elizabeth Duck, Mary Franks
Daniel and Elizabeth were married in Cabarrus Co.,
bond dated Jan 29, 1798, Melchor Fogelman, bondsman.

Daniel and Mary Franks were married July 8, 1800: in
Cabarrus Co., bondsman, Henry Huber.
1800: Daniel house hold consisted of himself and
wife 16-25, and 2 females -10. Listed next to
Christian Morris, George Moyer, Godfred Uery, Philip
Barnhart, Godfred Lype, and Andrew Sides.
1810: Daniel 26-44, 1 female 45+, 1 female 26-44, 1
female 10-15, 1 male -10, 4 females -10.

Blackwelder, Isaac & Mary Anna Readling
1800: Isaac 26-44, 1 female 26-44, 2 males 16-25, 1
female 16-25, 1 male 10-15, 2 females 10-15, 1 male
-10, and 2 females -10. Listed next to Mathias
Moyer, Nicholas Ridenhour, Martin Harkey, George
Bost, Martin Blackwelder, and Mary Bostian.
1810: Isaac and wife 45+, 2 males 16-25, 1 male 10-
15, 2 females 10-15, 4 males -10, and 1 female -10.

Blackwelder, Isaac
Married in Cabarrus Co., bond dated June 1, 1796,
bondsman, Paul Phifer.
1810: Isaac and wife 26-44, 2 males -10, and 2
females -10.

1790 - Blackwelder, Jacob
1800: Jacob and wife 26-44, 2 males 10-15, 2 males -
10, and 3 females -10. Listed next to Mary Bostain,
Martin Blackwelder, George Bost, Alias Bostain, Owen
Dry, and Jacob Dry.
1810: Jacob and wife 26-44, 1 male 16-25, 2 females
16-25, 2 males 10-15, 1 male -10, and 3 females -10.

1790 - Blackwelder, Martin
1800: Martin 26-44, 1 male 10-15, 1 male -10, and 4
females -10. Listed next to George Bost, Isaac
Blackwelder, Mathias Moyer, Mary Bostian, Jacob
Blackwelder, and Alias Bostian.
Owned land on Rockhole Creek jointly with Jacob
Baust in 1806.
1810: Martin and wife 26-44, 1 male 16-25, 2 females
16-25, 1 male 10-15, 1 female 10-15, 2 males -10,
and 1 female -10.

*Blair, Samuel
Children: Clarinda (Harris Houston)
1800: Samuel and wife 26-44, 1 female 16-25, and 1
male -10. Listed next to Thomas Black, John Black,
Jr., James Black, Charles Dorton, Samuel Weddington,
and Jean White.

Bless/Pless, Henry
Henry bought land from Peter Pless on Dutch Buffalo
Creek in July 1806.

Bless, Joseph
1810: Joseph and wife 26-44, 2 males -10, and 3
females -10.

Bless/Pless, Peter

Peter sold land on Dutch Buffalo Creek to Henry
Pless in July 1806.

Bless, Philip
1800: Philip is listed as a resident of Concord. His
and wife 26-44, 1 male 16-25, and 2 males -10.
Listed with John Master, Lawrence Snapp, George
Smith, Jacob Hudson, and Samuel Hughey.

Bless/Pless, Philip
1800: Philip and wife 26-44, 1 male 16-25, and 2
males -10. Listed next to George Smith, Lawrence
Snapp, William Townsend, Jacob Hutson, Catherine
Shinn, and Lewis Townsend.

Boehm, John
John was overseer of a road from Double Island to
Anderson Creek in Oct 1798.

1790 - Boger, Daniel
1800: Daniel 45+, 1 female 26-44, 1 male 16-25, 2
females 10-15, 3 males -10, and 2 females -10.
Listed next to George Wilhelm, Eve Wilhelm, Hardin
Wiggins, Charles Barnhart, John Barnhart, and Jacob
Barnhart.
1810: Daniel 45+, 1 female 26-44, 2 females 16-25,
and 2 males 10-15.
Daniel owned land on Back branch of Cold Water Creek
in Jan 1807, sold to George Baust. He also bought
land on Rocky River and Hamby Run in July 1813.

Boager, Jacob
1800: Jacob and wife 26-44, 1 male 16-25, and 1
female 16-25. Listed next to Peter Boager, John
Cauddle, Henry Cress, Henry Pless, Martin Uery, and
Jacob Hodgeman.
1810: Jacob 45+, 1 female 45+, and 1 male 26-44.

Boger, Jacob
1810: Jacob 26-44, 1 female 16-25, 1 male -10, and 1
female -10.

1790 - Boger, Peter
1800: Peter 45+, 1 male 10-15, and 2 females 10-15.
Listed next to John Cauddle, Henry Cress, Jacob
Cassock, Jacob Boager, Henry Pless, and Martin Uery.

Boger, Daniel
Daniel died in Cabarrus Co. in April 1860 at the age
of 80 from pneumonia.
In 1813, Daniel Boger was declared a lunatic in the
Oct 1813 session of Pleas and Quarter Sessions. It
is not conclusive that this was the right Daniel.

Boiles, Peter
1800: Peter and wife 16-25, and 1 female -10. Listed
next to Henry Ludwick, Henry Walker, John Biggers,
John Ritchey, Michael Walker, and Leonard Cluttz.

Bolinger, Henry
Children: Susannah

Bosshart, John

John died before April 1798.
Bost, Daniel & Elizabeth Nussman
Married April 13, 1799 in Cabarrus Co., George Bost
bondsman.
1800: Daniel household consisted of just himself and
Elizabeth, and wife 16-25. Listed next to Harmon
Moyer, Daniel Faggot, Henry Fite, Dorothy Petry,
Francis Funderburk, and Andrew Slough.
1810: Daniel 26-44, 1 female 16-25, 1 male -10, and
4 females -10.
1790 - Bost, Elias
Son of William Bost & Catharine Goodhart.
Children: John
Owned land on Whitford branch of Rocky River, and on
Rocky River.
1800: Elias 16-25, 1 female 26-44, 1 male 16-25, and
2 females 10-15. Listed next to Jacob Barnhart, John
Barnhart, Charles Barnhart, Philip Dry, Martin Dry,
and Jacob Effrit.
Bost, Elias
1810: Elias and wife 45+, 1 female 16-25, and 1 male
10-15.
1790 - Bost, George
1800: George and wife 26-44, 3 males 10-15, 2 males
-10, and 2 females -10. Listed next to Isaac
Blackwelder, Mathias Moyer, Nicholas Ridenhour,
Martin Blackwelder, Mary Bostian, and Jacob
Blackwelder.
Son of William Bost & Catharine Goodhart.
George bought land on Back branch of Cold Water
Creek, from Daniel Boger in Jan 1807.
 Bost, George
1810: George 16-25, 1 female 26-44, 3 other males
16-25, 2 males 10-15, 2 males -10, and 1 females -
10.
1790 - Bost, Jacob
1800: Jacob 45+, 1 female 26-44, 1 female 16-25, 1
male 10-15, 2 females 10-15, 3 males -10, and 1
female -10. Listed next to Solomon Davis, John
Barringer, Valentine Faggot, Paul Barringer, Martin
Harkey, and Nicholas Ridenhour.
1810: Jacob 45+, 1 female 26-44, 2 males 16-25, 1
female 16-25, and 2 males 10-15.
Son of William Bost & Catharine Goodhart.
Bost, John
Children: Elizabeth(born-1791)
John owned land on Whitford branch of Rocky River,
and on Rocky River. He died before April 1798.
Son of Elias Bost
Bost, John
1810: John and wife 26-44, 2 males -10, and 1 female
-10.

Bost, John
        1810: John household consisted of just himself 16-
        25.
Bost, William
        1810: William and wife 26-44, 2 males -10, and 4
        females -10.
Bost, William
        Married in Rowan Co., bond dated Jan 19, 1762.
        Bought land on Anderson Creek from Jonathan Osborn
        in Oct 1805.
Bostian, Alias
        1800: Alias' and wife 26-44, 1 male 16-25, 2 males
        10-15, 1 male -10, and 1 female -10. Listed next to
        Jacob Blackwelder, Mary Bostain, Martin Blackwelder,
        Owen Dry, Jacob Dry, and Andrew Dry.
Bostian, Mary
        1800: Mary 26-44, 2 females 16-25, 2 females 10-15,
        2 males -10, and 1 female -10. Listed next to Martin
        Blackwelder, George Bost, Isaac Blackwelder, Jacob
        Blackwelder, Alias Bostian, and Owen Dry.
1790 - Bouchfriend/Brackfriend, George
        1800: George and wife 45+. Listed next to James
        Bell, Walter Bell, Samuel Brown, Robert Biggers,
        John Coruthers, and Widow Caragin.
Bowers, Adam, Jr
        1800: Adam and wife 16-25, and 1 male -10. Listed
        next to Adam Bowers, Sr., Christian Blackwelder,
        Christian Barnhart, John Chamberlin, Mark Coleman,
        and Henry Furor.
        1810: Adam 26-44, 1 female 45+, 1 female 26-44, 1
        male 10-15, 1 female 10-15, 1 male -10, and 1 female
        -10.
Bowers, Adam, Sr
        1800: Adam and wife 45+. Listed next to Christian
        Blackwelder, Christian Barnhart, John Suther, Adam
        Bowers, Jr., John Chamberlin, and Mark Coleman.
Boyd, Peter
        1810: Peter household consisted of 1 male and 1
        female, and wife 45+, 1 male 16-25, and 1 female 16-
        25.
Brackfriend, George
        1800: George and wife 45+. Listed next to James
        Bell, Walter Bell, Samuel Brown, Robert Biggers,
        John Coruthers, and Widow Caragin.
Brackfriend/Berickfriend, John
        1810: John 26-44, 1 female 45+, and 1 female 16-25.
Bradford, David & Mary Chambers
        Married in Cabarrus County on Feb 1, 1803, Michael
        Bradford, bondsman.
        1800: before David and Mary were married, David and
        another male, and wife 26-44.

1810: David and Mary, and wife 26-44, and 1 male 16-
25.
Bradford, James
1810: James 45+, 1 female 45+, 1 female 26-44, 4
males -10, and 2 females -10.
1790 - Bradford, Mary
1800: Mary 45+, and 1 female 26-44. Listed next to
Moses Andrews, Robert Andrews, Joseph Alexander,
David Bradford, John Brown, and Samuel Brown.
Bradly, Isaiah
1810: Isaiah 45+,1 female 26-44, 1 male 16-25, 2
females 16-25, 1 female 10-15, 1 male -10, and 3
females -10.
Bradly, Josiah & Ann
1800: Josiah and wife 26-44, 1 male 16-25, 1 male -
10, and 4 females -10. Listed next to John Rumple,
George Overcash, Charles Bane, David McKinly,
Frances Linse, and John Goodman.
Josiah died before April 1813.
Bradshaw, David
1810: David 26-44, 1 female 16-25, 1 male -10, and 2
females -10.
Bradshaw, Eli
1810: Eli 16-25, 1 female 45+, and 1 female 10-15.
1790 - Bradshaw, James, Sr.
1800: James and wife 45+, 2 males 16-25, 3 females
16-25, and 2 males 10-15. Listed next to Josiah
Spears, Samuel McCurdy, John Black, Jr., Martha
Watson, Archibald White, and Samuel White.
James was born 1742, died Feb 19, 1809
Buried in Spears Cemetery of Rocky River Church.
Bradshaw, James Watson & Sarah Morrison
Children: Elias, Jane, Amzi (Hannah Brown), Hannah,
Elam (died young), Robert Elam (Margaret Appleby),
James Edward (Amanda Dryden), Thomas Watson
1800: James' and Sarah, and wife 26-44, 2 males -10,
and 1 female -10. Listed next to Francis Newell,
Hannah McFaddon, William Johnston, John Cromwell,
Archibald McCurdey, and Charles McKinley.
1810: James 26-44, 1 female 16-25, 2 males 10-15, 1
female 10-15, 2 males -10, and 1 female -10.
James and Sarah moved to TN and are buried near
Shelbyville.
Sarah was the daughter of Robert and Sarah Morrison.
Bradshaw, John
Lived in the Rocky River Church area
1810: John and wife 26-44, 2 males -10, and 1 female
-10.
Brandon, Isaac
1800: Isaac 45+, 1 female 26-44, 2 females 16-25, 2
males 10-15, 1 female 10-15, 2 males -10, and 3
females -10. Listed next to Mary Cagle, Cistra

Brint, George Tucker, Jr., Joshua Tucker, John Reed,
   and George Long.
Brian/Bryan, Henry
      1810: Henry 16-25, 1 female 26-44, 2 males 10-15, 2
      females 10-15, and 2 females -10.
Brians, William & Hannah Milnster
      Married in Cabarrus County, bond dated Jan 24, 1811,
      bondsman, Frederick Michael Milnster
      William had a child with Rachel Long in 1809.
      Children: Thomas F., Harriet E., daughter (?
      Plotte), John H. (not proven), Ann (not proven)
      William is listed in the 1850 Cabarrus Co. census as
      62 and Hannah is listed as 60.
1790 - Briges, James
      Heirs: Pemberton, James, Agnes
      Owned land on Cold Water Creek.
      James died between Jan 1804 and July 1805 in
      Cabarrus County.
Bridges, James
      1800: James 45+, 1 female 26-44, 3 males 16-25, 1
      female 16-25, 3 females 10-15, 2 males -10, and 2
      females -10. Listed next to Aaron Houston, John
      Goodman, Frances Linse, Henry Brines, Joseph Shinn,
      and John Culpepper.
      Sold land on Cold Water Creek and Irish Buffalo
      Creek to James Townsend and Michael Goodman in Oct
      1805.
Brines, Henry
      1800: Henry and wife 26-44, 1 male 10-15, 2 females
      10-15, 3 males -10, and 2 females -10. Listed next
      to James Bridges, Aaron Houston, John Goodman,
      Joseph Shinn, John Culpepper, and John Shaver.
Brint, Cistra
      1800: Cistra household consisted of 1 male 26-44, 1
      female 26-44, 1 male 16-25, 2 males -10, and 4
      females -10. Listed next to George Tucker, Jr., John
      Polk, John Brown, Mary Cagle, Isaac Brandon, and
      Joshua Tucker.
Brothers, Philip
      Bought land from John Houston on Rubens branch of
      Buffalo Creek in 1805.
Brown, Armistead & Susannah McEachern
      Married April 13, 1805 in Cabarrus Co., James
      Plunket, bondsman.
      Susannah was the daughter of John and Mary
      McCachron.
Brown, George
      1810: George and wife 16-25, and 2 females -10.
Brown, John & Milly Osbourne
      Children: Sarah, Evan
      Married in Cabarrus Co., bond dated Nov 12, 1799,
      bondsman, Samuel McCurdy.

1800: John and wife 16-25, and 1 female -10. Listed
next to Douglass Winchester, Charles Freeman, Andrew
Freeman, John Polk, George Tucker, Jr., and Cistra
Brint.
John died 1804, his orphans are named as Sarah and
Evan in Jan 1805.
Brown, John
     In the 1860 Cabarrus Co. census John is listed as 78
     years old.
1790 - Brown, John
     1800: John 26-44, 1 male 16-25, 1 female 16-25, and
     2 females 10-15. Listed next to David Bradford, Mary
     Bradford, Moses Andrews, Samuel Brown, Walter Bell,
     and James Bell.
 Brown, Samuel
     1800: Samuel and wife 45+, and 1 male 16-25. Listed
     next to John Brown, David Bradford, Mary Bradford,
     Walter Bell, James Bell, and George Brackfriend.
Brown, Samuel & Nancy Jamison
     Children: James
1790 - Bugg, William
     1800: William and wife 45+, 1 male 16-25, 2 females
     16-25, 1 male 10-15, 1 female 10-15, 1 male -10, and
     1 female -10. Listed next to David Wisner, Henry
     Howell, John Howell, Henry Cagle, James Clay, and
     Dennis Clay.
1790 - Burns, James & Penelope
     Children: Penelope C., Samuel
     1800: James 26-44, Penelope 16-25, and 3 males -10.
     Listed next to Daniel Bean, Alexander Allin,
     Valentine Kirkpatrick, John Crumwell, James
     Crumwell, and John Cochrin.
     1810: James 26-44, 1 female 45+, 1 female 26-44, 1
     male 16-25, 1 female 16-25, 1 male 10-15, 1 female
     10-15, 3 males -10, and 2 females -10.
     James born 1768, died 1817
     Penelope born 1771, died 1830
     Buried in Old Rocky River Cemetery
Bushard, Jacob
     1810: Jacob 45+, 1 female 26-44, 1 male 10-15, 1
     female 10-15, 2 males -10, and 2 females -10.
Buzzard, Jacob
     1800: Jacob 24-44, 1 female 45+, 1 female 26-44, 1
     male -10, and 1 female -10. Listed next to Jesse
     Herrin, Thomas Allin, Randle Studevant, Martin
     Harkey, Lewis Fouts, and Christopher Beaver.
Ceagle, David
     1810: David and wife 16-25, 2 males -10, and 1
     female -10.
1790 - Caegle, Henry
     1800: Henry and wife 26-44, 1 male 16-25, 2 males
     10-15, 1 female 10-15, and 1 female -10. Listed next

to William Bugg, David Wisner, Henry Howell, James
Clay, Dennis Clay, and John Ford.
1810: Henry 45+, 1 male 16-25, 1 female 16-25, and 1
female 10-15.
Ceagle, Henry, Jr
1810: Henry and wife 16-25.
Cagle, Mary
1800: Mary 45+, 4 females 10-15, and 1 male -10.
Listed next to Cistra Brint, George Tucker, Jr.,
John Polk, Isaac Brandon, Joshua Tucker, and John
Reed.
Callahan, William
Owned land on Rocky River in 1782.
Coleman, Jacob
Children: Margaret, George
Caldwell, Daniel & Jean Morrison
Jean was the daughter of Robert and Sarah Morrison.
Caldwell, John & Elizabeth
Caldwell, Robert & Phoebe Morrison
Children: John (Mary Allen), Robert (Serena
Houston), Daniel (Isabella E. Shields), Margaret
(Joshua Teeter-no children), James (Polly Dixon),
Silas (Matilda Evaline Query, Lyde Cochran), William
(Elizabeth E. Query)
Robert was born 1757, died Nov 6, 1832
Buried in Spears Cemetery in Cabarrus County, the
whereabouts of his wife are unknown.
Phoebe was the daughter of Robert and Sarah
Morrison.
Callens, James
Bought land on the south side of Coddle Creek from
Levi Russel in Jan 1807.
Callon, John
1800: John and wife 26-44, 2 males -10, and 2
females -10. Listed next to George Campbell,
Jeremiah Johnston, James Harris, Charles Campbell,
James Creatton, and William Vietch.
Callon, William, Jr & Sarah Alexander
1800: William 26-44, 1 female 45+, and 1 female -10.
Listed next to William Callon, Sr., Ezekiel Sharpe,
Robert McMurray, George Alexander, Thomas Gray, and
Nelson Gray.
Callon, William, Sr
1800: William and wife 45+. Listed next to Ezekiel
Sharpe, Robert McMurray, William Vietch, James
Creatton, William Callon, Jr., George Alexander, and
Thomas Gray.
Calhoun, James
Children: William
Calvin/Calvian, John
1810: John 45+, 3 males 16-25, 1 female 16-25, 1
female 10-15, and 3 males -10.

1790 - Campbell, Andrew
        Son of Andrew Campbell
        Children: Andrew, Lewis, Eugenia, Cirus, 2
        Unreadable
        Andrew died in 1798.
Campbell, Cevilia
Campbell, Charles & Charlotte Morris
        Married Oct 9, 1793 in Cabarrus County, Daniel Bean,
        bondsman.
        1800: Charles 26-44, his wife 16-25, 2 males -10,
        and 1 female -10. Listed next to John Callon, George
        Campbell, Jeremiah Johnston, James Creatton, William
        Vietch, and Robert McMurray.
        Owned land on Coddle Creek near James Callens and
        Levi Russel in Jan 1807.
        1810: Charles 45+, his wife, 26-44, 2 males 10-15, 1
        female 10-15, 2 males -10, and 2 females -10.
Campbell, Cyrus & Hannah Wiley
        Children:
        Son of Andrew Campbell
        Married Aug 1812
        Appointed guardian of Charles Campbell, son of James
        Campbell in 1813.
Campbell, George & Mary Russel
        Children: James H., Robert C., Addison H
        Married in Mecklenburg County, bond dated Jan 24,
        1791, bondsman, Robert Ervin
        George Campbell was bondsman for Levi Russell, son
        of James and Susannah Russell, and Sinthe (Jinsey?)
        Russell and Samuel McCracken.
        1800: the only George Campbell in Cabarrus Co. had
        the following in his household. Himself and wife 26-
        44, 1 male 10-15, 4 males -10, and 1 female -10.
        Listed next to Jeremiah Johnston, James Harris,
        Elisha Spears, John Callon, Charles Campbell, and
        James Creatton.
        Lands of George Campbell on the east side of Rocky
        River, sold under execution to Adam Meek in April
        1807.
        A George Campbell appointed guardian of his own
        children in 1814 Cabarrus County Pleas and Quarter
        Sessions.
Campbell, Hugh
        Owned land on Reedy Creek and Anderson Creek in
        1782.
Campbell, James
        Children: Charles, James, George, Berry, Ann, Sinah,
        Eugenios, Colliston
Campbell, John
        Owned land on Reedy Creek and Anderson Creek in
        1774. Probably a brother of Hugh Campbell.
Campbell, Joseph

Owned land on Coddle Creek in 1785.

Campbell, Martha
    1800: Martha 16 -25, 2 males 10-15, and 3 males -10.
    Listed next to Thomas White, Even Jones, Charles
    Tounsend, George Voiles, Signe Seales, and Stephen
    Mayfield.

Campbell, Matthew
    1800: Matthew and wife 45+, 2 females 26-44, and 1
    male 16-25. Listed next to James Stafford, Thomas
    Davis, Robert Harris, Jr., Griffin Morris,
    Cunningham Harris, and Elisha Spears.

Campbell, Murdoch
    1800: Murdoch household consisted of just himself,
    45+. Listed next to Lewis Townsend, Catherine Shinn,
    Jacob Hutson, John McKinley, Joseph White, and Jean
    Russle.

Cammel/Campbell, Robert & Jane Turner
    Children: Robert
    Owned land on Rocky River and Coddle Creek in 1779.

1790 - Cannon, James, Sr
    James died before April 1813, Aaron Townsend was the
    administrator of his estate.

Cannon, James & Ann Black
    Married in Cabarrus Co., bond dated July 29, 1790,
    bondsman, John Allison.
    1800: James and wife 26-44, 1 male -10, and 1 female
    -10. Listed next to David Suther, Dudly Tounsend,
    John Winecough, John Smith, John Baker, and
    Alexander Patterson.
    1810: James and wife 26-44, 2 males 10-15, 1 female
    10-15, 4 males -10, and 1 female -10.
    In the 1850 Cabarrus Co. census, Ann is listed as 79
    years old.

1790 - Cannon, John
    1800: John 26-44, 1 female 16-25, 1 male 16-25, 1
    male -10, and 1 female -10. Listed next to James
    Christopher, Abram Alexander, Hezekiah Alexander,
    Moses Alexander, Arthur Donelson, William Gardenor,
    and Robert Hope.

Carl, Daniel
    1810: Daniel 26-44, 1 female 16-25, and 2 males -10.

Carlock, Frederick & Clary
    Children: Rachel(? Williams), Elena, John,
    Margaret, Samuel, Moses, Frederick. Children named
    as minors in court records, 1798.
    Frederick owned land on Cold Water Creek and Buffalo
    ·Creek next to Isaac Lofton and William Waggoner in
    1784.
    Frederick died before April 1798.

Carlock, Frederick & Isabell
    Sold land to John Davis in 1805.

Carson, John

1810: John 16-25, 2 females 16-25, 1 male 10-15, 1
female 10-15, and 3 males -10.
Cassock, Jacob
1800: Jacob and wife 26-44, 2 males 10-15, 1 female
10-15, 2 males -10, and 2 females -10. Listed next
to David Speck, George Speake, Henry Lineboh, Henry
Cress, John Cauddle, and Peter Boager.
1790 - Cerlaugh (Carlock), George & Millison
Children: Esther
1800: George and wife 26-44, 1 female 16-25, 1 male
10-15, 2 females 10-15, 2 males -10, and 1 female -
10. Listed next to Levi Curzine, Thomas Clark, John
Lee, Charles Tounsend, Even Jones, and Thomas White.
George died before 1814 leaving Esther and orphan
whose appointed guardian was Abraham Alexander.
Carlock, John
1800: John 16-25, 1 male 16-25, 2 females 16-25, and
1 male -10. He listed next to John Vossel, Michael
Watters, John Gray, Jacob Self, Sr., Jacob Self,
Jr., and David Self.
1790 - Carrigan, James
James was fined on April 20, 1803 with David Russell
for contempt of court.
1800: James and wife , and wife 26-44, 1 male 10-15,
and 2 males -10. Listed next to Hugh Heare, Robert
Stanford, Josiah Deweast, John Caragin, James
Purviance, and Thomas Voiles.
Caragin, James
1800: James 26-44, 2 females 16-25, 1 female 10-15,
and 1 male -10. Listed next to Samuel Kenly, John
Gilmore, Robert Alexander, Benjamin Alexander, John
Jones, and Duncan Smith.
1810: James and wife 26-44, 1 male 16-25, 2 males
10-15, and 2 females -10.
Caragin, John
1800: John and 1 female 16-25. Listed next to James
Caragin, Sr., Hugh Heare, Robert Stanford, James
Purviance, Thomas Voiles, and John McGraw.
1810: John household consisted of 1 male 45+, 1 male
26-44, 1 female 16-25, and 3 males -10.
Caragin, Mark
1810: Mark 26-44, 1 female 16-25, 2 females 10-15, 2
males -10, and 1 female -10.
Caragin, Widow
probably widow of Thomas or William.
Carrigan, William
1810: William and wife 45+, 3 males 16-25, and 1
female -10.
1790 - Carriger/Cariker, Andrew
1800: Andrew and wife 26-44, 3 males 10-15, 2
females 10-15, 4 males -10, and 3 females -10.
Listed next to Philip Cariker, Jr., George Cariker,

Philip Cariker, Sr., David Fink, Henry Plylor, and
Peter Misenheimer.
Andrew owned land on Plum Branch.
1790 - Carriger/Cariker, George
       1800: George 45+, 1 female 26-44, 2 males 16-25, 2
       males 10-15, 2 females 10-15, 1 male -10, and 2
       females -10. Listed next to Philip Cariker, Sr.,
       Elias House, Daniel Little, Philip Cariker, Jr.,
       Andrew Cariker, and David Fink.
       George owned land on and wife sides of Plum Branch
       in July 1812.
1790 - Carriger/Cariker, Philip, Jr
       1800: Philip and wife 26-44, 2 males 10-15, 3 males
       -10, and 1 female -10. Listed next to George
       Cariker, Philip Cariker, Sr., Elias House, Andrew
       Cariker, David Fink, and Henry Plylor.
       Philip owned land on Plum Branch in July 1812.
1790 - Carriger/Cariker, Philip, Sr
       1800: Philip 45+, and 1 male 26-44. Listed next to
       Elias House, Daniel Little, Stephen Mayfield, George
       Cariker, Philip Cariker, Jr., and Andrew Cariker.
       Philip owned land on Plum Branch.
Carruthers, Hugh & Sarah Purviance
       Children: John, Robert, Esther (Francis Ross), Sarah
       (James Purviance), Hugh, James
       Hugh owned land on Buffalo Creek and Coddle Creek
       near Wolf Meadow Branch in 1763.
       Hugh died in 1782 and is buried in Rocky River
       Cemetery.
1790 - Carruthers, Hugh G & Mathe Irvin, Margaret
       Carruthers
       Children: Peggy, Ann, Jenny
       Owned land on Buffalo Creek and Coddle Creek
       Hugh died before April 1806.
       1800: Hugh and wife 26-44, 1 male 16-25, 2 males 10-
       15, 1 female 10-15, 2 males -10, and 3 females -10.
       Listed next to Alexander Patterson, John Baker, John
       Smith, Alexander McClary, Levi Russell, and John
       Rogers.
1790 - Carruthers, James
       Children: Peggy, Ann
       Owned land on Reedy Creek in 1779.
       James died before July 1805. Provisions for widow
       were laid off by James Scott, James Plunkett, Jr.
       and James Walker.
1790 - Carruthers, John & Elinor   102
       Children: Mary, Isobel, Sarah
       Owned land on Muddy Creek and Anderson Creek in
       1771.
       1800: John and Elinor, and wife 45+. Listed next to
       John Powell, Able Powell, John Ford, Michael Garmon,
       Travis Gullino, and Leonard Mire.

1810: John and wife 45+, 2 males 16-25, 1 male 10-
15, 1 female 10-15, and 2 females -10.
1790 - Carruthers, John
1800: John and wife 45+, 1 male 26-44, and 1 male
16-25. Listed next to Robert Biggers, George
Brackfriend, James Bell, Widow Caragin, Thomas
Erwin, and Mitchel Flemmon.
1790 - Corruthers, Robert C. & Margaret
Margaret born 1754, died Aug 12, 1794, buried in Old
Rocky River Cemetery.
Carriker/Carker, Andrew & Eleanor Kiser
1810: Andrew and wife 45+, 3 males 16-25, 2 females
16-25, 1 male 10-15, 1 female 10-15, and 1 female -
10.
Carriker, Paul
1810: Paul household consisted himself 16-25, 1
female 26-44, 1 male -10, and 1 female -10.
Carrithers, Thomas & Margaret Neely
Married Jan 1, 1813 in Mecklenburg Co., James
Carothers, bondsman.
Caruthers, Margaret
1810: Margaret 45+, and 2 females 16-25.
Caruthers, Thomas
1800: Thomas and 1 female, and wife 26-44. Listed
next to Moses Rogers, William Means, John Rogers,
Richard Marlin, William Corell, and John Weddington.
1810: Thomas' and wife 26-44, 2 males -10, and 3
females -10.
1790 - Carson, John Kelly & Mary McBroom, Sarah Staven
John and Mary were married in Rowan in 1767.
John and Sarah were married in Rowan in 1775. John
lived on Lot 1, NW SQ Concord in 1807. John also
bought land from James Russel in July 1806.
John will was probated in Nov 1812 naming wife
Sally, brother James, aunt and uncle James and Sarah
McIntire. No children named.
John sold land on and wife sides of Three Mile
Branch in April 1813.
Carson, James
1800: James 16-25. Listed next to Mathias Phifer,
James Hughey, Samuel Hughey, John Russell, David
Russle, and Mary Russle.
Carson, Widow
1810: her 45+, 1 male 26-44, 1 male 16-26, and 1
female 16-25.
Carter, Charles
1800: Charles 45+, 1 male 45+, 1 female 45+, 1
female 26-44, 1 male 10-15, 1 male -10, and 2
females -10. Listed next to Drury Rogers, Peter
Troutman, Joseph Woolever, Henry Melchor, John
Cauble, Nicholas Rough, and John Barger.
Casey, Henry

Children: Solomon-born Nov 1782
Cassock, Jacob
Caster, Henry
        1810: Henry 16-25, 3 females 16-25, and 2 females -
        10.
Caster, Henry
        1810: Henry 45+, 1 female 26-44, 2 females 10-15,
        and 3 males -10.
Cauble, John & Peggy Carlock
        1800: John and Peggy, and wife 26-44, 1 male -10,
        and 1 female -10. Listed next to Henry Melchor,
        Charles Carter, Drury Rogers, Nicholas Rough, John
        Barger, and Charles Clover.
Cauble/Coble, Peter & Christina Dry
 Cauble, Peter
        1800: Peter 45+, 1 male 26-44, 1 female 16-25, and 1
        male -10. Listed next to Peter Limeboh, George
        Clontz, Jacob Hodgeman, Jacob Pines, John Edleman,
        and John File.
Cauble/Cable, Peter
        1810: Peter and wife 26-44, 1 male 10-15, and 1
        female 10-15.
Cauple, Peter
        1810: Peter and wife 26-44, and 2 females -10.
Cauddle, John
        1800: John and wife 26-44, 1 male 16-25, 2 males 10-
        15, and 2 females 10-15. Listed next to Henry Cress,
        Jacob Cassock, David Speck, Peter Boager, Jacob
        Boager, and Henry Pless.
1790 - Chamberlain, John
        Owned land on the west side of Cold Water Creek near
        Voils' branch in 1784.
        1800: John 45+, 1 female 26-44, 1 male 16-25, 4
        females 16-25, 1 male 10-15, and 1 male -10. Listed
        next to Adam Bowers, Jr., Adam Bowers, Sr.,
        Christian Blackwelder, Mark Coleman, Henry Furor,
        and Frederick Frank.
        1810: John and wife 45+, 2 males 16-25, 1 female 16-
        25, and 1 female -10.
Chambers, Maxwell & Margaret
        Maxwell sold land to Samuel Brown in April 1798.
Charles, John
        Owned land on Dutch Buffalo Creek near Meeting House
        Branch in 1783.
Cheek, Elisha
        1810: 26-44, 1 female 16-25, 1 male -10, and 3
        females -10.
Cheek, Joshua
        1800: Joshua and wife 16-25. Listed next to Abigel
        Griffin, Rabeckah Ford, Stephen Self, Rabeckah
        Mitchell, George Garmon, and Henry Smith, Jr.
Chitley, Hardin

1800: Hardin and wife 26-44, 2 males -10, and 1
female -10. Listed next to Mary Russle, David
Russle, John Russell, John Martin, James Hadley, and
Cevilia Campbell.
Probably the son of Isaiah Chittin who owned land on
Sugar Creek in Mecklenburg Co. in 1780.

Christman, George & Elizabeth
George sold land to Frederick Limbach in April 1798.

Christman, Michael
Owned land on Dutch Buffalo Creek in 1768.

Christopher, James & Isabella Wilson
1800: James and Isabella 16-25, 3 males -10, and 1
female -10. Listed next to Abram Alexander, Hezekiah
Alexander, Moses Alexander, John Cannon, Arthur
Donelson, and William Gardenor.

Chives, John
1810: John 26-44, 1 female 16-25, 1 male -10, and 1
female -10.

Clark, Thomas & Esther Barringer
Married July 13, 1805 in Cabarrus Co., Paul
Barringer bondsman. This Thomas could be the one
listed in the 1800 census, but further research is
needed. If they are one and the same, this would be
a second marriage for one of and wife of them.

Clark, Thomas
1800: Thomas 45+, 1 female 26-44, 1 male 10-15, and
2 females 10-15. Listed next to John Lee, Margret
Curzine, Nicholas Curzine, Levi Curzine, George
Carlock, and Charles Tounsend.

Clause, Michael
Owned land on Dutch Buffalo Creek in 1782.

Clay, Dennis
1800: Dennis and wife 16-25, and 2 males -10. Listed
next to James Clay, Henry Cagle, William Bugg, John
Ford, Able Powell, and John Powell.

1790 - Clay, James & Mary Carithers
1800: James and Mary, and wife 26-44, 1 male 10-15,
3 males -10, 1 female -10. Listed next to Henry
Cagle, William Bugg, David Wisner, Dennis Clay, John
Ford, and Able Powell.
Mary was the daughter of James Carithers.

1790 - Clay, Isham
1800: Isham and wife 26-44, 2 females 10-15, and 3
males -10. Listed next to George Teater, John
Stuart, James Love, George Kizer, Andrew Watts, and
John Walls.
Isham owned land on Big Meadow Creek.

Cline, Daniel
1800: Daniel and wife 26-44, 3 males -10, and 2
females -10. Listed next to John Soseman, Jonathan
Hartzell, Christopher Leigh, William Goodwin,
Godfred Uery, and George Moyer.

Cline, Daniel & Lea Blackwelder
        Married Jan 19, 1795 in Cabarrus Co., Frederick
        Milnster?, bondsman.
        1800: Daniel and Lea, and wife 26-44, 2 males -10,
        and 2 females -10. Listed next to William Croner,
        Jacob Croner, Christian Goodnight, John Long, Jacob
        Lewis, and Mathias Mitchell, Sr.
        1810: Daniel and wife 26-44, 1 male 10-15, 1 female
        10-15, 1 male -10, and 4 females -10.
Cline, David
        1810: David and wife 16-25, 1 male -10, and 2
        females -10.
Cline, George
        1810: George 26-44, 1 female 45+, 3 males 16-25, 1
        female 16-25, 1 male 10-15, 2 females 10-15, 1 male
        -10, and 1 female -10.
Cline, Henry & Elizabeth Furr
        Married in Cabarrus County, bond dated Dec 9, 1800:
        bondsman, John Mitchler.
        1800: Henry and 1 female, and wife 16-25, and 1 male
        -10. Listed next to Conrod Hise, Henry Cuthezen,
        Tobias Cress, George Goodman, Jr., Peter Weaver, and
        Michael Goodman(Big).
        1810: Henry and wife 26-44, 1 male 10-15, 2 males -
        10, and 1 female -10.
1790 - Cline, Michael
        Owned land on Dutch Buffalo Creek near Lick Branch
        and Jacob Misenhimer in 1783.
1790 - Clonts, George
        1800: George and wife 26-44, 1 male 10-15, 2 females
        10-15, 2 males -10, and 2 females -10. Listed next
        to Jacob Hodgeman, Martin Uery, Henry Pless, Peter
        Limeboh, Peter Cauble, and Jacob Pines.
1790 - Clots/Clutz, Tobias
        1800: Tobius' and wife 26-44, 1 female 10-15, 2
        males -10, and 1 female -10. Listed next to Caleb
        Douss, John Ridley, George Fink, Rabeckah Heninger,
        Henry Fite, and Daniel Faggot.
Clonts/Cluttz, Leonard & Elizabeth Lefler
        1800: Leonard 16-25, 1 female 26-44, 2 males -10,
        and 2 females -10. Listed next to Michael Walker,
        John Ritchey, Peter Boiles, John Cluttz, Jacob
        Lingle, and Thomas Goodman.
Clonts/Cluttz, John
        1800: John 16-25, and wife 26-44. Listed next to
        Leonard Cluttz, Michael Walker, John Ritchey, Jacob
        Lingle, Thomas Goodman, and Jacob Slough.
Clover, Charles
        1800: Charles 26-44, 1 female 16-25, 2 males -10,
        and 1 female -10. Listed next to John Barger,
        Nicholas Rough, John Cauble, Jacob Hoover, Rinehold
        Overshine, and John Lippard.

1790 - Cochran, Benjamin
        Owned land on Clear Creek in 1783.
        1800: Benjamin 45+, 1 female 26-44, 1 male 16-25, 2
        males 10-15, 3 females -10, and 1 male -10. Listed
        next to Thomas White, Sr., Robert White, Jean White,
        William Newell, John Newell, and Joseph Bigger.
1790 - Cochran, John
Cochran/Cokran, John
        1810: John 26-44, 1 male 16-25, 1 female 16-25, 1
        male -10, and 1 female -10.
Cochran, Martha
        Martha died before Oct 1798. Her LWT was proven by
        Robert Harris of Fuda Creek.
1790 - Cochran, Paul
        Owned land on Rocky River in 1784.
1790 - Cochran, Robert (M) & Anne
        Children: Cyrus H., Elam W., Martha
        Owned land on Back Creek
        1810: Robert and wife,   and wife 45+, 1 male
        16-25, 1 female 16-25, 1 male 10-15, and   1
        female 10-15.
Cochran/Cokran, Robert
        1810: Robert 45+, 1 female 26-44, 1 male 16-25, 1
        female 10-15, 2 males -10, and 1 female -10.
Cochran, Robert
        1810: Robert and wife 26-44, 2 males 10-15, and 3
        males -10.
        Robert was born June 21, 1764, died July 28, 1837
        Buried in Spears Cemetery of Rocky River Church
Cochran, Robert Brice & Malinda Sarah Morrison
        Children: John Cunningham (Mary Davis), Elizabeth
        (Samuel A. Stewart), James Morrison (Sarah Cochran),
        A. Hope (Jane T. Harris), Margaret (Harvey
        Morrison), Martha (William Pringle Harris), Mary
        (Cicero Alexander), Robert Lee (Martha McGinnis,
        Catherine Matilda Irwin) (Robert Lee Morrison had no
        children)
        Robert B. was born 1793, died Nov 2, 1824
        Malinda was born 1792, died Jan 31, 1846
        Buried in Spears Cemetery of Rocky River Church
1790 - Cochran, William
        1810: William 45+, 1 female 26-44, 1 male 16-25, 2
        males 10-15, and 1 male -10.
        William was born 1752, died Oct 2, 1829
        Buried in Spears Cemetery of Rocky River Church
Cochrin, William & Mary McCreery
        Married Aug 20, 1795 in Mecklenburg Co., Thomas
        Cochran, bondsman.
Coleman, Daniel
        1810: Daniel and wife 26-44, 2 males 16-25, and 1
        male -10.
Coleman, Jacob

1810: Jacob and wife 26-44, 1 male 10-15, and 2
females -10.
Coleman, Jacob
1810: Jacob 26-44, 1 male 16-25, 1 female 16-25, and
2 females -10.
1790 - Coleman, Mark
1800: Mark and wife 45+, 2 males 16-25, 1 female 16-
25, 2 males 10-15, 3 males -10, and 1 female -10.
Listed next to John Chamberlin, Adam Bowers, Jr.,
Adam Bowers, Sr., Henry Furor, Frederick Frank, and
Christian Goodnight.
Owned land on Big Cold Water Creek in Jan 1806.
1790 - College/Coledg, Henry
Owned land at the head waters of Cane Branch in
1785.
1800: Henry and wife 45+, and 1 female 16-25. Listed
next to Peter Tucker, Peter Long, Valentine, Watts,
John Tucker, Thomas Ingram, and David Cowell.
1810: Henry and wife 45+.
Collins, James
1810: James and wife 26-44, 2 males 10-15, 1 female
10-15, and 3 females -10.
Collins, Lewis
1810: Lewis and wife 16-25, and 2 females -10.
Common, John
1810: John 26-44, 1 female 45+, 1 female 26-44, 1
male 10-15, 1 female 10-15, 1 male -10, and 3
females -10.
Conder, John & Margaret Mack/Mock
Married March 26, 1799 in Cabarrus Co., Mathias
Winekauf, bondsman.
1800: John 26-44, Margaret 16-25, and 1 male -10.
Listed next to James Scott, Michael Awalt, John
Neshler, Sr., Michael Young, William Wagoner, and
John Winecough.
Conder, Peter
1810: Peter and wife 26-44, 1 male -10, and 1 female
-10.
Conkrite, Hardy/Harkles
Owned land on Cold Water Creek and Three Mile Branch
in 1783.
Cook, Jacob
Owned land on Cold Water Creek in 1783.
Cook, John
Owned land on Mallard Creek in 1780.
Cook, John & Elizabeth Coleman
Married in Cabarrus Co., bond dated Nov 6, 1797,
bondsman, Jacob Murphy.
1800: John and wife 26-44, and 1 male -10. Listed
next to Henry Plott, Peter Overcash, John Yoman,
Mathias Cook, Jacob Overcash, and David Nishler.

1810: John and wife 26-44, 1 female 16-25, 1 male
10-15, 1 male -10, and 5 females -10.
Cook/Kook, Mathias
1810: Mathias 45+, 1 male 26-44, 1 female 10-15, 2
males -10, and 2 females -10.
1790 - Cook, Nicholas & Dorothea.
Owned land on Cold Water Creek before 1783.
Sold land to John Shinn in 1799
1790 - Cook, Jacob
Children: Jacob, Nicolas
Cook, Mathias
1800: Mathias and wife 45+, and 1 male 16-25. Listed
next to John Cook, Henry Plott, Peter Overcash,
Jacob Overcash, David Nishler, and Martin Slough.
Cook, Mathias & Mary Friesland
Married in Cabarrus Co., bond dated July 20, 1802,
bondsman, John Suther.
Coram, Henry
1810: Henry 26-44, 1 female 16-25, 2 males 10-15, 1
male -10, and 1 female -10.
Correll/Currel, Daniel
1810: Daniel and wife 16-25, and 2 males -10.
Correll, John
1810: John 45+, 1 female 26-44, 1 male 16-25, 2
females 16-25, and 1 male 10-15.
Correll, William
1800: William and wife 26-44, 3 males -10, and 1
female -10. Listed next to Richard Marlin, Thomas
Caruthers, Moses Rogers, John Weddington, Vachel
Holbrooks, and John Overcast.
Corzine, Abel & Polly Klutz
1810: Abel 26-44, 1 male 16-25, 1 male 10-15, 2
females 10-15, 1 male -10, and 1 female -10.
Married Feb 14, 1814 in Cabarrus Co., John Corzine,
bondsman.
Abel bought land on Coddle Creek from John Shinn in
July 1806, and also from Duncan Morrison on the
north side of Coddle Creek.
Corzine, George & Mary Ann Russell
Children: James C. (Holly L. Hudson)
Mary Ann was the daughter of David and Elizabeth
Morrison Russell.
Buried in Coldwater Baptist Church Cemetery along
with other members of the Corzine family.
1790 - Corzine, George, Jr
1800: George and wife 26-44, 1 male 16-25, 1 female
16-25, 1 male 10-15, 1 female 10-15, 1 male -10, and
3 females -10. Listed next to William Atkinson, John
McGraw, Thomas Voiles, John Wilson, Charles Bane,
and George Overcash.
1810: George and wife 26-44, 2 males 16-25, 2
females 16-25, 1 female 10-15, and 1 female -10.

1790 - Corzine, George, Sr., & Margaret
        Children: George, Rachel, Abigail.
        Son of John Corzine and Leah Shinn
        Owned land on Cold Water Creek and Buffalo Creek in
        1783.
        Brother of Nicholas Corzine.
        George died before Oct 1798, leaving George as an
        orphan. George Carlock appointed guardian.
        1800: Margret 45+, 1 male 16-25, and 1 female 10-15.
        Listed next to Nicholas Curzine, William McGraw,
        James McGraw, John Lee, Thomas Clark, and Levi
        Curzine.
Corzine, John & Leah Shinn
        Children: George, Nicholas
        John is believed to have died before 1790.
        Leah was born in 1740, died in 1788??
Corzine, John & Mary
        Children: George, Samuel, William, and 7 unnamed
        daughters.
        Owned land on Buffalo Creek.
        John was bondsman, along with Henry Horrah, for
        Robert Russell and Mary Willson who were married in
        Rowan Co. on March 17, 1762. He was also bondsman
        for Eleanor Russell and Robert Black in Rowan on
        March 5, 1762.
        John died in 1776.
Corzine, John & Polly Gibson
        Married May 3, 1810 in Cabarrus Co., Benjamin
        Robbins, bondsman.
        1810: John 16-25, and wife 26-44.
Corzine, John & Rachel Corzine
        Married May 9, 1801 in Cabarrus Co., John Shinn,
        bondsman.
        1810: John and wife 16-25, and 1 female -10.
1790 - Corzine, Levil(Levi)
        1800: Levi 26-44, 1 female 45+, 1 male 16-25, 1
        female 16-25, 2 males 10-15, and 4 females -10.
        Listed next to Thomas Clark, John Lee, Margret
        Curzine, George Carlock, Charles Tounsend, and Even
        Jones.
        Owned land on Little Coldwater Creek.
Corzine, Levi & Prudence Shinn
        Children: Reuben
        Married April 20, 1801 in Cabarrus Co., James
        Purviance, bondsman.
1790 - Corzine, Nicholas
        1800: Nicholas and wife 26-44, 2 females 16-25, 2
        males 10-15, 1 female 10-15, 1 male -10, and 2
        females -10. Listed next to William McGraw, James
        McGraw, John Plott, Margret Curzine, John Lee, and
        Thomas Clark.
        Son of Nicholas Corzine.

Corzine, Nicholas
        Children: Levi, Nicholas
        Brother: George
        Nicholas died in 1769.
Corzine, Noah & Jenny Russell
        Married Sept 21, 1810 in Cabarrus Co., Robert
        Russell bondsman.
        Children: John R. (Betsy Madans or McLain),
        Elizabeth (Solomon Snider), Moses H., David M. (Mary
        A. Hudson), Mary Ann (James W. Collier), Nelly
        Clementine (Henry Winecoff), George W. (Claressa
        Emeline Johnston), James O. (I.A. Watho/Walter?)
        Buried in Coldwater Baptist Church Cemetery.
1790 - Corzine, Samuel
        1800: Samuel and wife 26-44, 1 male 10-15, 1 female
        10-15, 1 male -10, and 3 females -10. Listed next to
        Joshua Hadley, Robert Purviance, John Shaver, Martha
        Ferguson, Alexander Ferguson, and Samuel Ferguson.
        1810: Samuel 45+, 1 female 45+, 2 females 10-15, 1
        male -10, and 3 females -10.
Cotton, Elijah
        1810: Elijah 26-44, 1 male 16-25, 1 female 16-25,
        and 1 male -10.
        Elijah sold to Richard Brandon on Bach Branch in Jan
        1814.
Cowell/Coul, David
        1800: David and wife 26-44, and 2 females -10.
        Listed next to Thomas Ingram, John Tucker, Henry
        Coledg, Abraham Leftenburg, Joseph Howell, Jr., and
        Joseph Howell, Sr.
Cowden, Robert
        Owned land between Rocky River and Coddle Creek in
        1778.
Cox, John
        1800: John and wife 26-44, 2 females 10-15, 2 males
        -10, and 1 female -10. Listed next to John Culp,
        John Barringer, George Barringer, William Cox, Moses
        Cox, and George Culp.
        1810: John 45+, 1 female 45+, 2 males 10-15, and 2
        females 10-15.
Cox, Moses
        1800: Moses and wife 45+. Listed next to William
        Cox, John Cox, John Culp, George Culp, Peter Keply,
        and Peter Keply, Jr.
Cox, William
        1800: William and wife 26-44, 1 female 10-15, 3
        males -10, and 3 females -10. Listed next to John
        Cox, John Culp, John Barringer, Moses Cox, George
        Culp, and Peter Keply.
1790 - Creaton/Craton, James & Isabel
        Children: Mary (Moses or Oliver Wiley)
        1790: James and wife.

1800: James and wife 45+.
1810 James 45+
Sold land on Rocky River to Robert W. Smith in Oct
1805.
Cratton, William
Sold land on Meadow Creek to John Reed in Oct 1805.
1810: William and wife 45+, 1 female 26-44, 1 male
16-25, 1 female 16-25, and 1 male -10.
Crawford, David
1800: David and wife 45+, 1 male 26-44, and 2
females 16-25. Listed next to Joseph Young, Andrew
Alexander, Nelson Gray, William Wallace, Ludwick
Wallace, and Josiah Wallace.
1810: David and wife 45+, and 2 males 16-25.
Crawford, James
1810: James and wife 26-44, 1 male 10-15, 3 males -
10, and 3 females -10.
Crawford, Joseph
Appointed deputy register of county in Oct 1797.
Cress/Kress, Adam
Owned land on Coddle Creek and Wolf Meadow Branch of
Coddle Creek in 1784.
Cress, Henry
1800: Henry and wife 26-44, 1 male 16-25, 2 males -
10, and 2 females -10. Listed next to Jacob Cassock,
David Speck, George Speake, John Cauddle, Peter
Boager, and Jacob Boager.
Cress, Jacob
1810: Jacob 45+, 1 male 16-25, 1 female 10-15, and 1
male -10.
Cress, John
John was accused of a shooting disturbance in the
courthouse in the April term of court in 1812, along
with John Weddington and Thomas Benson.
Cress, Nicholas
Owned land near Adams Creek and Dutch Buffalo Creek
1790 - Creps/Cress, Philip
1810: Philip 45+, 1 female 26-44, 1 male 16-25, 2
females 16-25, 1 male 10-15, 1 female 10-15, and 1
female -10.
1790 - Creps/Cress, Tobias
1800: Tobias 26-44, 1 male 26-44, 1 female 26-44, 1
female 16-25, 1 male 10-15, 2 females, 2 males -10,
and 3 females -10. Listed next to Charles Seffrid,
Asemus Peninger, George File, Henry Cuthezen, Conrod
Hise, and Henry Cline.
Crimble, Murey
Patent dated March 3, 1745 for land in what was
known as the Great Tract, or Welsh Tract on the
south side of Rocky River near the Rocky River
community.
Crockett, Andrew

Andrew owned land on Irish Buffalo Creek.
Crommel, John, Sr.
          John sold land on Reedy Creek in April 1813.
Croner, Christian
          1810: Christian and wife 26-44, 4 males -10, and 1
          female -10.
Croner, Jacob
          Owned land on Three Mile Branch of Cold Water Creek
          near Umberford branch in 1778.
          1800: Jacob and wife 45+, 3 males 16-25, and 2
          females 16-25. Listed next to Christian Goodnight,
          Frederick Frank, Henry Furor, William Croner, Danil
          Cline, and John Long.
          1810: Jacob and wife 45+, 2 males 26-44, 1 female
          16-25, 2 males -10, and 1 female -10.
Croner, William
          1800: William and wife 26-44, 1 male -10, and 1
          female -10. Listed next to Jacob Croner, Christian
          Goodnight, Frederick Frank, Daniel Cline, John Long,
          and Jacob Lewis.
Crowell, John & Isbel McWilliams
          Married Feb 2, 1797 in Mecklenburg Co., Joseph
          McQu??, Simon Crowell, bondsmen.
          Located in Dollen militia district in Oct 1801.
Crowell, Peter & Catherine
          Children: George, Deiterich, Simon, William
          (Wilhelm)
          Peter died about 1763. He was born in Germany and
          arrived in PA on the ship Loyal Judith, Nov 25,
          1740.
          Peter owned land on the east side of Buffalo Creek,
          bought from Conrad Haraha, part of a tract formerly
          granted to Paul Barringer in 1762.
1790 - Croul/Croll, Peter
          Peter died before July 1805 in Cabarrus County.
          Son of Samuel & Margaret Sell Crowell.
Crumwell, Andrew
          1810: Andrew 26-44, 1 female 16-25, and 1 male -10.
Crumwell, James
          1800: James and wife 26-44, 1 female 10-15, 2 males
          -10, and 2 females -10, Listed next to John
          Crumwell, James Burns, Daniel Bean, John Cochrin,
          William Cochrin, and Robert Cochrin, Jr.
Crumwell, John & Mary Dorton
          Married in Cabarrus Co., bond dated April 2, 1802,
          bondsman, Jonathan Dorton.
          1800: John over 45, and 2 males -10. Listed next to
          James Burns, Daniel Bean, Alexander Allin, James
          Crumwell, John Cochrin, and William Cochrin. A
          branch of Reedy Creek was known as John Cromwell
          branch as early as 1782.

1810: John and wife 45+, 1 male 26-44, 1 female 26-44, 1 female 16-25, and 1 male -10.
Crumwell, John, Sr.
    1800: John and wife 45+, 2 females 16-25, and 1 male 10-15. Listed next to William McArnulty, Noah Sandiford, Robert McEchron, John Black, Jr., and Samuel McCurdy.
Cromwell, John, Jr.
    1800: John 16-25, 1 female 26-44, and 1 male -10. Listed next ot James Bradshaw, Jr., Francis Newell, Hannah McFaddon, Archibald McCurdey, Charles McKinley, and Dorothy Scott.
Cruse, Adam
    1800: Adam and wife 26-44, 1 male 10-15, 2 females 10-15, 3 males -10, and 1 female -10. Listed next to George Goodman, Sr., George Fisher, Jacob Fisher, Andrew Cruse, John Misenheimer, and William Mensinger.
    1810: Adam 45+, 1 female 26-44, 2 males 16-25, 1 female 16-25, 1 male 10-15, and 3 males -10.
Cruse, Andrew
    1800: Andrew and wife 26-44, 1 male 10-15, 3 males -10, and 1 female -10. Listed next to Adam Cruse, George Goodman, Sr., George Fisher, John Misenheimer, William Mensinger, and Henry Pence.
    1810: Andrew 26-44, 2 males 16-25, 1 female 16-25, 2 males 10-15, 1 female 10-15, 3 males -10, and 1 female -10.
Cruse, Andrew
    1810: Andrew 45+, 1 male 16-25, 1 female 16-25, 2 males 10-15, 1 female 10-15, 3 males -10, and 1 female -10.
Cruse, Henry
    1810: Henry and wife 26-44, 1 male 10-15, 1 female 10-15, 3 males -10, and 3 females -10.
Cruse, Tobias
    1810: Tobias' and wife 45+, 1 male 16-25, 2 females 16-25, 1 male 10-15, 1 female 10-15, 2 males -10, and 2 females -10.
Culp, Elisabeth
    1810: Elisabeth household consisted of just herself 45+.
Culp, George
    1800: George 26-44, 1 female 16-25, 2 males -10, and 1 female -10. Listed next to Moses Cox, William Cox, John Cox, Peter Keply, Peter Keply, Jr., and Kelin Keply.
    1810: George and wife 25-44, 2 males 10-15, 2 males -10, and 3 females -10.
Culp, George
    1810: George and wife 26-44, 1 male 10-15, 1 female 10-15, 2 males -10, and 3 females -10.

Culp, Henry
        1810: Henry 26-44, 1 female 16-25, 1 male -10, and 1
        female -10.
Culp, John
        1800: John and wife 45+, 2 males 16-25, and 1 female
        10-15. Listed next to John Barringer, George
        Barringer, Mathias Barringer, John Cox, William Cox,
        and Moses Cox.
        John died before July 1809.
Culp, Peter
        1810: Peter and wife 16-25, and 2 females -10.
        Peter was the executor of John Kulp estate along
        with John Berringer, Sr.
Culp, Peter
        1810: Peter 26-44, 1 female 16-25, and 2 females -
        10.
Culpepper, John
        1800: John and wife 26-44, 1 male 10-15, 2 males -
        10, and 2 females -10. Listed next to Joseph Shinn,
        Henry Brines, James Bridges, John Shaver, Robert
        Purviance, and Joshua Hadley.
Curry, Aaron
        1800: Aaron and wife 26-44, 1 male -10, and 3
        females -10. Listed next to Sarah Neely, Isaac
        McClennon, Joseph McNeely, Valentine Faggot, John
        Barringer, and Solomon Davis.
Curry, Robert & Sarah Taylor
        Married in Mecklenburg Co., March 6, 1790, Robert
        Sloane, bondsman.
        1800: Robert over 45, Sarah 26-44, 1 female 16-25, 2
        male 10-15, 3 males -10, and 1 female -10. Listed
        next to Isaac McClellan/McLennon, Mark Evans, James
        Snell, George Harris, Robert Harris, Jr., and Thomas
        Davis.
        1810: Robert age is not shown. His household
        consisted of 1 female 26-44, 2 males 16-25, and 1
        male 10-15.
Cuthbertson/Cuthezen, Henry
        1800: Henry and wife 26-44, 1 male -10, and 1 female
        -10. Listed next to Tobias Cress, Charles Seffrid,
        Asemus Peninger, Conrod Hise, Henry Cline, and
        George Goodman, Jr.
Dacton, Charles
        Owned land on Rocky River near the head of the
        Meadow Spring in 1782.
Daniels, Susannah
        Owned land on Muddy Creek in 1782.
1790 - Davidson, John, Majr
        Owned land on Rocky River in 1784.
Davis, Aaron
        1810: Aaron 26-44, 1 female 16-25, and 2 males -10.
Davis, Andrew

1800: Andrew age 26-44, presumably his wife at over
45, 2 males 16-25, 3 females 16-25, and 2 females
10-15. Listed next to Robert and William Bain, John
Davis, Sarah Shelby, and David Taylor.
1810: Andrew and wife 45+, 3 females 16-25, 1 male -
10, and 1 female -10.

Davis, Andrew, Jr.
1810: Andrew and wife 26-44, 1 male -10, and 1
female -10.

Davis, Andrew, Jr & Ann Carrothers
1800: Andrew and Ann 26-44, 1 female 16-25, 3 males
-10, and 1 female -10. Listed next to Robert
Cochrin, Jr., William Cochrin, John Cochrin, Samuel
Harris, Robert Harris, and Alexander Hughey.

Davis, Andrew
1810: Andrew 26-44, 1 female 16-25, 3 males -10, and
3 females -10.

Davis, Caleb
1810: Caleb and wife 26-44, 1 male 16-25, 2 females
16-25, 1 male 10-15, 1 female 10-15, 1 male -10, and
4 females -10.

Davis, David
Owned land on Rocky River in 1781.

1790 - Davis/Davies, George
Owned land on Rocky River and Coddle Creek in 1784.
1800: George and wife 45+, 3 males 16-25, 1 female
16-25, 1 female 10-15. Listed next to Agness
Listenbay, William W. Spears, David White, Robert
Davis, Alexander Scott, and Joseph Welsh.
1810: George and wife 45+, and 1 male 26-44.

David, George
1810: George and wife 26-44, and 3 females -10.

1790 - Davis, James & Jean
Owned land on the south side of Rocky River in 1782.
Possibly the son of Thomas and Amelia Davis.

Davis, John
1800: John and wife 26-44, 1 male -10, and 3 females
-10. Listed next to Robert and William Bain, Andrew
Davis, and Sarah Shelby.

Davis, John
1810: John 26-44, his wife 45 +, 1 male -10, and 3
females -10.

Davis, Jonathan
1810: Jonathan and wife 26-44, 1 male -10, and 2
females -10.

Davis, Moses
1810: Moses 26-44, and 1 female 16-25.

1790 - Davis/Davies, Robert
Owned land on Rocky River in 1782.
1800: Robert over 45, 4 males 16-25, 3 females 16-
25, 2 males 10-15 and 1 female 10-15. Listed next to

George Davis, Agness Listenbay, William W. Spears,
Alexander Scott, Joseph Welsh, Edward Neil.
Davis, Robert
    1810: Robert 16-25, and 2 females 16-25.
Davis, Robert
    1810: Robert 16-25, and 2 females 16-25.
Davis, Samuel
    Samuel sold land in April 1813 to Andrew Davis on
    Reedy Creek, formerly property of Thomas Davis.
Davis, Solomon
    1800: Solomon and wife 26-44, 1 female 16-25, 2
    males -10, and 3 females -10. Listed next to John
    Barringer, Valentine Faggot, Aaron Curry, Jacob
    Bost, Paul Barringer, and Martin Harkey.
1790 - Davis, Thomas & Amelia
    Children: Elam Harvey (Malinda E. Gingles), James N.
    Thomas owned land on Reedy Creek in 1777.
    1800: Thomas and wife 45+, 1 male 26-44, 2 males 16-
    25, 2 females 16-25, 1 female 10-15, and 1 male -10.
    Listed next to Robert Harris, Jr., George Harris,
    Robert Curry, James Stafford, Matthew Campbell, and
    Griffin Morris.
    1810: Thomas and wife 45+, 1 male 26-44, 2 males 16-
    25, and 2 females 16-25.
    Thomas was born 1777, died Aug 7, 1819
    Amelia remarried to John Gingles in 1828
    Amelia was born Jan 3, 1782, died July 2, 1853
    Amelia and John Gingles are buried in Spears
    Cemetery with and wife of their first spouses.
Davis, Thomas
    1810: Thomas 26-44, 1 female 16-25, and 2 males -10.
Dean, Jacob
    Owned land on Hamby Branch, a branch of Rocky River
    in 1784.
Deaton, Thomas
    1810: Thomas 45+, 1 female 26-44, and 4 males -10.
Delph, Peter & Eve
    Owned land on Lick Branch of Dutch Buffalo Creek in
    1777.
Dennis, Eli P. & Sarah Shinn
    Married in Cabarrus Co., bond dated April 19, 1810:
    bondsman, Thomas D. Murray.
    1810: Eli and Sarah 26-44.
    Eli and Sarah moved to Pope Co., AR.
Dewalt/Dewatt, Jacob
    1800: Jacob and wife 45+, 1 male 16-25, 1 male 10-
    15, 1 female 10-15, 2 males -10, and 3 females -10.
    Listed next to William Sefred, Michael Fesperman,
    Henry Fesperman, Henry Gatchey, Michael Gatchey, and
    Marin Penninger.

1810: Jacob 45+, 1 female 26-44, 2 males 16-25, 1
male 10-15, 1 female 10-15, 1 male -10, and 1 female
-10.
Dewault, Michael
1810: Michael and wife 26-44, and 3 females -10.
Deweast, Josiah
1800: Josiah and wife 26-44, 5 females 10-15, and 3
females -10. Listed next to Robert Miller, Peter
Miller, James Gailor, Robert Stanford, Hugh Heare,
and James Caragin, Sr.
Dickey, James
Owned land on Coddle Creek in 1778
1790 - Dickson, James
Owned land on Clear Creek in 1778.
Dickson, James
1810: James and wife 16-25, and 1 female -10.
Dickson, James M.
1810: James 26-44, 1 female 16-25, and 1 female -10.
Dickson, Robert
1810: Robert and wife 26-44, 2 males -10, and 1
female -10.
Dickson, Widow
1810: the widow 45+, 1 male 16-25, 2 females 16-25,
1 female 10-15, and 1 male -10.
Dikens, James
1810 James 45+, 1 male 26-44, 5 males 16-25, and 1
female 16-25.
Dixon, Hugh
Son of Elizabeth Dixon
Owned land on Reedy Branch of Rocky River.
Dobbs, Arthur & Justina
Owned land between Dutch Buffalo Creek and Little
Coldwater Creek in 1764.
Dobson, Thomas
1800: Thomas and wife 26-44, 4 males -10, and 1
female -10. Listed next to Daniel Doherty, Martin
Shive, John Simeoner, John Smith, John Tagert, and
Joseph Ross.
1810: Thomas and wife 26-44, 1 female 10-15, and 4
females -10.
Doherty, Daniel
1800: Daniel and wife 45+, 1 male 26-44, 1 female
26-44, and 5 females -10. Listed next to Martin
Shive, John Simeoner, Francis Ross, Thomas Dobson,
John Smith, and John Tagert.
1810: Daniel and wife 45+, 1 male 45+, 1 female 26-
44, 1 male 16-25, 2 females 16-25, 1 male 10-15, 1
female 10-15, 1 male -10, and 3 females -10.
1790 - Daugherty/Doherty, David (& Rebecca ?)
Owned land on Rocky River in 1777.
Rebecca Daherty was a witness to Robert Morrow will.
Daugherty/Doherty, James

1810: James and wife 45+, 2 males 16-25, 1 male 10-
15, 2 females 10-15, 1 male -10, and 1 female -10.
Doland/Doolin, Henry
1800: Henry and wife 45+, and 2 males 16-25. Listed
next to John Kepple, Kelin Keply, Peter Keply, Jr.,
Timothy Doland, Samuel Graver, and Ephraim D.
Harris.
1810: Henry and another male, and wife 45+, 1 female
45+, 1 female 26-44, 2 males -10, and 1 female -10.
Doland, Timothy
1800: Timothy and wife 16-25. Listed next to Henry
Doland, John Kepple, Kelin Keply, Samuel Graver,
Ephraim D. Harris, and William Louder.
Donaldson, Arthur & Jane Frazer
1800: Arthur 26-44, 1 female 45+, 1 female 26-44,
and 2 females -10. Listed next to John Cannon, James
Christopher, Abram Alexander, William Gardenor,
Robert Hope, and William Harris, the tailor.
Owned land near Coddle Creek on Rocky River in 1784.
1810: Arthur and wife 26-44, 2 males -10-15, 1 male
-10, and 2 males -10.
1790 - Donaldson, John
Owned land on Coddle Creek
Donnell, John
Owned land on Coddle Creek before 1785.
Donnell, Thomas
Owned land on Coddle Creek in 1785.
Dorlan, Charles
1810: Charles 45+, 2 males 16-25, and 1 female 16-
25.
Dorton, Charles
1800: Charles 45+, 1 female 26-44, 1 male 16-25, 2
males 10-15, 1 male -10, and 1 female -10. Listed
next to Samuel Blair, Thomas Black, John Black, Jr.,
Samuel Weddington, Jean White, and Robert White.
Dorton, David
David was born 1777, died Feb 9, 1847
Buried in Spears Cemetery of Rocky River Church.
Douglas, George
1810: George 26-44, 1 female 16-25, and 2 males -10.
Douglass, William
1800: William 26-44, 1 female 16-25, and 2 males -
10. Listed next to Samuel Keilough, William
Keilough, Oliver Harris, James McCaleb, Samuel
Martin, and Widow Neil.
Douss, Caleb
1800: Caleb 26-44, 1 male 10-15, 1 female 10-15, 1
male -10, and 2 females -10. Listed next to John
Ridley, George Fink, John Furor, Jr., Tobius Clutz,
Rabeckah Heninger, and Henry Fite.
Dresser, Manasah

1800: Manasah and wife 26-44, 2 males 10-15, and 2
females -10. Listed next to Jacob Krider, Jr.,
Michael Overcash, Daniel Krider, Jacob Krider, Sr.,
Jacob Murph, and Paul Walton.

Dry, Andrew & ? Teem (daughter of Jacob Teem)
    1800: Andrew 26-44, 1 female 26-44, 1 male 10-15, 2
    females 10-15, and 2 males -10. Listed next to Jacob
    Dry, Owen Dry, Alias Bostain, Martin Everit, William
    Folk, and Jacob Harky.
    1810: Andrew and wife 45+, 1 female 26-44, 2 males
    16-25, 2 males 10-15, and 2 females -10.

Dry, Charles & Christine
    Charles' LWT was proven in Oct 1797.

Dry, Christian
    1800: Christian 16-25, 1 female 16-25, and 1 female
    45+. Listed next to Hannah Voiles, Robert Lee,
    Roland Voiles, Isaac Loftin, John Plott, and James
    McGraw.

Dry, Daniel
    Daniel bought land on Stoney Branch of Little Bear
    Creek from Thomas Lowder of Montgomery County in
    July 1813.

Dry, George & Anna Phifer
    Anna was the daughter of Jacob Phifer.

Dry, Jacob & Catherine Hegler
    Married in Cabarrus Co., bond dated Aug 8, 1799,
    bondsman, Jonathan Hertze.
    1800: Jacob 26-44, 1 female 16-25, 1 female 10-15,
    and 1 female -10. Listed next to Owen Dry, Alias
    Bostain, Jacob Blackwelder, Andrew Dry, Martin
    Everit, and William Folk.
    1810: Jacob 26-44, 1 female 45+, 1 male -10, and 5
    females -10.

Dry, John
    1810: John and wife 16-25, 1 male -10, and 1 female
    -10.

Dry, Martin
    1800: Martin and wife 26-44, 3 males 10-15, 1 female
    10-15, 1 male -10, and 3 females -10. Listed next to
    Philip Dry, Elias Bost, Jacob Barnhart, Jacob
    Effrit, Paul Furor, and John Furor.
    1810: Martin and wife 45+, 2 males 16-25, 1 male 10-
    15, and 2 females 10-15.

Dry, Owen
    1800: Owen and wife 26-44, 1 male 10-15, 1 female
    10-15, and 1 male -10. Listed next to Alias Bostain,
    Jacob Blackwelder, Mary Bostain, Jacob Dry, Andrew
    Dry, and Martin Everit.
    1810. Owen and wife 45+, and 1 male 10-15.

Dry, Peter
    1810: Peter and wife 16-25.

Dry, Philip

1800: Philip 16-25, 1 female 26-44, 2 females 10-15,
2 males -10, and 1 female -10. Listed next to Elias
Bost, Jacob Barnhart, John Barnhart, Martin Dry,
Jacob Effrit, and Paul Furor.
1810: Phillip 16-25, 1 female 26-44, 2 females 16-
25, 2 males 10-15, 1 female 10-15, 1 male -10, and 1
female -10.
Philip was a wagon maker.
Duccant, Isaih
1810: Isaih 45+, 1 temale 26-44, 2 females 16-25, 2
females 10-15, 2 males -10, and 3 females -10.
Duke, John
1800: John and wife 45+, 2 males 16-25, 2 females
16-25, and 1 female 10-15. Listed next to Michael
Goodman(Big), Peter Weaver, George Goodman, Jr.,
Jacob Rimer, Tobias Stirewalt, and William Ryal.
Duke, Thomas
1810: Thomas 45+, 1 female 45+, 1 male 16-25, 2
females 16-25, and 1 female 10-15.
Dulen/Doolin, Rice
Bill of sale to Gideon Alemon for 1 Negro boy named
John, age 9 or 10, in Cabarrus County court in 1805.
Owned land on Cold Water Creek. Sheriff, Joseph
Young sold some of this land to Martin Phifer in Jan
1806.
1810: Rice 26-44, 1 female 45+, 1 female 26-44, 1
male 16-25, 2 males -10, and 1 female -10.
Dupley, Paul
Owned land on Dutch Buffalo Creek in 1782.
Earnhart/Ernhart, Peter
1810: Peter 16-25, 1 female 16-25, and 2 males 10-
15.
Eagle, John
Owned land on Hamby Branch, a branch of Rocky River
in 1784.
Edleman, John
1800: John and wife 26-44, 2 males -10, and 2
females -10. Listed next to Jacob Pines, Peter
Cauble, Peter Limeboh, John File, Jacob Fisher, and
George Fisher.
1810: John and wife 26-44, 2 males 16-25, 1 female
16-25, 1 male 10-15, 1 female 10-15, 2 males -10,
and 1 female -10.
Edmonton/Edmiston, John
1800: John and wife 26-44, 2 females 16-25, 1 male
10-15, 1 female 10-15, 2 males -10, and 1 female -
10. Listed next to Widow McClain, Robert Erwin,
Charles Harris (doctor), Samuel Meek, Alexander
Query, and John Scoles.
Edmiston, Samuel
1810: Samuel 26-44, 1 female 45+, 1 male 16-25, 3
females 16-25, 1 male 10-15, and 1 female 10-15.

Effrit/Seffrit, Jacob
        1800: Jacob 16-25, 1 female 16-25, 1 male 10-15, 2
        males -10, and 1 female -10. Listed next to Martin
        Dry, Philip Dry, Elias Bost, Paul Furor, John Furor,
        and Peter Hagler, Jr.
Effrit/Seffrit, Martin & Ann
        1810: Martin 45+, 1 female 26-44, 1 male 16-25, 1
        female 16-25, 1 female 10-15, and 1 female -10.
        Martin gave beloved friend, Henry Linker, Sr., land
        on Adam Creek for natural love and affection in
        April 1812.
Elliott, Andrew
        Owned land on Back Creek
England, Daniel & Martha
        Owned land on Coddle Creek in 1763.
Erwin, Elenor
        1800: Elenor household consisted of just herself 26-
        44. Listed next to John Robinson, William Gray,
        James Alexander, Ezekiel Wright, Elizabeth Posey,
        and William Wiley.
1790 - Erwin, Robert & Hannah
        Children: Samuel, James (Margaret Phifer?), William,
        John (Jane Harris?), Hannah?(Charles Parks)
        1800: Robert 45+, Hannah 26-44, 2 males 10-15, 1
        female 10-15, and 2 males -10. Listed next to
        Charles Harris (doctor), William Harris (tailor),
        Robert Hope, Widow McClain, John Edmonton, and
        Samuel Meek.
        Owned land on the north side of Long River in 1777.
        Robert died before April 1806. John Russel and John
        Masters appointed administrators of Robert estate,
        Charles Park was security.
Irwin/Erwin, Samuel L. & Rachel Huie
        Married Sept 22, 1802 in Cabarrus Co., Charles
        Parks, bondsman.
        Bought land on Coddle Creek in Oct 1805 from Azariah
        Alexander. Bought land on Coddle Creek from Josiah
        Alexander in July 1806.
Erwin, Samuel & Matilda Purvines
        Married March 2, 1808 in Cabarrus Co., David S.
        Purvince, bondsman.
        Samuel and Matilda are shown in the 1860 Cabarrus
        Co. census as 73 and 71 years old.
        Samuel was born in 1788, and Matilda was born in
        1790.
Erwin, Thomas
        1800: Thomas and wife 26-44, 2 males 10-15, and 3
        females 10-15. Listed next to Widow Caragin, John
        Coruthers, Robert Biggers, Mitchel Flemmon, David
        Farr, and Archibald Gilmore.
Erwin, William & Peggy Purvines

Married Sept 28, 1811 in Cabarrus Co., James Hudson,
bondsman.
Owned land on Coddle Creek
Evans, Mark
    1800: Mark and wife 26-44, and 2 females -10. Listed
    next to James Snell, Francis Greer, William Andrew,
    Isaac McLennon, Robert Curry, and George Harris.
Everit, Martin
    1800: Martin and wife 45+, 1 male 26-44, and 1
    female 10-15. Listed next to Andrew Dry, Jacob Dry,
    Owen Dry, William Folk, Jacob Harky, and John House.
    1810: Martin and wife 45+.
1790 - Ewart, Joseph & Agness
    Owned land on Rocky River in 1780.
    Son of Robert
Ewart, Robert
    Children: Joseph
    Owned land on Rocky River in 1764.
    Died before 1780.
Faggert, Daniel
    1800: Daniel 16-25, 1 male 16-25, 2 females 16-25,
    and 1 female -10. Listed next to Henry Fite,
    Rabeckah Heninger, Tobius Clutz, Harmon Moyer,
    Daniel Bost, and Dorothy Petry.
    Given land on Adams Creek from his father Jacob
    Faggert, Sr in 1805.
    1810: Daniel 16-25, 1 female 26-44, 1 female 10-15,
    3 males -10, and 2 females -10.
Faggert, Daniel
    1810: Daniel 26-44, 1 male 16-25, 1 female 16-25, 3
    males -10, and 2 females -10.
Fagot, George
    1810: George 45+, 1 male 16-25, 1 female 16-25, 1
    male -10, 1 female -10.
Fagot, George
    1810: George 26-44, 1 female 16-25, 1 male -10, and
    1 female -10.
1790 - Faggett, Jacob & Margaret Bost
    Children: Daniel
    Owned land on Coldwater Creek and Adams Creek, near
    Hamby Run in 1784.
    1800: Jacob 45+, 1 female 16-25, and 2 males -10.
    Listed next to Lewis Fisher, Peter Hagler, Jr., John
    Furor, Melchor Fogleman, John Hagler, Sr., and
    Leonard Hartsell.
    1810: Jacob and wife 26-44, 2 males 10-15, 1 female
    10-15, and 3 females -10.
Faggot, Valentine
    1800: Valentine and wife 26-44, 1 female 10-15, and
    3 females -10. Listed next to Aaron Curry, Sarah
    Neely, Isaac McClennon, John Barringer, Solomon
    Davis, and Jacob Bost.

1810: Valentine 45+, 1 female 26-44, 2 females 19-
15, 1 male -10, and 2 females -10.

Farer, Henry
1810: Henry 26-44, 1 female 45+, 2 males -10, and 1
female -10.

Farr, David D.
Owned land on Coddle Creek in 1805.
1800: David and wife 26-44, 1 male -10, and 2
females -10. Listed next to Mitchel Flemmon, Thomas
Erwin, Widow Caragin, Archibald Gilmore, William
Hunt, and John Houston.

Farr, Ephraim
Owned land on Coddle Creek and Rocky River in 1775.
Died in 1785.

Farr, Ephraim & Easter Latta
Married July 14, 1801 in Mecklenburg Co., Joseph
Latta, bondsman.
Owned land on Coddle Creek

Farr, Henry
Owned land on Cold Water Creek in 1784.

Farr, Henry
Bought land on Clear Creek in 1805 from Jacob Self.
Henry bought land on Caldwell Creek and Muddy Creek
in July 1806.
1810: Henry and wife 26-44, 5 males 10-15, 2 males -
10, and 2 females -10.

Farr, John & Margaret
Owned land on Coddle Creek near Afton Run in 1775.
John died before 1790.

1790 - Farr, John & Elizabeth Woodside
Owned land on English Buffalo Creek.

Farr/Pharr, John & Catharine McEachern/McCoheron
Married in Cabarrus County, bond dated Nov 4, 1799,
bondsman, Hector McCachern
Far, Robert
1810: Robert 26-44, 1 female 45+, 2 males 16-25, 2
females 16-25, and 1 female -10.

Farr, Samuel
1810: Samuel and wife 26-44, 2 males -10, and 2
females -10.

1790 - Farr, Walter
Children: John, Samuel, Robert. Will proven April
1801
Walter was born in 1740, died 1799
Buried in Old Rocky River Cemetery

Farris, Walter
Owned land on Coddle Creek in 1782.

1790 - Ferguson, Alexander & Mary
Children: Alexander, William, Mary?, Robert, Samuel?
Owned land on Cold Water Creek and Buffalo Creek in
1775.
Alexander died 1802.

Mary died before 1805.
Possibly the son of John Ferguson.
1800: Alexander and Mary, and wife 45+, 1 male 16-
25, 2 males 10-15, and 1 female 10-15. Listed next
to Martha Ferguson, Samuel Corzine, Joshua Hadley,
Samuel Ferguson, Samuel Hughey, and James Hughey.
Ferguson, Alexander & Eliza Harris
    Married in Cabarrus Co., bond dated June 30, 1808,
    John H. Brandon, bondsman.
    1810: Alexander 26-44, his wife, 16-25, and 1 male -
    10.
Ferguson, Robert & Hannah Hudson, Elizabeth Corzine
    Robert and Hannah were married in Cabarrus Co., bond
    dated Sept 17, 1800: bondsman, Samuel L. Irwin.
    Robert and Elizabeth were married in Cabarrus Co.,
    bond dated Aug 12, 1802, bondman, John Davis.
    Robert was bondsman for Samuel Ferguson and Agnes
    Berry in 1798.
    1810: Robert 26-44, his wife 16-25, 3 males -10, and
    1 female -10.
    He is listed in the 1850 Cabarrus Co. census as 71
    years old.
Ferguson, Samuel & Agnes Berry
    Married in Cabarrus Co., bond dated June 20, 1798,
    bondsman, Robert Ferguson.
    1800: Samuel 16-25, 1 male 16-25, 1 female 16-25,
    and 1 male -10. Listed next to Alexander Ferguson,
    Martha Ferguson, Samuel Corzine, Samuel Hughey,
    James Hughey, and Mathias Phifer.
1790 - Ferguson, Widow (Martha)
    1800: Martha , 45+, and 1 female 16-25. Listed next
    to Samuel Corzine, Joshua Hadley, Robert Purviance,
    Alexander Ferguson, Samuel Ferguson, and Samuel
    Hughey.
Ferguson, William
    1810: William and wife 16-25, and 1 female -10.
Forguson, William
    1810: William and wife 16-25.
Ferral, Catherine
    1810: Catherine 26-44, 1 male -10, and 1 female -10.
1790 - Ferrill, John
    Children: Hiram
1790 - Fesperman, Frederick
    Son of Henry and Christina Fesperman.
    1810: Frederick household consisted of 1 male 45+, 1
    male 26-44, 1 female 16-25, and 2 males -10.
Fesperman, Frederic & Rosina Hise
    Married Oct 14, 1802 in Cabarrus Co., David Suther,
    bondsman.
1790 - Fesperman, Michael
    Son of Henry and Christina Fesperman

1800: Michael 45+, 1 female 26-44, 1 male 16-25, 1
male 10-15, 1 female 10-15, and 3 females -10.
Listed next to Henry Fesperman, Michael Goodman,
John Lippard, William Sefred, Jacob Dewatt, and
Henry Gatchey.

1790 - Fesperman, John
Son of Henry and Christina Fesperman.
John sold land on Shaney Wolf Creek in Oct 1812.

Festerman, John & Elizabeth Phifer
Married Jan 16, 1798 in Cabarrus Co., Henry Prise,
bondsman.
1810: John 26-44, 1 female 16-25, 2 males -10, and 2
females -10.

Fesperman, Henry
Died in or before 1782.

1790 - Festerman/Fesperman, Henry & Christina
Children: Michael, John, Frederick, Henry, Margaret
(Henry Ritchie)
Henry will was probated in July 1791.
Christina LWT was proven in July 1797.

Fesperman, Henry
1800: Henry 16-25, 1 male 16-25, 1 female 16-25, 1
male -10, and 3 females -10. Listed next to Michael
Goodman, John Lippard, Rinehold Overshine, Michael
Fesperman, William Sefred, and Jacob Dewatt.
1810: Henry and wife 26-44, 1 male 16-25, 3 females
10-15, 1 male -10, and 3 females -10.

File, George
Owned land on Dutch Buffalo Creek in 1778.
George LWT was proven in April 1797.

File, George
1800: George 16-25, 1 female 45+, and 1 female -10.
Listed next to Mathias Beam, Michael Wiser, George
Seffred, Asemus Peninger, Charles Seffrid, and
Tobias Cress.
1810: George household consisted of 1 male 16-25, 1
female 45+, 1 female 26-44, 1 female 16-25, 4 males
-10, and 1 female -10.

File, Henry
1810: Henry and wife 26-44, 1 male 10-15, 2 males -
10, and 1 female -10.

File, Henry
1810: Henry age is not shown. His household
consisted of 1 female 26-44, 1 male 10-15, 3 males -
10, and 1 female -10.

File, Jacob
1810: Jacob 45+, 1 female 26-44, 1 male 26-44, 2
males 10-15, 3 males -10, and 2 females -10.

File, John
1800: John and wife 26-44, 2 females 10-15, 2 males
-10, and 2 females -10. Listed next to John Edleman,

Jacob Pines, Peter Cauble, Jacob Fisher, George
Fisher, and George Goodman, Sr.
1810: John and wife 45+, 3 males 10-15, 1 female 10-
15, and 2 males -10.
File, Philip
1800: Philip and wife 26-44, and 1 female -10.
Listed next to Jacob Slough, Thomas Goodman, Jacob
Lingle, John Cluttz, and Joseph Gray.
1810: Phillip 45+, 1 female 26-44, 1 male 16-25, 1
female 16-25, and 1 male -10.
Fink, David
1800: David and wife 26-44, 2 males 10-15, 1 female
10-15, 3 males -10, and 2 females -10. Listed next
to Andrew Cariker, Philip Cariker, Jr., George
Cariker, Henry Plylor, Peter Misenheimer, and George
Hartman.
Fink, George
1800: George and wife 26-44, and 1 male -10. Listed
next to John Furor, Jr., Arthur Underwood, Martin
Wedinhouse, John Ridley, Caleb Douss, and Tobius
Clutz.
1810: George 45+, 1 female 26-44, 1 male 16-25, and
1 male -10.
1790 - Fisher, Frederick
Owned land between Dutch Buffalo Creek and Little
Coldwater Creek in 1767, near Adam Creek.
Fisher, Frederick, Jr
Owned land on a ridge between Cold Water Creek and
Adam Creek in 1777.
1790 - Fisher, George
1800: George and wife 26-44, 1 female 10-15, 3 males
-10, and 2 females -10. Listed next to Jacob Fisher,
John File, John Edleman, George Goodman, Sr., Adam
Cruse, and Andrew Cruse.
1810: George and wife 45+, 1 male 16-25, 2 females
16-25, 1 male 10-15, 2 males -10, and 3 females -10.
Bought land from John Melchor on Rocky River in
1805, as well as land from Henry Fisher on Dutch
Buffalo Creek in July 1806.
George operated a ferry in 1797.
Fisher, Henry
Owned land on Dutch Buffalo Creek in 1806.
Henry bought land on Lick Branch of Dutch Buffalo
Creek in Jan 1814.
1810: Henry and wife 26-44, and 1 male -10.
Fisher, Lewis
1800: Lewis and wife 26-44, 2 females 10-15, 1 male
-10, and 1 females -10. Listed next to Peter Hagler,
Jr., John Furor, Paul Furor, Jacob Faggot, Melchor
Fogelman, and John Hagler, Sr.

1810: Lewis and wife, 45+, 2 females 16-25, 1 male
10-15, 2 females 10-15, 1 male -10, and 4 females -
10.
Fisher, Jacob
1800: Jacob and wife 26-44, 3 males -10, and 1
female -10. Listed next to John File, John Edleman,
Jacob Pines, George Fisher, George Goodman, Sr., and
Adam Cruse.
Fisher, Martin
Owned land between Dutch Buffalo Creek and Little
Coldwater Creek in 1767.
File, Philip
Fite, Henry
1800: Henry and wife 16-25, and 1 male -10. Listed
next to Rabeckah Heninger, Tobius Clutz, Caleb
Douss, Daniel Faggot, Harmon Moyer, and Daniel Bost.
Fleming, George
Owned land on Coddle Creek
Fleming, John
Children: Eleanor, Betsy, Jenny, John B., Ann,
Polly, William Lee, James, Sarah.
John died before Jan 1809. Mitchel and Allison
Fleming were administrators of his estate.
Fleming, Richard & Catharine
Children: Henry, William, Sarah, James
Richard died before 1800.
1800: Catherine 26-44, 1 male 10-15, 1 female 10-15,
2 males -10, and 1 female -10. Listed next to
William Young, Robert Smith, James Smith, Mary
Fulham, Susanna Russel, and Robert Alexander.
1810: Catey 45+, 1 male 16-25, 1 female 16-25, 2
males 10-15, and 1 female 10-15.
1790 - Flemming, Mitchell
Owned land on the east side of Coddle Creek in 1784.
1800: Mitchell and wife 26-44, 2 males 10-15, 2
females 10-15, and 3 females -10. Listed next to
Thomas Erwin, Widow Caragin, John Coruthers, David
Farr, Archibald Gilmore, and William Hunt.
1810: Mitchell 45+, 1 female 26-44, 1 male 16-25, 1
female 16-25, 3 females 10-15, 1 male unde 10, and 1
female -10.
Fleming, William
1810: William and wife 16-25, and 1 male -10.
Flinn, Ebenezer
Bought land on Coddle Creek from Stephen Alexander
in 1805.
1810: Ebenezer and wife 26-44, 3 males 16-25, 1
female 16-25, 3 males -10, and 2 females -10.
Fogelman, Christian & Polly Loftin
Children: Almina, Wilson
Christian bought land on Rocky River in Jan 1813.
Fogelman, Christopher

1810: Christopher household consisted of 4 males 26-
44, 1 female 16-25, 2 females 10-15, and 1 male -10.

Fogelman, George
    1810: George 16-25, and 1 female 10-15.
    George and Christian Fogelman sold land on Hamby Run
    of Rocky River, and on Adam Creek in Jan 1813.

1790 - Fogleman, Melchor
    1800: Melchor 45+, 3 males 16-25, 1 female 16-25,
    and 1 male 10-15. Listed next to Jacob Faggot, Lewis
    Fisher, Peter Hagler, Jr., John Hagler, Sr., Leonard
    Hartsell, and George Hartsell.
    Melchor sold on Adam Creek in April 1813.

Fogelman, Michael
    Owned land on Adam Creek near Hamby Run in 1784.

1790 - Foil/File, George
    Owned land on Dutch Buffalo Creek.
    George died before Oct 1798.

1790 - Foil/File, John

Folk, William
    1800: William 26-44, 1 female 45+, and 1 male 16-25.
    Listed next to Martin Everit, Andrew Dry, Jacob Dry,
    Jacob Harky, Martin Harky, and John House.

Ford, John
    1800: John 26-44, 1 female 16-25, 2 males -10, and 1
    female -10. Listed next to Dennis Clay, James Clay,
    Henry Cagle, Able Powell, John Powell, and John
    Carruthers.
    1810: John 26-44, 1 female 45+, 1 female 26-44, 1
    male 10-15, 1 female 10-15, 1 male -10, and 3
    females -10.

Ford, Henry
    Owned land on and wife sides of Clear Creek in 1785.

Ford, Rabeckah
    1800: Rabeckah household consisted of just herself
    45+.

Forrester, Owen
    Owned land on Long Branch of Cold Water Creek in
    1779.

Fostey, Lewis
    1810: Lewis 45+, 1 female 26-44, 2 males 10-15, 2
    females 10-15, 2 males -10, and 3 females -10.

Fouts, Lewis
    1800: Lewis and wife 26-44, 1 male 10-15, 1 female
    10-15, 2 males -10, and 3 females -10. Listed next
    to Martin Harkey, Jacob Buzzard, Jesse Herrin,
    Christopher Beaver, Peter Isenhour, and Michael
    Isenhour.

Frank, Frederick
    1800: Frederick 26-44, 1 female 26-44, 5 males 16-
    25, 2 males -10, and 1 female -10. Listed next to
    Henry Furor, Mark Coleman, John Chamberlin,

Christian Goodnight, Jacob Croner, and William
Croner.
1790 - Frank, Jacob
Children: John, Joseph, Susannah, Margaret, Jacob
Owned land on Little Coldwater Creek in 1782.
Jacob died before July 1799 and his children were
referred to as orphans in the court records.
Fraser/Frazure, Israel
1810: Israel 26-44, 1 female 16-25, and 1 male -10.
In the 1850 census of Cabarrus Co., Israel is listed
as 72 years old.
Frazer, John
1810: John and wife 26-44, and 1 female -10.
Fraser, William
1800: William and wife 45+, 3 males 16-25, 2 females
16-25, 2 females 10-15, and 1 male -10. Listed next
to Isaac Workman, Joseph Patton, Elizabeth
Patterson, Morgan Hall, William Hamilton, and
William McCray.
1810: William and wife 45+, 2 males 16-25, and 2
females 16-25.
Freeman, Andrew
1800: Andrew and wife 16-25, and 1 male -10. Listed
next to Henry Smith, Sr., Henry Smith, Jr., George
Garmon, Charles Freeman, Douglass Winchester, and
John Brown.
Freeman, Charles
1800: Charles and wife 26-44. Listed next to Andrew
Freeman, Henry Smith, Sr., Henry Smith, Jr.,
Douglass Winchester, John Brown, and John Polk.
Freeman, Clayborn
Clayborn died before July 1797.
Freisland, Frederick
1810: Frederick 16-25, and 2 females 16-25.
Frichey, John
1810: John 26-44, 1 female 45+, 1 male 10-15, 1 male
-10, and 2 females -10.
Frohock, John
Owned land on Coddle Creek at the Mill Creek Branch
and Afton Run in 1770.
Fulham, Mary
1800: Mary 45+, 2 females 16-25, 1 female 10-15, 1
male -10, and 1 female -10. Listed next to Catherine
Flemmon, William Young, Robert Smith, Susanna
Russel, Robert Alexander, and John Gilmore.
1810: Mary 26-44, 1 male -10, and 2 females -10. She
is close to Joseph Russel.
Funderburk, Francis
1800: Francis 45+, 1 female 26-44, 1 male -10, and 1
female -10. Listed next to Dorothy Petry, Daniel
Bost, Harmon Moyer, Andrew Slough, George Smith, and
William Stow.

1810: Francis 26-44, 1 female 26-44, 1 male 16-25, 1
male 10-15, 1 female 10-15, 1 male -10, and 2
females -10.

Furor, Henry
1800: Henry and wife 26-44, 1 male 10-15, 2 females
10-15, 2 males -10, and 2 females -10. Listed next
to Mark Coleman, John Chamberlin, Adam Bowers, Jr.,
Frederick Frank, Christian Goodnight, and Jacob
Croner.

Furor, John
1800: John 45+, 1 female 26-44, 2 males 16-25, 1
female 16-25, 1 male 10-15, and 3 females -10.
Listed next to Paul Furor, Jacob Effrit, Martin Dry,
Peter Hagler, Jr., Lewis Fisher, and Jacob Faggot.

Furor, John, Jr.
1800: John and wife 16-25, and 1 female -10. Listed
next to Arthur Underwood, Martin Wedinhouse, Peter
Teame, George Fink, John Ridley, and Caleb Douss.

Furor, Paul
1800: Paul 45+, 1 female 26-44, 1 male 16-25, 2
females 16-25, 1 male 10-15, 1 female 10-15, 3 males
-10, and 1 female -10. Listed next to Jacob Effrit,
Martin Dry, Philip Dry, John Furor, Peter Hagler,
Jr., and Lewis Fisher.

Fur, Henry
1810: Henry 45+, 1 female 26-44, 2 males 16-25, 2
females 10-15, 2 males -10, and 1 female -10.

1790 - Furr, John & Margaret
Owned land on Little Cold Water Creek in Jan 1806
and sold to Peter Overcash.

1790 - Furr, Paul
Owned land on Meadow Creek and Dutch Buffalo Creek
in 1786.
1810: Paul and wife 45+, 1 male 26-44, 3 males 16-
25, 3 females 16-25, 1 male 10-15, 1 female 10-15,
and 1 female -10.

Gallimore, John
1800: John and wife 45+, 1 male 16-25, 1 male 10-15,
and 2 females 10-15. Listed next to Leonard
Barberick, Henry Propst, Michael Pealer, John
Skilhouse, Henry Simmons, and George Harkman.

Gallimore, William
William bought on Coddle Creek in Jan 1814.

Gardner, James
1810: James and wife 26-44, 1 male 16-25, 1 male -
10, and 3 females -10.

1790 - Gardner, William
1800: William and wife 45+, 1 male 26-44, and 1
female 26-44. Listed next to Arthur Donelson, John
Cannon, James Christopher, Robert Hope, William
Harris (tailor), and Charles Harris.

Owned land between Rocky River and Coddle Creek in
1775.
Garmon, George
1800: George 26-44, 1 female 16-25, 1 male 16-25, 1
male -10, and 1 female -10. Listed next to Rabeckah
Mitchell, Joshua Cheek, Abigel Griffin, Henry Smith,
Jr., Henry Smith, Sr., and Andrew Freeman.
Owned land on Rocky River near James Love in Jan
1807.
1810: George and wife 26-44, 1 female 10-15, 2 males
-10, and 1 female -10.
Garmon, John
1800: John and wife 16-25, and 1 male -10. Listed
next to James Long, Frederick Kizer, Leonard Mire,
Beverly Gray, John Gray, and Michael Watters.
1810: John and wife 26-44, 1 female 10-15, 2 males -
10, and 3 females -10.
Garmon, Michael
1800: Michael and wife 45+, 1 female 16-25, 2
females 10-15, and 1 male -10. Listed next to John
Carruthers, John Powell, Able Powell, Travis
Gullino, Leonard Mire, and Frederick Kizer.
1810: Michael and wife 45+, 1 female 26-44, and 1
male 16-25.
Garretson, John
Children: Thomas, Lydia Ann
Garrison, Adam & Anney
Owned land on Rocky River in 1778.
Garrison, John
1810: John and another male 26-44, 4 males 16-25, 2
females 16-25, 2 males 10-15, and 1 male -10.
Garrison, Samuel R. & Martha Morrison
Children: Robert C. (Martha Buchanan), Sarah
(Archibald M. Pickens), Samuel R.(died at age 9)
Married March 13, 1811 in Mecklenburg Co., Thomas
Morrison, bondsman.
Samuel and Martha moved to TN with many other family
members and are buried near Shelbyville.
Martha was the daughter of Robert and Sarah
Morrison.
Garrison, Samuel & Esther
Samuel sold land in Oct 1797.
Gatchey, Henry
1800: Henry and wife 45+, 1 male 26-44, 2 males 10-
15, 3 males -10, and 1 female -10. Listed next to
Jacob Dewatt, William Sefred, Michael Fesperman,
Michael Gatchey, Martin Penninger, and George
Seffred.
Gatchey, Michael
1800: Michael and wife 26-44, 2 males -10, and 1
female -10. Listed next to Henry Gatchey, Jacob

Dewatt, William Sefred, Martin Penninger, George
Seffred, and Michael Wiser.
Gailor, James
    1800: James and wife 26-44, 3 males 10-15, 1 female
    10-15, 2 males -10, and 1 female -10. Listed next to
    James Sullivan, Robert Martin, Athen Almore, Peter
    Miller, Robert Miller, and Josiah Deweast.
    1810: James and wife 45+, 1 male 16-25, 1 female 16-
    25, 2 males 10-15, 1 female 10-15, 2 males -10, and
    1 female -10.
Gaylor, Theophilus & Polly Davis
    Son of James Gaylor
    Owned land on Rocky River
Gillimon, William
    1810: William 26-44, 1 female 16-25, 1 male -10, and
    3 females -10.
Gillim, William
    1810: William and wife 26-44, 1 male -10, and 3
    females -10.
1790 - Gilmore, Archabeld
    Owned land on Coddle Creek.
    1800: Archibald and wife 45+. Listed next to David
    Farr, Mitchel Flemmon, Thomas Erwin, William Hunt,
    John Houston, and Archibald Houston.
1790 - Gilmore, James & Margret
    Children: Josiah, Mary, Nathaniel, William
    Owned land on Rocky River in 1780.
    James died Oct 8, 1784 at the age of 40.
    Margaret died March 30, 1815 at the age of 63.
Gilmore, John
    1800: John 26-44 and another male 26-44, his wife
    26-44, 1 female 16-25, 1 male 10-15, 3 males -10.
    Listed next to Robert Alexander, Susanna Russel,
    Mary Fulham, Samuel Kenly, James Caragin, and
    Benjamin Alexander.
Gilmore, Josiah
    1810: Josiah household consisted of just himself,
    45+.
1790 - Gilmore, Nathaniel & Jane
    Children: Nathaniel - Father or son moved to Sumner
    Co., TN where he died in 1806. Others who moved with
    him were Zaccheus and James Wilson.
    Owned land on the south side of Rocky River and
    Sugar Creek in 1779.
Gilmore, Nat
    1810: Nat 15-25, and 1 male 16-25.
Gilpon, Henry & Sarah
    Children: Elizabeth, Eleanor, Nancy (born 1785),
    Susannah, Nelly, Sally, Ann, Alexander.
    Henry died before July 1797.
Gingles, Charles Harrison & Mary Morrison

Children: James Washington (Fannie Hutchinson),
Cynthia McKee (Dr. George O. Brosnahan), Rose (N.C.
Shackleford - Judge), Mary Harris (Richard Hill
Turner), Annie Gaston (Fillo della Rua), Sarah
Adelaide, Charles Harrison, Jr (Jessie McNeil),
Frances Fillmore.
Son of John & Rachel Morrison Gingles
1790 - Gingles, John & Rachel Morrison, Amelia Davis
Children: Jenny, Margaret (James S. Russell), Samuel
Harvey (Tirzah Morrison), Mary (? Parks), Rachel
(Samuel F. Morrison), Rosanna (William Morrison),
Elizabeth (Peter Roland McEachern), James, John
(Dorcas Morrison McGinnis, Martha Clementine
Purviance, Elizabeth Brice Cochran Harris), William
Lee (Rachel Russell), Charles Harrison (Mary
Morrison), Malinda E. (Elam Harvey Davis)
John and Rachel lived in No. 2 township in Cabarrus
County.
Son of Samuel and Margaret McAllister Gingles
John was born May 15, 1769, died July 28, 1831
Rachel was born April 18, 1772, died Oct 30, 1825
Buried in Spears Cemetery of Rocky River Church
Gingles, John & Dorcas Morrison McGinnis, Martha
Clementine Purvians, Elizabeth Brice Cochran Harris
Children: Margaret Matilda (Lawson A. Blackwelder),
Louisa C. (John Northern), Rachel Catherine M.
(Benjamin F. Glenn), James R., Charles M., Sarah J.
It is believed that the three girls were daughters
of John and Dorcas Morrison, and that the three boys
were sons of John and Martha Purvians.
Son of John and Rachel Morrison Gingles
Gingles, Samuel & Margaret McAllister
Children: Rosanna (John Caruth), Samuel (Eleanor
Beatty), James, John (Rachel Morrison, Amelia
Davis), Adlai, Isabella, Mary (Alexander McCarter),
Rachel (John Harris)
Owned land on Crowder Creek of Rocky River in 1763.
Samuel was from Scotland, though he may have been
born in Ireland. Samuel died on Jan 24, 1777.
Margaret died March 28, 1809.
Gingles, Samuel & Eleanor Beatty
Children: Samuel, Patsy (Gideon Robinson), Elizabeth
(Benaiah Gullick), Margaret (John Harris), Thomas H.
(Margaret B. Ewing), David, Adlai, female born 1804-
1810: female born 1794-1804
Samuel owned land on Duck Creek in 1783.
Moved to Lincoln Co., NC before 1790.
Son of Samuel & Margaret McAllister Gingles
Gingles, Samuel Harvey & Tirzah Morrison
Children: Harriet, Harvey, Jane, Caroline
Married about 1820

Moved to Lowndes dist., Lowndes Co., AL with Charles
Harrison Gingles before 1837.
Son of John and Rachel Morrison Gingles
Gingles, William Lee & Rachel Russell
    Children: Mary L. (died at the age of 12), David
    Harrison (drowned in Coddle Creek at the age of 7),
    Elizabeth M. (Evan Alexander Flowe), William Lee,
    Jr.
    Son of John and Rachel Morrison Gingles.
Glover, Hezekiah
    1800: Hezekiah 26-44, 2 females 16-25, 1 male -10,
    and 3 females -10. Heis listed next to John
    Overcast, Vachel Holbrooks, John Weddington, John
    Means, James Means, and Charles McNelond.
Glover, William
    1800: William and wife 26-44, 1 male -10, and 1
    female -10. Listed next to Susanna Morrison, John
    Patterson, Thomas Rogers, John Kesler, James Martin,
    and Robert Sullivan.
    1810: William 45+, 1 female 26-44, 1 male 10-15, 1
    female 10-15, 3 males -10, and 2 females -10.
Goodman, Christian
    Owned land on Dutch Buffalo Creek in 1775.
1790 - Goodman, Christopher
    Owned land on Blackwater Run, a branch of Dutch
    Buffalo Creek in 1784.
    Christopher died before 1798, his LWT was proven by
    Jacob Cline.
    Son of Michael Goodman.
Goodman, George, Sr.
    1800: George 45+, 1 female 26-44, 3 females 10-15, 3
    males -10, and 2 females -10. Listed next to George
    Fisher, Jacob Fisher, John File, Adam Cruse, Andrew
    Cruse, and John Misenheimer.
Goodman, George, Jr.
    1800: George 26-44, 1 female 45+, 1 female 26-44, 1
    male 10-15, 2 males -10, and 1 female -10. Listed
    next to Henry Cline, Conrod Hise, Henry Cuthezen,
    Peter Weaver, Michael Goodman(Big), and John Duke.
    1810: George and wife 26-44, 3 males 10-15, 2 males
    -10, and 1 female -10.
    George bought land on Dutch Buffalo Creek in July
    1813.
1790 - Goodman, Jacob & Mary
    Owned land on a branch of Dutch Buffalo Creek.
    Son of Michael Goodman.
Goodman, John
    1800: John 26-44, 3 males 16-25, 1 female 16-25, 2
    males -10, and 2 females -10. Listed next to Frances
    Linse, David McKinly, Josiah Bradly, Aaron Houston,
    James Bridges, and Henry Brines.
Goodman, Michael

Children: Christopher, Michael, Jacob, George, John
Michael died about 1777.
1790 - Goodman, Michael & Catherine
Michael was in Mecklenburg County in 1782.
1800: Michael 45+, 1 female 26-44, 1 male 16-25, 2
females 10-15, 3 males -10, and 2 females -10.
Listed next to Peter Weaver, George Goodman, Jr.,
John Duke, and Jacob Rimer.
1810: Michael and Catherine 45+, 1 male 16-25, 2
males 10-15, 2 females 10-15, and 1 female -10.
1790 - Goodman, Michael, Jr
Son of Michael Goodman.
1800: Michael and wife 26-44, 1 female 16-25, 1 male
10-15, 1 female 10-15, 3 males -10, and 3 females -
10. Listed next to John Lippard, Rinehold Overshine,
Jacob Hoover, Henry Fesperman, Michael Fesperman,
and Williem Sefred.
Michael owned land on Irish Buffalo Creek in 1805,
bought from James Bridgers.
Goodman, Michael
1810: Michael 26-44, 1 female 26-44, 1 female 16-25,
2 males -10, and 1 female -10.
Goodman, Staphel & Cathron
Owned land on a branch of Dutch Buffalo Creek in
1782.
Goodman, Tobias
Owned land on a branch of Dutch Buffalo Creek in
1784.
1810: Tobias 26-44, 1 female 45+, 2 males 16-25, 1
female 16-25, and 2 males -10.
Goodman, Thomas
1800: Thomas and wife 26-44, 1 male -10, and 1
female -10. Listed next to Jacob Lingle, John
Cluttz, Leonard Cluttz, Jacob Slough, Philip File,
and Joseph Gray.
1810: Thomas 26-44, 1 female 16-25, 1 male -10, and
1 female -10.
Goodnight, George & Catherine
Owned land on Coldwater Creek in 1779.
1790 - Goodnight, Christian 146
Owned land on Cold Water Creek next to Christian
Barnheart in 1783.
1800: Christian and wife 45+, 1 male 16-25, 2
females 16-25, 4 males 10-15, and 1 female -10.
Listed next to Frederick Frank, Henry Furor, Mark
Coleman, Jacob Croner, William Croner, and Daniel
Cline.
Goodnight, Michael
1810: Michael 45+, 1 male 26-44, 1 female 10-15, 2
males -10, and 1 female -10.
Son of George and Catherine Goodknight ?
Goodnight, Michael

1810: Michael and wife 26-44, 1 female 10-15, 2
males -10, and 1 female -10.
Goodwin, William
    1800: William household consisted himself 26-44, and
    wife 16-25. Listed next to Daniel Cline, John
    Soseman, Jonathan Hartzell, Godfred Uery, George
    Moyer, and Christian Morris.
Gordin, William
    1800: William 26-44, 1 female 45+, 1 male 16-25, and
    2 females 10-15. Listed next to Henry Linker George
    Hartman, Peter Misenheimer, Hardin Wiggins, Eve
    Wilhelm, and George Wilhelm.
Gorright, Fight
    Owned land on Dutch Buffalo Creek in 1782.
Gossage Daniel
    1810: Daniel and wife 26-44, 2 males -10, and 2
    females -10.
    Daniel sold to William Gallimore on Coddle Creek in
    Jan 1814.
Graham, John
    Owned land on Rocky River before 1784.
    John died before 1784.
Graver, Samuel
    1800: Samuel and wife 26-44, 2 males 10-15, 2 males
    -10, and 2 females -10. Listed next to Timothy
    Doland, Henry Doland, John Kepple, Ephraim D.
    Harris, William Louder, and Jacob Moose.
Gray, Beverly
    1800: Beverly 26-44, 1 female 16-25, and 1 male -10.
    Listed next to John Garmon, James Long, Frederick
    Kizer, John Gray, Michael Watters, and John Vossel.
    1810: Beverley 26-44, 1 female 16-25, 4 males -10,
    and 1 female -10.
Gray, James
    1810: James 45+, 2 females, 45+, 1 male 26-44, 3
    males 16-25, 2 females 16-25, 4 males 10-15, and 2
    males -10.
Gray, James
    1810: James and wife 26-44, 2 males -10, and 1
    female -10.
Gray, John
    1800: John and wife 45+, 1 male 16-25, 1 female 16-
    25, 1 male 10-15, and 1 female 10-15. Listed next to
    Beverly Gray, John Garmon, James Long, Michael
    Watters, John Vossel, and John Carlock.
Gray, Joseph
    1800: Joseph and wife 26-44, 1 male 16-25, 2 males
    10-15, 4 males -10, and 2 females -10. Listed next
    to Philip File, Jacob Slough, Thomas Goodman, Jacob
    Lingle, and John Cluttz.
Gray, Nelson

1800: Nelson and wife 26-44, 1 male 16-25, and 3
females -10. Listed next to Thomas Gray, George
Alexander, William Callon, Sr., Andrew Alexander,
Joseph Young, and David Crawford.

Gray, Thomas
    1800: Thomas and wife 26-44, and 1 male -10. Listed
    next to George Alexander, William Callon, Sr. and
    Jr., Nelson Gray, Andrew Alexander, and Joseph
    Young.

Gray, William
    1800: William and wife 26-44, 2 males -10, and 2
    females -10. Listed next to James Alexander, John
    Alexander, Hugh Pickens, John Robinson, Elenor
    Erwin, and Ezekiel Wright.

Green, Linard & Ann
    Owned land on the south bank of Rocky River in 1780.

Green, Needham & Polly Kiser
    Children: Margaret

Green, William
    1810: William and wife 26-44, 1 female 16-25, 2 male
    10-15, 2 females 10-15, 2 males -10, and 3 females -
    10.

Greer, Andrew
    Owned land between Horton Branch of Anderson Creek
    and Muddy Creek and Caldwell Creek in 1772.

Greer, Francis & Catherine Cromwell
    Married in Cabarrus County Sept 4, 1793, John
    Cromwell, bondsman.
    1800: Francis 26-44, 1 female 16-25, 1 male -10, 1
    female -10. Listed next to William Andrew, Edward
    Neil, Joseph Welsh, James Snell, Mark Evans, and
    Isaac McLennon.

Griffin, Abigel
    1800: Abigel 26-44, and 2 males 10-15. Listed next
    to Rabeckah Ford, Stephen Self, David Self, Joshua
    Cheek, and Rabeckah Mitchell.

Guiliams, William
    Owned a grist mill on Clear Creek.

Gun, Martin
    1800: Martin and wife 26-44, and 2 females -10.
    Listed next to Molly Peanix, Gallant Peanix, William
    McCray, Elizabeth Skiliton, Jean McLusky, and
    Elizabeth Holly.

Hadley, James
    1810: James and wife 26-44, 1 male 10-15, and 3
    females -10.

1790 - Hadley, Joshua
    Owned land on Irish Buffalo Creek at Coldwater Creek
    in 1783.
    1800: Joshua and wife 45+, 1 male 16-25, 2 females
    16-25, and 1 female 10-15. Listed next to Robert

Purviance, John Shaver, John Culpepper, Samuel
Corzine, Martha Ferguson, and Alexander Ferguson.
Hadley, Stephen
1810: Stephen and wife 26-44, 2 males 10-15, 3 males
-10, and 2 females -10.
Stephen died before April 1813.
Hagler ? & Catharine
Children: Charles (Sarah Linker), John, Leonard
(Elizabeth Hartsel), Jacob, Mary (William Anderson)
Hagler, James
James died in Cabarrus Co. in May 1860 at the age of
60.
1790 - Hagler, John
Owned land on the north side of Rocky River in 1786.
1800: John and wife 45+, 1 male 16-25, 1 female 16-
25, 1 male 10-15, 2 females 10-15, and 2 males -10.
Listed next to Melchor Fogelman, Jacob Faggot, Lewis
Fisher, Leonard Hartsell, George Hartsell, and
Frederick Plylor.
1810: John and wife 26-44, 3 males 16-25, 1 female
16-25, and 1 male -10.
Hagler, Peter, Jr.
1800: Peter and wife 16-25, and 2 males -10. Listed
next to John Furor, Paul Furor, Jacob Effrit, Lewis
Fisher, Jacob Faggot, and Melchor Fogelman.
Hall, John
1800: John 45+, 1 female 26-44, 2 females 16-25, and
2 males -10. Listed next to Robert Harris, Archibald
Houston, Jr., Archibald Houston, Hugh Hamilton,
Oliver Harris and William Kellough.
Hall, Morgan
1800: Morgan and wife 26-44, 1 female 16-25, 1 male
10-15, 1 female 10-15, 1 male -10, and 2 females -
10. Listed next to William Fraser, Isaac Workman,
Joseph Patton, William Hamilton, William McCray, and
Gallant Peanix.
1810: Morgan 45+, 1 female 16-25, and 2 males -10.
Hamilton/Hambleton, Hugh
Owned land on Rocky River in 1772.
Died in 1772.
Hamilton, Hugh
1800: Hugh and wife 26-44, 1 male 10-15, 1 female
10-15, 1 male -10, and 3 females -10. Listed next to
John Hall, Robert Harris, Archilbald Houston, Jr.,
Oliver Harris, William Keilough, and Samuel
Keilough.
Hamilton/Hambleton, John & Mary Skelington
Married Feb 22, 1791 in Mecklenburg Co., Jonas
McCullough, bondsman.
John Hambleton bought land on Coddle Creek from the
sheriff of Cabarrus in Jan 1806. Land formerly owned
by David D. Farr.

1810: John and wife 26-44, 2 males 16-25, 1 male 10-15, 1 female 10-15, 1 male -10, and 4 females -10.

Hamilton, Russell
Russell was overseer of Dutch Road from Hagler Ford to Anderson Creek in April 1813.

Hamilton, William
1800: William 26-44, 1 female 45+, 1 female 26-44, and 2 females -10. Listed next to Morgan Hall, William Faser, Isaac Workman, William McCray, Gallant Peanix, and Molly Peanix.

Harding, Ambrose
Owned land on a branch of Coddle Creek in 1769.

Hare, Peter
Owned land on Adams Creek

Harkey, David
1810: David 16-25, 1 female 26-44, 1 female 16-25, and 1 female -10.

Harkey, Henry
1810: Henry and wife 26-44, 3 males 10-15, 2 females 10-15, 4 males -10, and 1 female -10.

Harky, Jacob
1800: Jacob and wife 26-44, 2 males -10, and 2 females -10. Listed next to William Folk, Martin Everit, Andrew Dry, Martin Harky, John House, and Henry Ovestwald.
1810: Jacob and wife 26-44, 1 male 10-15, 2 females 10-15, 3 males -10, and 1 female -10.

1790 - Hargey/Harky, Martin & Caty
1800: Martin 26-44, 1 female 45+, 1 female 16-25, and 1 male 10-15. Listed next to Jacob Harky, William Folk, Martin Everit, John House, Henry Ovestwald, and Christian Hurlohor.
Martin died in Cabarrus County before Oct 1814.

Harkey, Martin, Jr.
1800: Martin and wife 26-44, 2 males -10, and 1 female -10. Listed next to Paul Barringer, Jacob Bost, Solomon Davis, Nicholas Ridenhour, Mathias Moyer, and Isaac Blackwelder.
Owned land on Dutch Buffalo Creek in 1806.

Harkey, Martin
1800: Martin and wife 26-44, 2 males -10, and 1 female -10. Listed next to Henry Heren, Christian Hurlohor, Jr., Christian Hurlohor, George Hise, Mary House, and Barbary Lype.

Harkey, Martin
1800: Martin 16-25, 1 female 45+, 1 female 16-25, 2 males -10, and 1 female -10. Listed next to Jacob Buzzard, Jesse Herrin, Thomas Allin, Lewis Fouts, Christopher Beaver, and Peter Isenhour.

Harkman, George
1800: George 26-44, 1 female 45+, 2 females 16-25, 1 male 10-15, 1 female 10-15, and 2 females -10.

Listed next to Henry Simmons, John Skilhouse, John
Gallimore, Phillip Shive, Daniel Krider(Crider), and
Michael Overcash.
1810: George and wife 45+.
Harris, Alexander W. & Penelope Morrison
    Children: Sarah Pharr (George W. Alexander),
    Elizabeth Matilda (David Newell, James Monroe
    Irwin), Isaac (Mary Morrison Burns of Camden, SC),
    Margaret Morrison, William Hope (Lulu Raybourn),
    James Alexander (Margaret E. Burns of Camden, SC,
    Margaret A. Johnston, Sarah T. Trainum of Salem, NC)
    Son of William Harris.
Harris, Andrew
    Andrew was referred to as an orphan in Jan 1813
    court and was bound to George Klutts to learn Tailor
    trade.
*Harris, Charles & Mary Barringer (doctor)
    1800: Charles 26-44, 1 female 26-44, 2 other males
    26-44, 1 male 16-25, 1 male -10, and 1 female -10.
    Listed next to William Harris (tailor), Robert Hope,
    William Gardenor, Robert Erwin, Widow McClain, and
    John Edmonton.
    1810: Charles 26-44, 2 females 26-44, 3 males 16-25,
    2 females 16-25, 1 male 10-15, and 1 male -10. He is
    close to William Harris and Catey Hope.
    Charles bought land on Rocky River from Robert Smith
    in Oct 1805.
    Charles died Sept 21, 1825
    Mary was the daughter of Paul & Elizabeth Peck
    Barringer.
Harris, Cunningham
    1800: Cunningham 45+ and 1 male 16-25. Listed next
    to Griffin Morris, Matthew Campbell, James Stafford,
    Elisha Spears, James Harris, and Jeremiah Johnston.
    Harris, Edward D.
    1810: Edward and wife 45+, 2 males 16-25, 2 females
    16-25, 2 males 10-15, 1 male -10, and 1 female -10.
Harris, Elizabeth
    In 1790 Elizabeth household contained XXX, and 1800:
    it consisted of herself over 45, 2 males 26-44, 1
    female 26-44, 1 female 16-25, and 1 female 10-15.
    Listed next to William Harris, David Taylor, James
    Plunkett, Sr., James Russell, and James Scott.
1790 - Harris, Ephraim Drake
    1800: Ephraim and wife 45+, 1 male 16-25, 1 male 10-
    15, 2 females 10-15, 2 males -10, and 1 female -10.
    Listed next to Samuel Graver, Timothy Doland, Henry
    Doland, William Louder, Jacob Moose, and James
    McMahon.
    Ephraim died between Jan and April 1816.
Harris, George & Elizabeth Alexander

Married March 24, 1796 in Cabarrus County, Nathaniel
Alexander, bondsman.
1800: George and Elizabeth 26-44, 1 male 26-44, 1
male -10, 1 female -10. Listed next to Robert Curry,
Isaac McLennon, Mark Evans, Robert Harris, Jr.,
Thomas Davis, and James Stafford.
George was the sheriff of Cabarrus County in 1804,
and he died before Jan 1814.
1810 George and Elizabeth, and wife 26-44, 1 male
10-15, 1 female 10-15, 3 males -10, and 2 females -
10.
Harris, James & Elizabeth
Children: Margaret, James, Robert, William H.,
Thomas C.
1800: James and Elizabeth 26-44, 1 male -10, 1
female -10. Listed next to Elisha Spears, Cunningham
Harris, Griffin Morris, Jeremiah Johnston, George
Campbell, and John Callon.
1810 James 26-44, 1 male 10-15, 1 female 10-15, and
1 male -10.
Harris, Joshua
Joshua owned land on Fuda Creek in 1814. He was the
son of William Harris, Sr.
He died in Cabarrus Co. in September 1860 at the age
of 76.
1790 - Harris, Oliver
Son of Robert and Margaret Harris
1800: Oliver and wife 26-44, 1 female 10-15, 3 males
-10, and 2 females -10. Listed next to Hugh
Hamilton, John Hall, Robert Harris, William
Keilough, Samuel Keilough, and William Douglass.
Harris, Plipper
1810: his and wife 45+, 1 male 26-44, 1 male 16-25,
2 males 10-15, 2 females 10-15, 3 males -10, and 2
females -10.
1790 - Harris, Robert, Jr. & Margaret
Children: Margaret, Mary, Hannah (? Wiley), Samuel,
Oliver, James
Robert will was probated in Jan 1795 in Mecklenburg
County
Owned land on Fuda Creek in 1782.
1790 - Harris, Robert, Esq & Frances
Children: Robert, Elizabeth, female, Martha (Samuel
Harris)
In Mecklenburg in 1782, Fuda Creek, died 1798
Harris, Robert, Esq.
1800: Robert and wife 45+. Listed next to Archibald
Houston, Jr., Archibald Houston, John Houston, John
Hall, Hugh Hamilton, and Oliver Harris. This could
be the Robert Harris below who married Agness Ross,
but further research is needed to confirm.
Harris, Robert & Agness Ross

Married in Cabarrus County, bond dated Sept 28,
1793, bondsman, John Callon.
1810: Robert and wife 26-44, 1 male 10-15, 1 female
10-15, 1 male -10, and 2 females -10.
Harris, Robert & Martha
    Owned land on Caldwell Creek
Harris, Robert & Margaret Robb
    Married Jan 16, 1793 in Mecklenburg Co., George
    Stafford, bondsman.
    Margaret was born 1774, may have died May 27, 1811.
    A Robert Harris sold land on the north side of Back
    Creek to Robert Cochran in July 1806. It is unclear
    if this is in fact the right Robert Harris.
    A Margaret Harris was listed in the 1860 Cabarrus
    Co. census as 81 years old.
1790 - Harris, Robert, Capt/Col
    Robert died before Oct 1798 in Cabarrus County. He
    lived in the Poplar Tent area of the county and his
    estate return was 10,000 pounds.
1790 - Harris, Samuel, Jr & Martha Harris
    Daughter of Robert & Frances Harris
    Martha was born 1768, died Aug 2, 1797.
    1800: Samuel 26-44, 2 females 10-15, and 2 males -
    10. Listed next to Andrew Davis, Jr., Robert
    Cochrin, Jr., William Cochrin, Robert Harris,
    Alexander Hughey, and William Morrison.
    Samuel sold to Samuel, Sr. on Caldwell Creek in Jan
    1813, and to his grandsons, Samuel C. Harris, and
    Elam Stanhope Harris, land on Caldwell Creek in Jan
    1814.
Harris, Samuel
    1810: Samuel 26-44, 1 male 16-25, 1 male 10-15, and
    1 female 10-15.
1790 - Harris, Thomas S., Majr & Mary
    Lived in the Rocky River Church area.
    1810: Thomas and wife 26-44, 1 male 26-44, 1 female
    45+, 1 male 16-25, and 1 female 16-25.
Harris, Thomas
    Owned land on the south side of Four Mile Creek in
    1779.
Harris, William & Martha Cochran
    Married March 10, 1795 in Cabarrus Co., Alexander
    McLarty, bondsman.
    1810: William and wife 26-44, 1 male 10-15, 1 female
    10-15, 3 males -10, and 1 female -10.
    Martha was born 1774, died Jan 25, 1818
    Buried in Spears Cemetery of Rocky River Church.
1790 - Harris, William, Jr.
    Owned land on Coldwater Creek.
    1800: his and wife age 26-44, 2 males 10-15, 2 males
    -10, and 3 females -10. Listed next to Sarah Shelby,

David Taylor, Elizabeth Harris, James Plunkett, Sr.,
and James Russell.
1810: William and wife 45+, 3 males 16-25, 3 females
10-15, 2 males -10, and 1 female -10.
1790 - Harris, William, Sr 135
Children: Joshua
1800: a William Harris' household contained William
26-44, 2 females 26-44, 1 male 16-25, 2 females 10-
15 and 1 male -10. Listed next to Robert Hope,
William Gardenor, Arthur Donelson, Charles Harris,
Robert Erwin, and Widow McClain.
Owned land on the north side of Fuda Creek in 1774.
1790 - Hartman, George
1800: George 45+, 1 female 26-44, and 1 female -10.
Listed next to Peter Misenheimer, Henry Plylor,
David Fink, Henry Linker, William Gordin, and Hardin
Wiggins.
George sold land on Dutch Buffalo Creek to Paul
Furrer, Sr. in July 1806.
1810: George and wife 45+, 1 male 16-25, 1 female
16-25, 1 female 10-15, and 1 male -10.
Hartsell, George
1800: George 26-44, 1 female 45+, 1 female 26-44, 1
female 10-15, 1 male -10, and 3 females -10. Listed
next to Leonard Hartsell, John Hagler, Sr., Melchor
Fogelman, Frederick Plylor, George M. Redling, and
Andrew Rinehart.
1810: George and wife 45+, 4 females 16-25, 1 male
10-15, 1 male -10, and 1 female -10.
Hartsell, George
1810: George and wife 26-44, 3 females 16-25, 1
female 10-15, 2 males -10, and 1 female -10.
Hartsell/Hartzell, Jonathan
1800: Jonathan and wife 26-44, and 2 males -10.
Listed next to Christopher Leigh, Peter Quilman,
Joseph Starns, John Soseman, Daniel Cline, and
William Goodwin.
1810: Jonathan and wife 26-44, 1 male 10-15, 1 male
-10, and 3 females -10.
Hartsell, Leonard
1800: Leonard and wife 26-44, 1 male -10, and 1
female -10. Listed next to John Hagler, Sr., Melchor
Fogelman, Jacob Faggot, George Hartsell, Frederick
Plylor, and George M. Redling.
1810: Leonard 26-44, 1 female 45+, 1 female 26-44, 1
male 10-15, 1 female 10-15, 2 males -10, and 1
female -10.
1790 - Hartwick, Conrad
Owned land in the fork of Meadow Creek and Canada
Branch in 1782.
Haynes, William
Owned land on Muddy Creek in 1779.

1790 - Hays, Patrick & Rachel Russel
        Children: William ?, James(Susan Fitz), Louise(John
        Cooper), Mary, Frances, Cynthia, Sarah
        Owned land on Wolf Meadow Branch of Coddle Creek in
        1785.
        Son of William and Frances Hays
        Rachel was the daughter of James and Jane Carson
        Russell.
        Patrick moved to Greene Co., GA, but when is
        unknown. He may have gone to Abbeville Co. SC first
        as there was a Patrick Hays there. Before 1808 he
        moved to Warren Co., TN and was there through 1812.
        He then moved to Shelby Co., AL where he was a
        judge. By 1820 he was in Dallas Co., AL which is
        where he died. Rachel and son James are in the 1830
        Shelby Co., AL census.
Hays, William & Frances
        Children: Patrick
        Owned land on Wolf Meadow Branch of Coddle Creek and
        English Buffalo Creek in 1782.
Headright, John
        Owned land near Longreen branch of Coldwater Creek
        in 1784.
Heare, Hugh
        1800: Hugh snd his wife, and wife 26-44, and 3 males
        -10. Listed next to Robert Stanford, Josiah Deweast,
        Robert Miller, James Caragin, Sr., John Caragin, and
        James Purviance.
Henderson, William
        1810: William household consisted of 2 males 45+, 1
        female 45+, 1 male 16-25, 1 male 10-15, 1 female 10-
        15, 1 male -10, and 1 female -10.
Heninger, Rabeckah
        1800: Rabeckah 45+, 1 female 16-25, 2 males 10-15, 1
        female 10-15, and 1 male -10. Listed next to Tobius
        Clutz, Caleb Douss, John Ridley, Henry Fite, Daniel
        Faggot, and Harmon Moyer.
1790 - Henry, Henry, Capt
        Owned land on Coddle Creek in 1784.
Heren, Henry
        1800: Henry and wife 45+, 3 females 10-15, 1 male -
        10, and 2 females -10. Listed next to Christian
        Hurlohor, Christian Hurlohor, Jr., Henry Ovestwald,
        Martin Harkey, George Hise, and Mary House.
Herrin, Jesse
        1800: Jesse over 45, 1 female 26-44, 2 males 16-25,
        2 females 16-25, 1 male 10-15, 1 female 10-15, and 2
        males -10. Listed next to Thomas Allin, Randle
        Studevant, George Miller, Jacob Buzzard, Martin
        Harkey, and Lewis Fouts.
Hertough, Frederick

Owned land on Hamby Branch, a branch of Rocky River
in 1784.
Hess, Daniel
    1810: Daniel 26-44, 1 female 16-25, 2 males -10, and
    1 female -10.
Hewit, James & Elizabeth
    Owned land on Three Mile Branch in 1783.
Hileman, Jacob
    Bought land on Great Cold Water Creek in 1805 from
    Gideon Aleman.
    Bought land on Cold Water Creek from Mark Coleman in
    Jan 1806.
    Jacob bought land on Dutch Buffalo Creek from
    Nicholas Shuping(of Rowan Co.) in Jan 1812.
    1810: Jacob and wife 16-25.
Hillman, Jacob
    1810: Jacob 45+, 1 female 26-44, 2 females 16-25, 1
    male 10-15, 3 males -10, and 2 females -10.
Hill, Joel
    1810: Joel 16-25, 1 female 26-44, 1 male -10, and 3
    females -10.
Hindman, Jacob
    1810: Jacob and wife 16-25.
1790 - Hise/Hese, Conrad
    1800: Conrad and wife 45+, 1 male 16-25, 2 females
    16-25, 1 male 10-15, 1 female 10-15, and 3 females -
    10. Listed next to Henry Cuthezen, Tobias Cress,
    Charles Seffrid, Henry Cline, George Goodman, Jr.,
    and Peter Weaver.
    Conrad bought land on Dutch Buffalo Creek from Adam
    Moyers in July 1806.
Hise, George
    1800: George and wife 45+, 1 male 16-25, 2 females
    16-25, 1 female 10-15, 1 male -10, and 1 female 10.
    Listed next to Martin Harkey, Henry Heren, Christian
    Hurlohor, Jr., Mary House, Barbary Lype, and Jonas
    Lype.
Hodgeman, Jacob
    1800: Jacob and wife 26-44, 3 males 10-15, and 3
    males -10. Listed next to Martin Uery, Henry Pless,
    Jacob Boager, George Clontz, Peter Limeboh, and
    Peter Cauble.
1790 - Holbrook, Caleb & Druscilla Baker
    Married in Rowan Co., bond dated April 1, 1780,
    bondsman, Ad Baker.
    Moved to Gwinett Co., GA, died there about 1814.
    Lived in Mecklenburg at time of Revolution and
    served.
    Son of John Holbrook
    Druscilla had strong ties with Elias Baker and
    Benjamin Baker who also moved to GA. She was born in
    1763.

Caleb died in 1814.
Drucilla applied for a pension in 1841.
1790 - Holbrook, John
    Children: Vachel, Caleb (Drucilla Baker), Sarah
    (Elias Baker), Elizabeth (Benjamin Baker), William
    (Sarah Baker), and possibly Margaret (Joseph
    Higdon), Catherine (William Baker), and Jacob.
    Owned land on English Buffalo Creek in 1782.
    Moved to Franklin Co., GA
Holbrook, Samuel & Elizabeth Russell
    Children: David Greenberry (Jane Ann Purvians, Jane
    Ann Robinson, Sarah C. Allison Young, Harriet Moore
    Allison, Mary Stafford, Virginia Moore), Elijah
    (Mary Frazier, Joseph Young), Harvey P., Robert
    Russell
    Son of Vachel Holbrook
1790 - Holbrook, Vaitch (Vachel) & Catherine
    Children: John, Samuel(Elizabeth Russell), Richard,
    Griffith
    Son of John Holbrook.
    1800: Vachel household consited of himself and wife
    26-44, 1 female 16-25, 2 males 10-15, 3 males -10,
    and 1 female -10.
    1810: Vachel 45+, 1 female 16-25, 2 males 16-25, 2
    males 10-15, 4 males -10, and 2 females -10.
1790 - Holbrook, William & Sarah Baker
    Married in Rowan Co., bond dated May 14, 1785,
    bondsman, Caleb Holbrooks.
    Sold land to William Correl 1800 and it is believed
    he moved to Georgia with his father and brother,
    Caleb.
Holly, Elizabeth
    1800: Elizabeth 45+, 1 male 26-44, 1 male 16-25, 1
    male 10-15, and 2 females 10-15. Listed next to Jean
    McLusky, Elizabeth Skiliton, Martin Gun, Thomas
    Rogers, John Patterson, and Susanna Morrison.
Holton, David
    1810: David 26-44, 1 female 16-25, and 1 female -10.
Hoover, Jacob
    1800: Jacob and wife 45+, 2 males 16-25, 2 females
    16-25, 1 male 10-15, 2 females 10-15, and 3 males -
    10. Listed next to Charles Clover, John Barger,
    Nicholas Rough, Rinehold Overshine, John Lippard,
    Michael Goodman, and Henry Fesperman.
Hoover, John
    1810: John and wife 16-25, and 2 females -10.
Hope, Abner
    Abner was overseer of Tuckasegee Road from Rocky
    River to the Mecklenburg Co. line in April 1813.
    1810: Abner and wife 26-44, 2 males -10, and 2
    females -10.
Hope, James

1810: James 26-44, 1 female 16-25, 3 males -10, and
1 female -10.

1790 - Hope, Robert & Catherine
    Children: Thomas (Ann Allison), John (Peggy
    Houston), James, Margaret (Joseph Alexander),
    Catherine (Joseph Crawford)
    These children of Robert are based on marriage
    records so the accuracy can not be guaranteed.
    1800: Robert and Catherine, and wife 45+, 3 males
    16-25, 1 male 10-15, and 2 males -10. Listed next to
    William Gardenor, Arthur Donelson, John Cannon,
    William Harris (tailor), Charles Harris, and Robert
    Erwin.
    Robert died before 1810.
    1810: Catey 45+, 1 male 16-25, 1 male 10-15, and 1
    female 10-15.
    Owned land on Clarke Creek, a branch of Rocky River

Hough, Jacob
    Owned land on Adams Creek and Dutch Buffalo Creek in
    1783.

House, Elias
    1800: Elias and wife 26-44, 1 male 16-25, 1 male -
    10, and 3 females -10. Listed next to Daniel Little,
    Stephen Mayfield, Signe Seales, Philip Cariker, Sr.,
    George Cariker, and Philip Cariker, Jr.
    1810: Elias and wife 45+, 1 male 10-15, 2 females
    10-15, 1 male -10, and 3 females -10.

House, John
    1800: John 26-44, 1 female 16-25, 1 male 10-15, and
    2 females -10. Listed next to Martin Harky, Jacob
    Harky, William Folk, Henry Ovestwald, Christian
    Hurlohor, and Christian Hurlohor, Jr.
    1810: John 45+, 2 males 16-25, 1 male 10-15, and 2
    females -10.

House, Margaret
    Children: Henry

House, Mary
    1800: Mary 45+, and 1 female 16-25. Listed next to
    George Hise, Martin Harkey, Henry Heren, Barbary
    Lype, Jonas Lype, and Philip Litaker.

Houston, Aaron
    1800: Aaron and wife 16-25, and 1 male -10. He
    listed next to John Goodman, Frances Linse, David
    McKinly, James Bridges, Henry Brines, and Joseph
    Shinn.

Houston, Andrew & Esther
    1810: Andrew 26-44, 1 male 26-44, 1 female 16-25, 1
    male -10, and 2 females -10.
    Andrew sold to George Basinger on Coddle Creek in
    Jan 1814.

1790 - Houstin, Archabeld, Capt
    Children: Archibald (Jeanne Crawford)

Owned land on Coddle Creek in 1776.
1800: Archibald and wife 45+. Listed next to John
Houston, William Hunt, Archibald Gilmore, Archibald
Houston, Jr., Robert Harris, and John Hall.
Houston, Archibald & Jeanne Crawford
    Married in Cabarrus Co. on April 16, 1794, John
    Simianer, bondsman.
    1800: Archibald and Jeanne and wife 26-44, 1 male -
    10, and 2 females -10. Listed next to Archibald
    Houston, John Houston, William Hunt, Robert Harris,
    John Hall, and Hugh Hamilton.
    1810: Archibald 45+, his wife, 26-44, 1 male 10-15,
    2 females 10-15, 2 males -10, and 1 female -10.
1790 - Houston, David
    On Little Buffalo Creek
    Son of William and Margaret Houston.
1790 - Houstin, David
    Owned land on the east side of Coddle Creek in 1784.
Houston, Eleanor
    1810: Eleanor 26-44, 1 male 16-25, 1 female 16-25, 2
    females 10-15, 3 males -10, and 2 females -10.
Houston, Nancy
    1810: Nancy household consisted of just herself 45+.
1790 - Houstin, John & Ann Howey
    Children: J. Thompson, Allen, Stephen, Peggy, Jane
    Owned land on Coddle Creek in 1778.
    Owned land on Coddle Creek and Reubens branch of
    Buffalo Creek. John also owned land on Third Branch,
    which he sold to John Rumple in July 1806.
    1810: John and Ann, and wife 45+, 1 male 16-44, 3
    females 16-25, 1 male 10-15, and 1 female 10-15.
    John died May 28, 1812
Houston ? & Agnes
    Children: John-born Dec 1793, Daniel-born Feb 1797
1790 - Houston, William, Jr
    1800: William and wife 26-44, and 3 males -10.
    Listed next to Robert Allison, Arthur McCree,
    William Wiley, Stephen Alexander, John Skilinton,
    and Joseph Alexander.
1790 - Houston, William, Sr & Margaret
    Children: William, David
    William died before 1805 and Margaret sold land
    along with her son William, Jr. to Michael Isenhour
    on Little Buffalo Creek in 1805.
    1800: William and wife 45+, 1 male 16-25, and 1
    female 16-25. Listed next to Thomas McCain, William
    Wallis, James Tanner, Benjamin Biggs, John Niehler,
    and Athen Almore.
Houston, William
    1810: William and wife 26-44, 1 male -10, and 1
    female -10.
Howell, Henry

1800: Henry 26-44, 1 female 16-25, and 1 male -10.
Listed next to James Little, John Misenheimer,
William Stow, James Love, John Stuart, and George
Teater.

Howell, Henry
1800: Henry and wife 16-25. Listed next to John
Howell, Joseph Howell, Sr., Joseph Howell, Jr.,
David Wisner, William Bugg, and Henry Cagle.

Howell, John
1800: John 26-44, 1 female 16-25, 1 male 10-15, and
3 males -10. Listed next to Joseph Howell, Sr.,
Joseph Howell, Jr., Abraham Leftenburg, Henry
Howell, David Wisner, and William Bugg.

Howell, Joseph, Jr.
1800: Joseph and wife 26-44, 1 male -10, and 2
females -10. Listed next to Abraham Leftenburg,
David Cowell, Thomas Ingram, Joseph Howell, Sr.,
John Howell, and Henry Howell.
1810: Joseph and wife 45+, 1 female 16-25, 1 female
10-15, 1 male -10, and 1 female -10.
In the 1860 Cabarrus Co. census Joseph is listed as
89 and an Elizabeth is listed as 67 years old.
Elizabeth must have been either Joseph second wife
or his daughter.

Howell, Joseph, Sr.
1800: Joseph and wife 45+, 4 males 16-25, 2 males
10-15, and 1 female 10-15. Listed next to Joseph
Howell, Jr., Abraham Leftenburg, David Cowell, John
Howell, Henry Howell, and David Wisner.
1810: Joseph and wife 45+, 1 male 16-25, 2 females
16-25, 1 male -10, and 1 female -10.

Hudson, Jacob and Eleanor Shinn
1800: Jacob is listed as a resident of Concord. His
26-44, 1 male 26-44, and 1 male -10. Listed with
John Master, Lawrence Snapp, George Smith, Philip
Bless, and Samuel Hughey.
Jacob and Eleanor were married in Cabarrus County,
bond dated June 4, 1801, bondsman, John Purviance.

Hughey, Alexander & Elizabeth McCachron
Married in Cabarrus County, bond dated Jan 28, 1795,
Hector McCachron, bondsman.
1800: Alexander and Elizabeth 26-44, and 1 female
10-15.
Elizabeth was the daughter of John & Mary McAhron.

Howey, James
Patent dated March 3, 1745 for land in what was
known as the Great Tract, or Welsh Tract on the
south side of Rocky River near the Rocky River
community.

1790 - Hughey, John G.L. & Jean Russel
Children:
John patrolled in Concord in 1804.

Huey, John G.L. & Mary Russell
    Married in Cabarrus County, bond dated Dec 9, 1806,
    bondsman, William A. Russell
    1810: John 26-44, Mary 16-25, 1 male -10, and 1
    female -10.
Huie, Alexander & Elizabeth McEachern/McCachron
    Married in Cabarrus County, bond dated Jan 28, 1795,
    Hector McEachern, bondsman.
*Huie, James
    Children: Catherine (James E. Kerr)
    1800: James and wife 26-44, 1 male 16-25, 3 males -
    10, and 2 females -10. Listed next to Samuel Hughey,
    Samusl Ferguson, Alexander Ferguson, Mathias Phifer,
    James Carson, and John Russell.
Huie, Samuel & Jane Morrison
    Children: John G.L. (Mary Russel), Pleasant M.,
    Josiah (Leah Cress), Silas, Robert C.
    Jane Morrison was the daughter of John & Mary
    Morrison. John died 1777, Mary died 1781. John &
    Mary were cousins and John brought Mary from
    Ireland. John was the brother of James and Robert C.
    Morrison and he settled on Caldwell Creek. He signed
    the petition for the pardon of the Cabarrus Black
    Boys in 1771. He was wounded in the Revolution and
    died as a result.
    1800: Samuel and Jane, and wife 26-44, 1 male 16-25,
    2 males 10-15, 1 female 10-15, and 2 males -10.
    Listed next to Samuel Ferguson, Alexander Ferguson,
    Martha Ferguson, James Hughey, Mathias Phifer, and
    James Carson.
    1810: Samuel and wife 45+, 1 male 10-15, and 2 males
    -10.
    Samuel died and left a will in 1817.
Hughey, Samuel
    1800: Samuel is listed as a resident of Concord. His
    and wife 45+, 1 male 26-44, 1 male 16-25, 1 female
    16-25, 2 males 10-15, and 2 males -10. Listed with
    John Master, Lawrence Snapp, George Smith, Philip
    Bless, and Jacob Hudson.
    1810: Samuel and wife 45+, 1 male 10-15, and 3 males
    -10.
Huey, Peter & Mary McAhron (widow of John)
    Children: Elizabeth (Hector McAhron)
    1800: Peter and Mary, and wife over 45, 1 female 16-
    25, 3 females 10-15, and 1 female -10. Listed next
    to William L. Alexander, James Scott, James Russell,
    Isaac Neeley, Hector McAharon, and Valentine
    Kirkpatrick.
    1810: Peter and wife 45+, 2 males 16-25, 2 females
    16-25, and 1 male -10.
Hughs, John

Owned land on Irish Buffalo Creek and Coddle Creek
in 1779.
Hughes, Samuel
Owned land on Coddle Creek and Buffalo Creek in
1779.
Humphrey, James
Owned land near the Muddy Branch of Coddle Creek in
1776.
Hunt, John
1810: John household consisted of 5 males 26-44.
Hunt, William
1800: William 45+, 2 males 10-15, and 1 male 16-25.
Listed next to Archibald Gilmore, David Farr,
Mitchel Flemmon, John Houston, Archibald Houston,
and Archibald Houston, Jr.
Hurlohor, Christian
1800: Christian and wife 45+. Listed next to Henry
Ovestwald, John House, Martin Harky, Christian
Hurlohor, Jr., Henry Heren, and Martin Harkey.
Hurlohor, Christian, Jr.
1800: Chrisitian and wife 26-44, 2 males -10, and 2
females -10. Listed next to Christian Hurlohor,
Henry Ovestwald, John House, Henry Heren, Martin
Harkey, and George Hise.
1810: Christian and wife 26-44, 1 female 16-25, 2
males 10-15, 1 female 10-15, and 4 females -10.
Hutson, Jacob
1800: Jacob 26-44, 1 male 26-44, and 1 male -10.
Listed next to Philip Pless/Bless, George Smith,
Lawrence Snapp, Catherine Shinn, Lewis Townsend, and
Murdoch Campbell.
Hutson, James
1810: James and wife 16-25, 1 male -10, and 2
females -10.
Hutson, Samuel
1810: Samuel and wife 26-44, 2 males -10, and 2
females -10.
Hutson, Seth
1810: Seth and wife 26-44, 1 male 10-15, 1 male -10,
and 2 females -10.
Hutson, William & Sarah Shinn
1810 William and wife 26-44, and 2 males -10.
Iagetser, William
1810: William and wife, 45+, 2 males 16-25, and 2
females 10-15.
Ingram, Thomas
1800: Thomas 26-44, and 1 female 45+.
Irwin, Lindsey
1810: Lindsey 26-44, 2 females 16-25, 1 male -10,
and 4 females -10.
Irwin, Samuel
1810: Samuel and wife 16-25, and 1 female -10.

Irwin, Thomas
        1810: Thomas and wife 45+, 1 male 16-25, 1 female
        16-25, and 1 male 10-15.
Isenhour, Michael
        1800: Michael 45+, 1 female 26-44, 1 female 10-15,
        and 2 females -10. Listed next to Peter Isenhour,
        Christopher Beaver, Lewis Fouts, John Barger,
        Mathias Barnhart, and Jacob Berry.
Isehoor, Michael
        1810: Michael 26-44, 1 female 10-15, 1 male -10, and
        2 females -10.
Isenhower, Nicholas
        1810: Nicholas and wife 26-44, 2 males -10, and 2
        females -10.
Isenhour, Peter
        1800: Peter and wife 45+, 2 males 26-44, 2 males 16-
        25, and 1 female -10. Listed next to Christopher
        Beaver, Lewis Fouts, Martin Harkey, Michael
        Isenhour, John Barger, and Mathias Barnhart.
        Peter owned land on Dutch Buffalo Creek near the
        Rowan county line.
        1810: Peter and 1 female, and wife 45+, 1 female 26-
        44, and 5 females -10.
1790 - Jarret, Daniel
        Children: Anthony
Jarret, John
        John LWT was proven in July 1812.
Jegler, Johanes
        Johanes was a witness for a deed between Paulser
        Ness and Paul Furrow on Dutch Buffalo Creek in 1786.
Jemison, Adam
        Adam bought and sold land in Jan 1814, but the
        location is not given.
Jemison, James
        1810: James 45+, 1 male 26-44, 2 females 26-44, 1
        male 10-15, 3 males -10, and 3 females -10.
        James bought land from John Jemison on the east side
        of Rocky River in April 1812.
Jemison, John
        John sold to James Jemison on the east side of Rocky
        River in April 1812.
Jamison, Samuel
        1810: Samuel and wife 26-44, 1 male 16-25, 1 male
        10-15, 1 male -10, and 2 females -10.
John, Robert
        Owned land on Muddy Creek in 1783.
        Son of Mary John
Johnston, Jeremiah
        1800: Jeremiah and wife 45+, 1 male 10-15, 1 male -
        10, and 1 female -10. Listed next to James Harris,
        Elisha Spears, Cunningham Harris, George Campbell,
        John Callon, and Charles Campbell.

Johnston, John
>   1810: John 16-25, 1 female 26-44, 1 male -10, and 2
>   females -10.

Johnston, Thomas
>   1810: Thomas and wife 26-44, 1 male -10, and 4
>   females -10.

Johnston, William
>   1800: William and wife 26-44, 1 male 10-15, 1 female
>   10-15, 1 male -10, and 5 females -10. Listed next to
>   Joseph Bigger, John Newell, William Newell, Hannah
>   McFaddon, Francis Newell, and James Bradshaw, Jr.

Jones, Even
>   1800: Even and wife 26-44. Listed next to Charles
>   Tounsend, George Carlock, Levi Curzine, Thomas
>   White, Martha Campbell, George Voiles, and Signe
>   Seales.

Jones, John
>   1800: John and wife and wife 45+, and 1 female 10-
>   15. Listed next to Benjamin Alexander, James
>   Caragin, Samuel Kenly, Duncan Smith, Hugh Pickens,
>   and John Alexander.

Justice, Hance & Mary
>   Owned land on Cufton Creek, a branch of English
>   Buffalo Creek in 1780.

Justice, Mannie
>   Owned land on Long Branch of Cold Water Creek in
>   1779.

Keever, Jacob
>   Children: Daniel (Mary Goodnight)

Kegel, Peter & Elizabeth
>   Peter sold land to Martin Dry in Jan 1799.

Kenly, Joshua
>   1810: Joshua household consisted of 1 male and 1
>   female and wife 45+, 1 male 16-25, 1 female 16-25, 2
>   males 10-15, 2 females 10-15, and 1 female -10.

Kenly, Samuel
>   1800: Samuel 45+, 1 female 26-44, 1 female 16-25, 1
>   male 10-15, 3 males -10. Listed next to John
>   Gilmore, Robert Alexander, Susanna Russel, James
>   Caragin, Benjamin Alexander, and John Jones.

Kepple, John
>   1800: John household consisted of 2 males 26-44, 1
>   female 16-25, and 2 males -10. Listed next to Kelin
>   Keply, Peter Keply, Jr., Henry Doland, Timothy
>   Doland, and Samuel Graver.
>   1810: John household consiste of himself and wife
>   26-44, 2 males -10, and 3 females -10.

Keply/Cepple, Kelin
>   1800: Kelin and wife 26-44, 2 males -10, and 2
>   females -10. Listed next to Peter Keply, Jr., Peter
>   Keply, George Culp, John Kepple, Henry Doland, and
>   Timothy Doland.

1810: Kelian 45+, 1 female 26-44, 2 males 10-15, 1
female 10-15, 2 males -10, and 2 females -10.
1790 - Kepple/Capley, Peter & Cillian
    Children: Margaret (George Earnhart), Elizabeth
    (John Grub), Catharine (Martin Dry), Peter, Henry,
    John (Sarah Crowell)
    1800: Peter and wife 45+. Listed next to George
    Culp, Moses Cox, William Cox, Peter Keply, Jr.,
    Kelin Keply, and John Kepple.
Keply, Peter, Jr.
    1800: Peter and wife 26-44, 1 male -10, and 2
    females -10. Listed next to Peter Keply, George
    Culp, Moses Cox, Kelin Keply, John Kepple, and Henry
    Doland.
    1810: Peter and wife 26-44, 1 male 10-15, 2 females
    10-15, 2 males -10, and 3 females -10.
Kepple/Cepple, William
    1810: William and wife 26-44, 1 male 10-15, 1 female
    10-15, 3 males -10, and 2 females -10.
Killough, Samuel
    Owned land on Rocky River in 1784.
    1800: Samuel 45+, 1 female 26-44, 2 females 16-25, 1
    male 10-15, 1 female 10-15, 2 males -10, and 4
    females -10. Listed next to William Keilough, Oliver
    Harris, Hugh Hamilton, William Douglass, James
    McCaleb, and Samuel Martin.
    1810: Samuel 45+, 2 females 26-44, 1 male 26-44, 1
    male 16-25, 3 females 16-25, 4 females 10-15, 3
    males -10, and 1 female -10.
Killpatrick, Robert
    1810: Robert and wife 16-25.
Keilough, William
    1800: William 26-44, 1 female 16-25, 3 males -10,
    and 1 female -10. Listed next to Oliver Harris, Hugh
    Hamilton, John Hall, Samuel Keilough, William
    Douglass, and James McCaleb.
    1810: William and wife 26-44, 1 female 16-25, 2
    males 10-15, 2 males -10, and 4 females -10.
Kesler/Keisler, John
    1800: John and wife 26-44, 2 males -10, and 1 female
    -10. Listed next to William Glover, Susanna
    Morrison, John Patterson, James Martin, Robert
    Sullivan, and Celia Russell.
    1810: John 45+, 1 female 26-44, 1 male 10-15, 2
    females 10-15, 2 males -10, and 1 female -10.
Kimmons/Cimmons, Andrew
    1810: Andrew 45+, 1 female 26-44, 1 male 16-25, 1
    male 10-15, 2 males -10, and 2 females -10.
Kimmons, Elizabeth
    Elizabeth was born 1780, died Oct 15, 1850
    Buried in Spears Cemetery of Rocky River Church
1790 - Kimmins, Hugh

Children: John
Owned land on Reedy Creek in 1782.
1810: Hugh and another male, and wife 45+, 1 female
45+, 2 males 16-25, 3 females 16-25, and 2 males 10-
15.

Kimmons, John & Margaret Morrison
Children: Abigail Erixena (Daniel McFarland), Hugh
Harvey (Cornelia Jane Hope), William Morrison
(Catherine C. Hope), Martha Ann (John Pinckney
Morrison), John Alexander (Mary Walker, Ellen Wiley,
Martha Jones, Annie Devall), James McEwen (Martha
Falls McCorkle), Robert Hall
John and Margaret moved to Mississippi in 1837.
Margaret was the daughter of William and Abigail
McEwen Morrison.

Kimmons, Margaret
Margaret was born 1787, died Nov 22, 1852
Buried in Spears Cemetery of Rocky River Church

Kirkpatrick/Killpatrick, James
Owned land on Irish Buffalo Creek and Coddle Creek
in 1773.

Kiripatrick, Robert
In the 1860 Cabarrus Co. census, Robert is listed as
74 years old. His son S.C., born 1810: married to
Margaret C., born 1812, is living with him.

1790 - Kirkpatrick, Valentine
Lived in the Rocky River Church area.
1800: his 26-44, his wife 26-44, 1 male 16-25, 1
female 16-25, 1 male 10-15, 1 female 10-15, 3 males
-10, and 1 female -10. Listed next to Hector
McAharon, Isaac Neeley, Peter Huey, Alexander Allin,
Daniel Bean, and James Burns.
1810: Valentine and wife 45+, 3 males 16-25, 2
females 16-25, 1 male 10-15, and 1 male -10.

Kiser, David & Rachel Kisor
Married in Cabarrus Co., bond dated Oct 17, 1804,
bondsman, Michael Clingman.
Children: Susannah, unknown female, John Mark,
Margaret Melissa, Irvin, William L., Ellen (Noah W.
Hartsell), Thomas P., Matlida.
Owned land on Rocky River in 1805.
1810: David 26-44, Rachel 16-25, 1 male -10, and 2
females -10.
David is listed in the Cabarrus Co. census as 69 and
Rachel is listed as 67 years old.

1790 - Kiser, Frederick & Rebecca
Owned land on both sides of Meadow Creek, a branch
on the north side of Rocky River in 1773.
1800: Frederick 26-44, Rebecca 45+, 2 females 16-25,
1 male 10-15, 1 female 10-15, 1 male -10, and 2
females -10. Listed next to Leonard Mire, Travis

Gullino, Michael Garmon, James Long, John Garmon,
and Beverly Gray.
1810: Frederick and Rebecca 45+, 2 males 16-25, and
3 females 10-15.
Kiser, George Alexander & Debbie Weatherford
Children: Susannah (Parrot Evans), Sarah (Joseph
Heinseman), Archibald (Lucinda Daniels), George Mark
(Mary Crayton), Deborah (John Mark Kiser), Phoebe
(Green Collins)
George was the son of George Alexander Kiser and
Mary Dove.
Kiser, George Alexander & Mary Dove
Children: George Alexander (Debbie Weatherford),
Elizabeth (George Long), David W. (Rachel Kiser),
Levi, Esther (Andrew Carriker), Marcus (Polly Kiser
- Blanche Kiser Taylor Moore, convicted of murder in
Alamance Co., NC in 1990, is a descendent of
Marcus), John Kiser (Eleanor Howell), Thomas Dove
(Mary Gurley), Mary Polly (Nathan Green).
1790 - Kiser, George & Mary
Owned land in the fork of Meadow Creek and Canada
branch on the north side of Rocky River in 1779.
Conveyed land to David Kiser in Oct 1805 on Rocky
River.
1800: George and wife 45+, 1 male 16-25, 2 males 10-
15, 1 female 10-15, 1 male -10, and 1 female -10.
Listed next to Isham Clay, George Teater, John
Stuart, Andrew Watts, John Walls, and Valentine
Watts.
1810: George and Mary 45+, 3 males 16-25, and 1
female 16-25.
Kizer, George, Jr.
1810: George 26-44, 1 female 16-25, 2 males -10, and
1 female -10.
Kiser, John & Eleanor Howell
Married in Cabarrus Co., April 27, 1814.
Children: Madison Washington, Pinkney Lafayette,
James Madison, John Franklin, Adeline, Eleanor,
Wiley Jackson, Merewether Posey, Mary Ann.
John and Eleanor moved to Campbell Co., GA.
Kiser/Kizer, Mark & Mary
Mark bought land adjacent to the Montgomery Co. line
in April 1812.
In the 1860 Cabarrus Co. census Mark is listed as 72
and Mary is listed as 67 years old.
Kiser, Michael
Michael sold land in Cabarrus Co. to George Kiser in
July 1806, location unknown.
Kiser, Peter & Fanny Garman
Children: Frederick, Margaret (? Teeter),
Catherine, Peter, Rachel, Elizabeth (Alexander

Klingman), George Alexander (Mary Dove), Sarah (John
Reed - owner of the Reed Gold Mine)
Peter died about 1785.
Kline, George
Children: Jacob
Klutz, George & Rosanah Furr
Married in Cabarrus Co., bond dated May 13, 1807,
bondsman, Richard S. Tate.
1810: George 26-44, 2 males 16-25, 1 female 16-25,
and 1 female -10.
Klutz/Cluts, John
1810: John and wife 26-44, 1 male 10-15, and 3 males
-10.
Klutz, Leonard
Bought land on Little Buffalo Creek from John
Melchor in 1805.
1810: Leonard and wife 45+, 1 female 26-44, 1 female
16-25, 1 male 10-15, 1 female 10-15, 1 male -10, and
3 females -10.
Klutts/Clutz, Tobias
1810: Tobias' 45+, 1 female 26-44, 1 female 10-15,
and 4 males -10.
Krider/Crider, Daniel
1800: Daniel and wife 26-44, 2 females 10-15, and 3
males -10. Listed next to Phillip Shive, George
Harkman, Henry Simmons, Michael Overcash, Jacob
Krider, Jr., and Manasah Dresser.
1810: Daniel and wife 26-44, 3 males 10-15, 3 males
-10, and 1 female -10.
Krider/Crider, Jacob, Jr.
1800: Jacob and wife 26-44, and 2 males -10. Listed
next to Michael Overcash, Danile Krider, Phillip
Shive, Manasah Dresser, and Jacob Krider, Sr.
Krider/Crider, Jacob, Sr.
1800: Jacob and wife 45+, 1 male 16-25, 1 female 16-
25, 2 males 10-15, and 1 female -10. Listed next to
Manasah Dresser, Jacob Krider, Jr., Michael
Overcash, Jacob Murph, Paul Walton, and Sarah Nowls.
Lance, John
Owned land on Coldwater Creek in 1783.
Landis, Christopher & Ruth
Owned land on Three Mile Creek in 1764.
Christopher died in or before 1771.
Lawrie, Samuel
Samuel was licensed as an attorney in April 1798.
Leigh/Lee, Christopher
1800: Christopher and wife 26-45, 1 male 10-15, 1
male -10, and 3 females -10. Listed next to Peter
Quilman, Joseph Starns, Robert Williams, Jonathan
Hartzell, John Soseman, and Daniel Cline.
Lee, James

1810: James and another male 16-25, 1 female 16-25,
and 1 male -10.
James sold to Mathias Barringer on the Sugar Run
Branch of Cold Water Creek in Jan 1814.

Lee, John
1800: John 45+, 1 female 26-44, 1 female 16-25, 2
males 10-15, and 1 female 10-15. Listed next to
Margret Curzine, Nicholas Curzine, William McGraw,
Thomas Clark, Levi Curzine, and George Carlock.

Lee, Robert & Catherine Plott
Married Feb 26, 1794 in Cabarrus Co., George Plotte
bondsman.
1800: Robert 16-25, 1 female 26-44, 1 male -10, and
2 females -10. Listed next to Roland Voiles, Mary
White, Henry Potts, Hannah Voiles, Christian Dry,
and Isaac Loftin.
Owned land on Three Mile Creek and the east side of
Dutch Buffalo Creek near John Barringer in April
1807.
1810: Robert and wife 26-44, 1 male 10-15, 1 female
10-15, 1 male -10, and 2 females -10.

Lee, William
1810: William household consisted of 1 female 16-25,
1 male 10-15, 2 males -10, and 1 female -10.

Lefler, Thomas
1810: Thomas' and wife 16-25, and 1 male -10.

Leftenburg, Abraham
1800: Abraham and wife 26-44, 4 males -10, and 1
female -10. Listed next to David Cowell, Thomas
Ingram, John Tucker, Joseph Howell, Jr., Joseph
Howell, Sr., and John Howell.

Leopard, William & Christina
Owned land on Dutch Buffalo Creek before 1783.
Christina estate settlement took place in July 1797.

Letsinger/Setsinger, John
Owned land on Coldwater and Buffalo Creeks in 1783.

Leviston, Robert
Owned land on Coddle Creek in 1782.

Lewis, Delphie
1800: Delphie 45+, and 1 male -10. Listed next to
Elizabeth Young, Gideon Almon, John Still, Noah
Sandiford, William Mc Anulty, and John Crumwell, Sr.

Lewis, Henry
1810: Henry and wife 26-44, 2 females 10-15, and 3
males -10.

Lewis, Jacob
1800: Jacob and wife 45+, 2 males 16-25, 1 female
16-25, 1 male 10-15, 2 females 10-15, and 1 male -
10. Listed next to John Long, Daniel Cline, William
Croner, Mathias Mitchell, Sr., Mathias Mitchell,
Jr., and Jacob Mitchell.

Lewis, Jacob

1810: Jacob household consisted of 2 males 16-25, 1
female 45+, 1 female 16-25, and 1 male 10-15.

Lewis, Michael & Caty Coon
Licht, Christopher
    Children: William
    1810: Christopher 26-44, 2 females 26-44, 3 males
    16-25, 1 female 16-25, 1 male -10, and 3 females -
    10.
1790 - Lidaker, Conrad
    Conrad bought land from Rolin, Thomas & Abel Voyls
    on Cold Water Creek in 1805.
Ledeker, George
    Indicted for murder in 1813
1790 - Lidaker/Lydecker, Philip & Rosina
    Children: Mary, Christina, Peter, George, Elizabeth
    Sides (John) After John death, Elizabeth married
    Elijah Perry of Montgomery Co.
    In Mecklenburg Co. in 1784.
Lincer, Henry
    1810: Henry and wife 16-25, and 1 female -10.
Lineboh, Henry
    1800: Henry and wife 26-44, 3 males -10, and 1
    female -10. Listed next to William Ryal, Tobias
    Stirewalt, Jacob Rimer, George Speake, David Speck,
    and Jacob Cassock.
Limeboh, Peter
    1800: Peter and wife 26-44, 1 male -10, and 3
    females -10. Listed next to George Clontz, Jacob
    Hodgeman, Martin Uery, Peter Cauble, Jacob Pines,
    and John Edleman.
1790 - Lingle, Conrad
    Children: Barbara, Elizabeth, Conrad
    son of Lorentz Lingle
Lingle, Francis
    1810: Francis and wife 45+, 3 males 16-25, 2 females
    10-15, 2 males -10, and 1 female -10.
1790 - Lingle, Jacob
    son of Lorentz Lingle
    1800: Jacob and wife 26-44, 1 female 16-25, 2 males
    10-15, 1 female 10-15, 1 male -10, and 3 females -
    10. Listed next to John Cluttz, Leonard Cluttz,
    Michael Walker, Thomas Goodman, Jacob Slough, and
    Philip File.
    Bought land on Little Buffalo Creek in 1805 from
    John Melchor.
    Sold land on Dutch Buffalo Creek to Henry Fisher in
    July 1806.
    Moved to Ohio before 1809.
Lingle, Paul
    1810: Paul and wife 16-25, and 1 female -10.
Linker, Henry

1800: Henry and wife 45+, 1 male 10-15, 1 female 10-
15, 4 males -10, and 2 females -10. Listed next to
George Hartman, Peter Misenheimer, Henry Plylor,
William Gordin, Hardin Wiggins, and Eve Wilhelm.
1810: Henry and wife 26-44, 2 males 16-25, 2 males
10-15, 2 females 10-15, 1 male -10, and 1 female -
10.
Linkker, Henry
1810: Henry and wife 16-25, 1 male -10, and 1 female
-10.
Linse, Frances
1800: Frances' , 26-44, and 1 female -10. Listed
next to David McKinly, Josiah Bradly, John Rumple,
John Goodman, Aaron Houston, and James Bridges.
Linse/Lence, Jacob
1810: Jacob and wife 26-44, 1 female 16-25, 1 male
10-15, 1 male -10, and 2 females -10.
Linton, Samuel
Owned land on Mallard Creek and King Branch, near
and on Rocky River in 1778.
Leppard, Frederick
1810: Frederick 26-44, 1 female 45+, 1 female 26-44,
1 female 16-25, 2 males -10, and 1 female -10.
Lippard, John
1800: John and wife 45+, 1 male 26-44, 1 male 16-25,
and 1 female 16-25. Listed next to Rinehold
Overshine, Jacob Hoover, Charles Clover, Michael
Goodman, Henry Fesperman, Michael Fesperman, and
William Sefred.
Lippard/Leppard, Peter
1810: Peter 26-44, 1 female 16-25, 2 males -10, and
1 female -10.
Lirely, John
John bought land from Peter Treece on Bear Creek in
July 1812.
Listenbay, Isaiah & Agness
1800: Agness 26-44, 1 male 10-15, and 3 females -10.
Listed next to William W. Spears, David White,
Solomon Spears, George Davis, Robert Davis, and
Alexander Scott.
Isaiah died before Oct 1798.
Litaker, Conrad
1800: Conrad 45+, 1 female 26-44, 1 male 10-15, and
1 female -10. Listed next to Philip Litaker, Jonas
Lype, Barbary Lype, George Misenheimer, John
Melchor, and Jacob Miller.
1810: Conrad 45+, 1 male 16-25, 1 female 16-25, 3
males -10, and 1 female -10.
Conrad bought land on Cold Water Creek from Abel,
Thomas, and Rolin Voyls in July 1805. He bought on
Adam Creek in April 1813.
Ledeker, George

George was indicted for murder in Oct 1813.

Liteker, Jacob
1810: Jacob 26-44, 1 female 45+, 1 female 10-15, 1
male -10, and 1 female -10.

Litaker, Philip
1800: Philip and wife 45+, 1 male 26-44, 1 male 16-
25, and 1 female 16-25. Listed next to Jonas Lype,
Barbary Lype, Mary House, Conrad Litaker, George
Misenheimer, and John Melchor.

Little, Daniel
1800: Daniel 45+, 1 female 26-44, 1 male 16-25, 1
male 10-15, 2 females 10-15, 4 males -10, and 2
females -10. Listed next to Stephen Mayfield, Signe
Seales, George Voiles, Elias House, Philip Cariker,
Sr., and George Cariker.

Little, Daniel & Mary
In the 1860 census, Daniel is listed as 70 and Mary
is listed as 60 years old.

Little, James
1800: James and wife 26-44, 1 male 10-15, 4 males -
10, and 1 female -10. Listed next to John
Misenheimer, William Stow, George Smith, Henry
Howell, James Love, and John Stuart.

1790 - Lock, Francis & Blanche
Owned land on a ridge between Coddle Creek and
Buffalo Creek in 1777, before Cabarrus became a
county.
Near Samuel Patton in 1783, sold land to Caleb
Phifer in 1798.

Lock, Matthew & Margaret Phifer, Elizabeth Crawford
Owned land on Irish Buffalo Creek in 1777.

1790 - Loften, Isaac
Owned land on Irish Buffalo Creek and Coldwater
Creek in 1784.
1800: Isaac 45+, 2 males 16-25, 1 female 16-25, and
1 male 10-15. Listed next to Christian Dry, Hannah
Voiles, Robert Lee, John Plott, James McGraw, and
William McGraw.

Long, George
1800: George and wife 16-25, and 1 female -10.
Listed next to John Reed, Joshua Tucker, Isaac
Brandon, William Polk, William Smith, and George
Tucker, Sr.
1810: George 26-44, 1 female 16-25, and 3 females -
10.
George bought land on the west side of Rocky River
from Michael Howell and George Reed in Jan 1812.

Long, Jacob & Christina
In the 1850 Union Co. census Jacob is listed as 81
and Christina is listed as 77 years old.

Long, James

1800: James and wife 26-44, 2 males -10, and 2
females -10. Listed next to Frederick Kizer, Leonard
Mire, Travis Gullino, John Garmon, Beverly Gray, and
John Gray.
1810: James 45+, 1 female 26-44, 1 male 16-25, 3
females 10-15, 3 males -10, and 1 female -10.

Long, John
1800: John and wife 26-44, 1 male 16-25, 2 females
16-25, 1 male 10-15, 2 females 10-15, 2 males -10,
and 3 females -10. Listed next to Daniel Cline,
William Croner, Jacob Croner, Jacob Lewis, Mathias
Mitchell, Sr., and Mathias Mitchell, Jr.
Owned land on Muddy Creek bordering Thomas Black,
David McKinley and Joseph McClelland in Oct 1806.
1810: John and wife 45+, 1 male 26-44, 1 male 16-25,
3 females 16-25, 1 male 10-15, 1 female 10-15, and 2
males -10.

Long, Peter
1800: Peter and wife 26-44, 2 males -10, and 1
female -10. Listed next to Valentine Watts, John
Walls, Andrew Watts, Peter Tucker, Henry Coledg, and
John Tucker.

Lootey, Jacob
1810: Jacob and wife 26-44, 1 female 16-25, 1 male
10-15, 2 males -10, and 1 female -10.

Louder, Thomas
Thomas moved to Montgomery Co. and sold land on
Stoney Branch of Little Bear Creek to Daniel Dry in
July 1813.

Louder, William
1800: William and wife 26-44, 1 male 16-25, 1 male
10-15, 3 males -10, and 2 females -10. Listed next
to Ephraim D. Harris, Samuel Graver, Timothy Doland,
Jacob Moose, James McMahon, and Frederick Peck.

Love, James & Elizabeth
Owned land on Coddle Creek and on Rocky River near
George Garmon and opposite David Purviance in 1778.
1800: James and wife 45+, 1 male 16-25, 1 female 16-
25, and 1 female 10-15. Listed next to Henry Howell,
James Little, John Misenheimer, John Stuart, George
Teater, and Isham Clay.
1810: James and wife 45+.

Love, Jonah
1810: Jonah 26-44, and 4 females -10.

Love, Thomas
Owned land on the south side of Clear Creek and on
both sides of Goose Creek about 1810. This area
later became Union County.

Ludwick, Henry
1800: Henry 26-44, 1 male 16-25, 1 female 16-25, 2
males -10, and 1 female -10. Listed next to Henry

Walker, John Biggers, Peter Simmons, Peter Boiles,
John Ritchey, and Michael Walker.
1810: Henry and wife 26-44, 2 males 10-15, 1 female
10-15, 1 male -10, and 1 female -10.

Ludwick, Nicholas & Barbara Ritchey
Owned land on Dutch Buffalo Creek in 1784.

Ludwick, Nicholas
1810: Nicholas and wife 26-44, 1 male 10-15, 3 males
-10, and 2 females -10.

Lufferd, Barn
1810: Barn and wife 26-44, 2 males 10-15, 2 females
10-15, 2 males -10, and 2 females -10.

Luther, John
Owned land between Dutch Buffalo Creek and Little
Coldwater Creek in 1784.

Lype, Barbary
1800: Barbara 45+, 1 male 16-25, and 1 female 10-15.
Listed next to Mary House, George Hise, Martin
Harkey, Jonas Lype, Philip Litaker, and Conrad
Litaker.

Lipe, George
1810: George and wife 16-25, and 1 male -10.

Lype, Godfred
1800: Godfred and wife and wife 26-44, 1 male 10-15,
1 male -10, and 2 females -10. Listed next to Philip
Barnhart, Daniel Blackwelder, Christian Morris,
Andrew Sides, George Miller, and Randle Studevant.
1810: Godfred and wife 26-44, 1 male 16-25, 1 female
10-15, 2 males -10, and 4 females -10.

Lipe, John
1810: John household consisted of himself and wife
26-44, 3 males 16-25, 2 males 10-15, and 4 males -
10.

Lype, Jonas
1800: Jonas' and wife 26-44, 2 females 16-25, 1 male
10-15, 2 females 10-15, 3 males -10, and 1 female -
10. Listed next to Barbary Lype, Mary House, George
Hise, Philip Litaker, Conrad Litaker, and George
Misenheimer.

Mann, John
Owned land on Half Meadow Branch, a branch of Coddle
Creek in 1780.

Margedand, John
John's LWT was proven in April 1798 by Michael
Winekauf.

Marlin, Richard
1800: Richard and wife 45+, 2 males 16-25, 3 females
16-25, 1 male 10-15, 1 male -10, and 4 females -10.
Listed next to Thomas Caruthers, Moses Rogers,
William Means, William Corell, John Weddington, and
Vachel Holbrooks.

Martin, James

1810: James 26-44, 1 male 16-25, 2 females 16-25, 4
males -10, and 1 female -10.
Martin, James & Peggy Kerr
Children: Hannah, Samey, Peggy L., James D., Robert
N., Billy, Thomas
Married Feb 27, 1797 in Mecklenburg Co., Richard
Kerr, bondsman.
1800: James 26-44, Peggy, 16-25, 1 female 10-15, and
1 male -10. Listed next to John Kesler, William
Glover, Susanna Morrison, Robert Sullivan, Celia
Russell, and Joseph Russell.
James' will was probated in April 1810 in
Mecklenburg. Executors were Alexander Stinson, John
Kerr, Thomas McGin and wife.
Martin, John
1800: John 26-44, 1 male 16-25, 1 female 16-25, and
1 female -10. Listed next to Hardin Chitley, Mary
Russle, David Russle, James Hadley, Cevilia
Campbell, and William Townsend.
1790 - Martin, Richard
Owned land on Muddy Branch and Stoney Run, branches
of Coddle Creek in 1778.
1790 - Martin, Robert
Owned land on Coddle Creek in 1780.
1800: Robert and wife 45+, 1 male 26-44, 1 female
26-44, 1 male 16-25, and 1 female 16-25. Listed next
to Athen Almore, John Niehler, Benjamin Biggs, James
Sullivan, James Gailor, and Peter Miller.
Martin, Samuel
1800 Samuel 26-44, and 1 female 45+. Listed next to
James McCaleb, William Douglass, Samuel Keilough,
Widow Neil, John Neil, and Samuel Pickens.
Mary, Thomas
Owned land on Muddy Creek in 1783.
1790 - Masters, George
Owned land on Coddle Creek in 1782.
1810: George 45+, 1 female 26-44, 1 male 10-15, 2
males -10, and 2 females -10.
Masters, John & Elizabeth Erwin
1800: John is listed as a resident of Concord. His
household consisted of 1 male 26-44, 1 female 16-25,
1 male 16-25, and 1 female -10. Listed with Lawrence
Snapp, George Smith, Philip Bless, Jacob Hudson, and
Samuel Hughey.
1810: John and wife 26-44, 2 females 16-25, 1 male
10-15, and 2 females -10.
Masters, Richard
1810: Richard household consisted a male and female,
and wife 45+, a male and a female, and wife 26-44, 3
females 16-25, 1 male 10-15, 2 females 10-15, 1 male
-10, and 1 female -10.
1790 - Maxwell, James & Elizabeth

Owned land on Rocky River in 1774.

Mayfield, Stephen
        1800: Stephen 26-44, 1 female 16-25, 1 male -10, and
        1 female -10. Listed next to Signe Seales, George
        Boiles, Martha Campbell, Daniel Little, Elias House,
        and Philip Cariker, Sr.

McAbley/McAiley, John
        Owned land on Coddle Creek in 1779, next to John
        Hughs, Ephraim Farr, and David Wilson.
        Owned land on and wife sides of the Muddy Branch and
        Stony Run of Coddle Creek in 1779.

1790 - McAhron/McEachern, John & Mary ? (Widow
        McCachron in 1790)
        Children: Ann (Isaac R. Shinn), Susannah (Armistead
        Brown), Mary (William Allison Russell), Hector
        (Elizabeth Huie), Elizabeth (Alexander Huie), Nancy
        (Benjamin Shinn), Ruth (? Robinson) Catharine (John
        Pharr), Thomas ?, William ? , James ?
        Owned land on Anderson Creek and Back Creek,
        branches of Rocky River.
        John was orphaned in Cumberland Co., NC in, or
        before 1757.
        James Simpson was appointed his guardian in April
        1757.
        John was born about 1742, died about 1788
        He was bondsman for James Plunket and Agness Houston
        in 1783 in Mecklenburg Co.
        John died in Cabarrus Co. in 1789. Robert Harris,
        Sr. or Jr., on Fuda Creek was the administrator of
        his estate.
        Mary remarried to Peter Huie, father of her
        daughter-in-law Elizabeth.

McAhron/McCachron/McEachern, Hector & Elizabeth Huie
        Children: Peter Roland
        Married July 26, 1791 in Mecklenburg Co., Peter
        Huie, bondsman.
        Son of John and Mary McCachron.
        1800: Hector and Elizabeth 26-44, 1 male -10, and 2
        females -10. Listed next to Isaac Neeley, Peter
        Huey, Valentine Kirkpatrick, Alexander Allin, and
        Daniel Bean.
        1810: Hector and wife 26-44, 1 male 10-15, 3 males -
        10, and 2 females -10.
        Lived in the Rocky River Church area

McAhron/McCachron/McEachern, James & Martha McKinley
        Married in Cabarrus County, bond dated Dec 28, 1802,
        bondsman, Thomas McClellan
        James bought land on Anderson Creek in April 1812.

McAhron/McCachron/McEachern, Robert
        Owned land on Anderson Creek, a branch of Rocky
        River in 1782.

1800: Robert and wife 45+, 2 males 16-25, 3 females
16-25, and 1 male 10-15. Listed next to John
Crumwell, Sr., William McAnulty, Noah Sandiford,
John Black, Jr., Samuel McCurdy, and Josiah Spears.
McAhron/McCachron/McEachern, Thomas & Jeane Caldwell
Married in Cabarrus County, bond dated Feb 4, 1803,
bondsman, Samuel White
Owned land on Anderson Creek and bought land on
Muddy Creek in April 1812.
McAhron/McCachron/McEachern, William & Martha Brown
Married in Cabarrus County, bond dated May 10, 1797,
bondsman, Archibald White
McAnnulty, Joseph
Overseer of road from Samuel Waddington ford on
Rocky River to David Taylor in Oct 1803.
1810: Joseph 26-44, 1 female 45+, 1 female 26-44, 1
female 16-25, 1 male 10-15, 1 female 10-15, 2 males
-10, and 3 females -10.
McAnulty, William
Owned land on the Long Branch of Clear Creek next to
Archibald McCurdy in 1782, and on Reedy Creek.
1800: William and wife 45+, 2 males 16-25, 1 female
16-25, 1 male 10-15, 1 female 10-15, and 1 female -
10. Listed next to Noah Sandiford, Delphie Lewis,
John Crumwell, Sr., Robert McEchron, and John Black,
Jr.
McAnulty, William
1810: William 26-44, 1 female 45+, 1 female 16-25, 1
male -10, and 2 females -10.
McBride, Malcolm
1810: Malcolm 26-44, 1 male 10-15, 1 female 10-15, 2
males -10, and 1 female -10.
Malcolm sold to Robert McMurry on Reedy Creek in
July 1812.
McCain, Thomas
1800: Thomas' household consisted himself 16-25, 1
female 45+, and 1 female -10. Listed next to William
Wallis, James Tanner, David Templeton, William
Houston, Sr., Benjamin Biggs, and John Niehler.
McCaleb, James
Children: John S.(Ann McCree), Jean(Silas Hunter),
Olivia(James Irwin), Polly(Evan Shelby Wiley)
Owned land on Rocky River in 1805.
1800: James and wife 26-44, 1 male 10-15, 2 females
10-15, 1 male -10, and 3 females -10. Listed next to
William Douglass, Samuel Keilough, William Keilough,
Samuel Martin, Widow Neil, and John Neil.
1810: James and wife 45+, 1 male 16-25, 1 female 16-
25, 2 females 10-15, and 1 male -10.
McCaleb, John S. & Ann McCree
Married in Cabarrus Co., bond dated Feb. 27, 1809,
Moses McCree, bondsman.

1810: John and wife 16-25, and 1 male -10.
1790 - McCammon/ McCommon/McCarmon, Charles & Sarah
Owned land on a ridge known as Poplar Ridge between
Coddle Creek and English Buffalo Creek in 1771.
Charles' LWT was proven in April 1799.
McCarron, James
1810: James age is not given, 1 female 16-25, 1 male
-10, and 2 females -10.
McCarron, Robert
1810: Robert 45+, 1 female 45+, 2 males 16-25, 3
females 16-25, and 2 females 10-15.
McCarron, Thomas
1810: Thomas and another male 16-25, 1 female 26-44,
1 female 16-25, 1 male -10, and 1 female -10.
McCaughey, John
Owned land on Rocky River and the north fork of
Stoney Creek and Back Creek in 1785.
McClain, Hugh
1810: Hugh and wife 16-25.
McClain, James & Ruth
Owned land on Three Mile Branch of Coldwater Creek
in 1764.
McClain, James & Elenor Baker
Elenor was the daughter of John Baker
Owned land on Three Mile Branch of Coldwater Creek
1790 - McClain, Allen & Martha
Children: John
Allen died before April 1798.
1790 - McClartey, Alexander, Jr & Jenny Morrison
Married Sept 18, 1776.
Children: James (Sarah Ellen Shelby, Deborah
Freeman), Archibald (Elizabeth Hasty, Ellen Beckman
Collins), Nancy (Isaac Helms), Polly (William
Weddington), Sallie (Archibald Brown), Catharine
"Caty" (Thomas Jerome), Jean (Johnston N. Bigger),
Mary, Elizabeth, Jane
1800: Alexander and Jenny, and wife 26-44, 1 male
16-25, 2 males 10-15, 2 females 10-15, 1 male -10,
and 4 females -10. Listed next to Hugh Carrithers,
Alexander Patterson, John Baker, Levi Russell, John
Rogers, and William Means.
1810: Alexander and Jenny 45+, 1 male 16-25, 1
female 16-25, 1 male 10-15, 2 females 10-15, and 2
females -10.
After Alexander's death in 1824, Jenny moved to
Arkansas with her son James. His will is filed in
Mecklenburg County, but he appears in the Cabarrus
County court records in 1805 declaring the mark of
his cattle, sheep, hogs.
Son of Alexander McLarty, born abt 1730 in Kintyre,
Scotland.
Jenny was the daughter of James and Jennet Morrison.

1790 - McClartey, Archabeld & Agness White??
        1800: Archibald 45+, 1 female 26-44, 2 females 10-
        15, 1 male -10, and 3 females -10. Listed next to
        Charles McNelond, James Means, John Means, Thomas
        Mock, Thomas Penenger, and John Patterson.
        Bought land on Anderson Creek from the legatees of
        Thomas McFaddin in Oct 1805.
        1810: Archibald and wife 45+, 2 males 10-15, 2
        females 10-15, 2 males -10, and 1 female -10.
        Son of Alexander McLarty, born abt 1730 in Kintyre,
        Scotland.
McLarty, James
        1810: James and wife 16-25.
McClellan/Miclelan, Charles
        1810: Charles 26-44, 1 female 16-25, 1 male 10-15, 1
        male -10, and 2 females -10.
McClelland/McLallen, Isaac
        Sold land 'to John White, Jr. between Rocky River and
        Cane Run in Oct 1805.
        1810: Isaac and wife 26-44, 2 males -10, and 4
        females -10.
1790 - McClelland, John & Sarah
        1810: John and wife 45+, and 2 females 10-15.
        Lived in the Rocky River Church area
McClelen, Joseph & Mary Laurens/Lawrence?
        Married Jan 25, 1792 in Mecklenburg Co., William
        McRee, bondsman.
        Joseph owned land on Muddy Creek bordering David
        McKinley, Thomas Black and John Long.
        1810: Joseph and Mary 26-44, 1 female 16-25, 1 male
        10-15, 2 females 10-15, and 4 males -10.
1790 - McClelland, Robert & Rebecca
        Robert died before 1790
        Owned land on a ridge known as Poplar Ridge between
        English Buffalo Creek and Coddle Creek in 1767.
McClellan, Thomas Harris & Sarah P. McKinly
        Thomas was born 1782, died Nov 29, 1807
        Buried in Old Rocky River Cemetery.
McClelan, William
        1810: William and wife 16-25, and 1 male -10.
McClenehan, Alexander
        Alexander died before July 1813.
McClennahan, Andrew
        Owned land on Long branch of Coldwater Creek in
        1779.
McClennon, Isaac
        1800: Isaac and wife 16-25, and 1 male -10. Listed
        next to Joseph McNeely, Aaron Wallis, John
        McClennon, Sarah Neely, Aaron Curry, and Valentine
        Faggot.
McClennon, John

1800: John 26-44, 1 female 45+, 1 male 16-25, 1
female 16-25, 2 males 10-15, 1 female 10-15, and 1
female -10. Listed next to Jacob Smith, Caleb
Woolfe, John White, Jr., Aaron Wallis, Joseph
McNeely, and Isaac McClennon.
1790 - McCoy, John & Catherine (Meck-1780)
Owned land on Three Mile Branch of Coldwater Creek
in 1780.
McCray, William
1800: William and wife 45+, 1 male 16-25, 2 females
16-25, 1 male 10-15, 2 females 10-15, 3 males -10,
and 1 female -10. Listed next to William Hamilton,
Morgan Hall, William Fraser, Gallant Peanix, Molly
Peanix, and Martin Gun.
McCullough, Henry Eustace
Owned land in the Poplar Tent area on Rocky River in
1765.
Henry came to Mecklenburg Co. from Halifax Co., NC.
He, or possibly a son or nephew, owned land on
McCalpin Creek and Sugar Creek.
McCulloch, John
Owned land on Muddy Creek a branch of Coddle Creek
in 1780.
McCurdy, Archibald
1810: Archibald and wife 26-44, 1 male -10, and 1
female -10.
1790 - McCurdey, Archabeld, Capt, & Maggie Sellers
Children: Archibald, Jr, Sophia, John (Cynthia
McCree), Mary (John Morrison), Samuel, Eleanor ?
(Alexander Allen), Margaret ? (Charles Allen)
Probably the son of Henry McCurdy, in Mecklenburg in
1769.
1800: Archabald and Margaret, and wife 45+, 2 males
16-25, and 2 females 10-15. Listed next to John
Cromwell, James Bradshaw, Jr., Francis Newell,
Charles McKinley, Dorothy Scott, and John Scott.
1810: Archibald and Maggie 45+, 1 male 26-44, 1
female 26-44, 1 female 16-25, 2 males -10, and 1
female -10.
Owned land on the Long Branch of Clear Creek
Archibald had two children with Mary Morrison
Russell, in the late 1790's. Zachariah McCurdy and
Stewart McCurdy. Court records name him as their
father. In 1850, Zachariah is shown as 51 years old
and living in the poor house for being cripple.
Archibald was born 1751, died Nov 10 1843.
McCurdy, John & Cynthia McCree
1810: John 26-44, Cynthia 16-25, and 1 male -10.
McCurdy, Samuel
1800: Samuel and wife 16-25, and 1 male -10. Listed
next to John Black, Jr., Robert McEchron, John

Crumwell, Sr., Josiah Spears, James Bradshaw, Sr.,
and Martha Watson.
1810: Samuel and wife 26-44, 1 male 10-15, 1 male -
10, and 2 females -10.
1790 - McFadian, Thomas & Hannah.
Thomas died May 24, 1799. Will proven by John &
Samuel Black in July court 1799.
Legatees: Benjamin McDowell, Margaret McDowell,
James Harris as guardian, Jeane Logan (Isaac Logan),
George McDowell, Hannah McFadden. Owned land on
Anderson Creek, a branch of Rocky River.
1800: Hannah , 45+, 2 males 16-25, and 1 female 16-
25. Listed next to William Johnston, Joseph Bigger,
John Newell, Francis Newell, James Bradshaw, Jr.,
and John Cromwell.
Hannah remarried to ? Wardlaw and lived in South
Carolina in Oct 1805.
McGinnis, Charles
1800: Charles and wife 45+, and 1 male 16-25. Listed
next to Enoch Morgan, James Morrison, John Morrison,
William Morrison, Aaron Townsend, and Solomon
Spears.
1810: Charles and wife 45+.
McGinnis, John
1810: John 26-44, his wife 16-25, 3 males -10, and 3
females -10.
McGraw, Enoch
1810: Enoch and wife 26-44, and 1 male -10.
1790 - McGraw, James
Owned land on Irish Buffalo Creek and Voil branch of
Coldwater Creek in 1778.
1800: James and wife 45+, 1 male 26-44, 2 males 16-
25, 2 males 10-15, and 1 female -10. Listed next to
John Plott, Isaac Loftin, Christian Dry, William
McGraw, Nicholas Curzine, and Margret Curzine.
1810: James and wife 45+, and 1 male -10.
McGraw, John & Sarah Corzine
Married Sept 7, 1795 in Cabarrus Co., Eli Corzine
bondsman.
1800: John and Sarah, and wife 16-25, 2 males -10,
and 1 female -10. Listed next to Thomas Voiles,
James Purviance, John Caragin, William Atkinson,
George Carosine(Corzine), and John Wilson.
1810: John and Sarah 26-44, 1 male 10-15, 1 female
10-15, 1 male -10, and 2 females -10.
McGraw, John
1810: John and wife 26-44, 2 males -10, and 4
females -10.
McGraw, Nicholas
1810: Nicholas and wife 26-44, and 1 female -10.
1790 - McGraw, William

1800: William and wife 26-44, 2 males 10-15, and 4
males -10. Listed next to James McGraw, John Plott,
Isaac Loftin, Nicholas Curzine, Margret Curzine, and
John Lee.
1810: William and wife 26-44, 2 males 16-25, 2 males
10-15, 1 female 10-15, and 2 males -10.
McKay, Arthur
Owned land on Connerford Branch of Coldwater Creek
in 1764.
McKeay, William
1810: William and wife 45+, 3 males 16-25, 1 female
10-15, and 1 male -10.
McKinley, Charles & Jean
1800: Charles and wife 26-44, 1 male 16-25, 1 male
10-15, 1 female 10-15, 2 males -10, and 1 female -
10. Listed next to Archibald McCurdey, John
Cromwell, James Bradshaw, Jr., Dorothy Scott, John
Scott, and John White.
1810: Charles' age is apparently not given. 1 female
26-44, 1 male 16-25, 1 male 10-15, 1 female 10-15,
and 2 males -10.
1790 - McCinley/McKinley, David
Owned land on Reedy Creek and Anderson Creek in
1783.
1790 - McKinley, David
Owned land on Muddy Creek bordering Thomas Black,
Joseph McClelland and John Long in Oct 1806.
1800: David and wife 26-44, 1 male 10-15, 2 females
10-15, 3 males -10, and 2 females -10. Listed next
to Josiah Bradly, John Rumple, George Overcash,
Frances Linse, John Goodman, and Aaron Houston.
1810. David and wife 45+, 3 males 16-25, 2 females
16-25, 1 male 10-15, and 1 female 10-15.
McKinley, David
1810: David and wife 45+.
McKinley, James & Rebecca McClellan
Married March 14, 1804 in Cabarrus Co., Thomas
McClellan, bondsman.
James was born Oct 19, 1783, died Jan 5, 1810
1810: Rebecca 16-25, 1 male -10, and 2 females -10.
Rebecca was born Nov 5, 1781, died Sept 20, 1825
Buried in Old Rocky River Cemetery.
1790 - McKinley, John
1800: John and wife 26-44, 1 male 10-15, 1 female
10-15, 2 males -10, and 2 females -10. Listed next
to Murdoch Campbell, Lewis Tounsend, Catherine
Shinn, Joseph White, Jean Russle, and John Wiley.
1810: John 45+, 1 female 26-44, 1 male 16-25, 1 male
10-15, 1 female 10-15, 2 males -10, and 2 females -
10.
McKinley, Samuel
Children: Elias

McKnight, James
> Owned land on the south side of Rocky River at the
> barony line in 1785. Deed states he is of Rowan Co.
> in 1785.

McLennon/McClellan, Isaac & Margaret Neely
> Married in Cabarrus County on Sept 21, 1799, Thomas
> Neely, bondsman.
> 1800: Isaac and Margaret 16-25, and 1 male -10.
> Listed next to Mark Evans, James Snell, Francis
> Greer, Robert Curry, George Harris, and Robert
> Harris, Jr.

McLoskey, Hugh
> 1810: Hugh 26-44, and 1 female 16-25.

McLusky, Jean
> 1800: Jean 16-25, 1 male 16-25, and 1 male -10.
> Listed next to Elizabeth Skiliton, Martin Gun, Molly
> Peanix, Elizabeth Holly, Thomas Rogers, and John
> Patterson.

McMahon, Andrew
> 1810: Andrew 26-44, 1 female 16-25, and 1 male -10.

McMahon, James
> 1800: James and wife 45+, 2 males 10-15, and 1 male
> -10. Listed next to Jacob Moose, William Louder,
> Ephraim D. Harris, Frederick Peck, Joseph Woolever,
> and Peter Troutman.
> 1810: James 45+, 1 female 26-44, and 2 males 16-25.

1790 - McMurray, James
> James' household begins the 1800 census. He lived
> next to his mother, Elinor.
> 1800: James and wife 45+, 1 male 16-25, 1 male 10-
> 15, 2 females 10-15, and 3 females -10.
> Son of Robert & Elinor

McMurry, John
> Evan L. Wiley was bondsman for John McMurray in
> Mecklenburg Co. in 1804.

McMurry, Laird
> Laird sold land on Caldwell Creek in April 1813.

1790 - McMurray, Robert & Elinor
> Owned land on and wife sides of John Cromwell spring
> branch, a branch of Reedy Creek in 1782.
> Robert will was proven in April 1800.
> 1800: Elinor 45+. Listed next to her son James and
> Robert Robb, Oliver Wiley, and Moses Wiley.

McMurray, Robert
> Son of Robert & Elinor
> 1800: Robert 26-44, 1 female 16-25, 1 male 16-25, 1
> male -10, and 1 female -10. Listed next to William
> Vietch, James Creatton, Charles Campbell, Ezekiel
> Sharpe, William Callon, Sr. and William Callon, Jr.
> Robert erected a mill on Mallard Creek in 1802 and
> owned land on Reedy Creek. He also served as sheriff
> in 1812.

1810: Robert and wife 26-44, 1 male 16-25, 1 female
16-25, 1 female 10-15, and 2 males -10.
McNair, Gilbert & Margaret
Owned land on Dowell Creek, a branch of Rocky River
in 1777.
McNeely, Joseph
1800: Joseph and wife 26-44, 1 male -10, and 1
female -10. Listed next to Aaron Wallis, John
McClennon, Jacob Smith, Isaac McClennon, Sarah
Neely, and Aaron Curry.
McNelond, Charles
1800: Charles and wife 26-44, 1 female 10-15, 2
males -10, and 2 females -10. Listed next to James
Means, John Means, Hezekiah Glover, Archibald
McLarty, Thomas Mock, and Thomas Penenger.
McQuown, Alexander
Owned land on Coddle Creek in 1777.
Son of Thomas & Elizabeth McQuown.
McQuown, Hugh
Owned land on Reedy Creek in 1779.
McQuown, Thomas & Elizabeth
Owned land on Coddle Creek in 1752.
McRee, Abraham & Barbara Phifer
Married in Cabarrus Co., bond dated Sept 22, 1809.
No bondsman named.
1810: Abraham and Barbara, and wife 16-25, and 1
male -10.
1790 - McRea/McRee, Arthur
Owned land on Muddy Branch, a branch of Coddle Creek
in 1783.
1800: Arthur and wife 26-44, 1 male 16-25, 1 female
16-25, 1 female 10-15, and 2 males -10. Listed next
to William Wiley, Elizabeth Posey, Ezekiel Wright,
Robert Allison, William Houston, and Stephen
Alexander.
McRee, Hugh
Owned land on Coddle Creek in 1778.
McRee, Martin
Owned land on Coddle Creek in 1780.
McRee, William & Jane
William died in or before 1822.
McWhorter, William
Owned land between Coddle Creek and English Buffalo
Creek in 1779.
Meade, David
Owned land on Rocky River in 1783.
Mealer, Peter
1810: Peter household consisted of 1 male 45+, 1
male 26-44, and 1 female 26-44.
Means, James
Owned land on Black branch to the banks of Wolf
Meadow Branch on Coddle Creek in 1782.

Died in or before 1792.
*Means, James A., Col
        Sheriff of Cabarrus County
        Owned land on Coddle Creek
        James died May 14, 1826
Means, James & Susanna Morrison
        Married in Cabarrus Co., bond dated May 13, 1801,
        bondsman, Hezekiah Glover.
        1800: James 16-25. Listed next to John Means,
        Hezekiah Glover, John Overcast, Charles McNelond,
        Archibald McLarty, and Thomas Mock.
        Susanna shows up in the 1850 census of Cabarrus Co.
        as 74 years old.
1790 - Means, John
        Owned land on Wolf Meadow branch of Coddle Creek and
        between Coddle Creek and English Buffalo Creek in
        1778.
        1800: John 45+, 1 female 26-44, 1 female 16-25, 1
        male 10-15, and 1 male -10. Listed next to Hezekiah
        Glover, John Overcast, Vachel Holbrooks, James
        Means, Charles McNelond, and Archibald McLarty.
Means, John
        1810: John and wife 16-25, and 1 male -10.
1790 - Means, William & Sarah
        William owned land on the head branches of Rocky
        River in the Welsh Tract in 1778 and he also owned
        land between Coddle Creek and Wolf Meadow Branch in
        1783. 1800 there is only one William Means listed in
        the census showing himself and 1 female 26-44, and 2
        males -10. It appears that this may have been a
        different William, but further research is needed to
        determine whether this William is the same William
        who was married to Sarah.
        William was sheriff in 1797.
        1810: William and Sarah, and wife 26-44, 2 males 16-
        25, 3 males 10-15, 1 female 10-15, 4 males -10, and
        1 female -10.
1790 - Meek, James, Esq & Mary
        Owned land on Rocky River in 1777.
        Son of Adam and Elizabeth Meek.
1790 - Meek, Moses, Jr & Margaret
        Owned land on Rocky River in the Welsh Tract, and on
        Stoney Creek, a branch of Mallard Creek in 1778.
Meek, Samuel & Jean
        Children: William Lee, Jean, Elizabeth
        1800: Samuel and Jean 26-44, and 2 males -10. Listed
        next to John Edmonton, Widow McClain, Robert Erwin,
        Alexander Query, John Scoles, and James Smith.
Meek, Thomas
        Owned land on English Buffalo Creek in 1782.
Melchor, Christian

Christian and George Fogelman sold land to George
and Henry Keriker on Hamby Run in Oct 1812.
Melcher/Melker, Henry & Nancy Abernathy
    Married in Cabarrus Co., bond dated March 27, 1795,
    bondsman, George Bost.
    1800: Henry age is not shown in the enumeration, but
    his household consisted of 1 female 16-25, 1 male
    10-15, 2 males -10, and 1 female -10. Listed next to
    Charles Carter, Drury Rogers, Peter Troutman, John
    Cauble, Nicholas Rough, and John Barger.
    Nancy is listed in the 1850 Cabarrus Co. census as
    73 years old.
1790 - Melcher, John
    1800: John and wife 45+, 2 females 16-25, 1 male 10-
    15, 1 male -10, and 1 female -10. Listed next to
    George Misenheimer, Conrad Litaker, Philip Litaker,
    Jacob Miller, Abram Misenheimer, and Peter Quilman.
    Owned land on Rocky River and Little Buffalo Creek
    in 1805.
Mensinger, William
    1800: William and wife 26-44, 1 female 10-15, and 1
    female -10. Listed next to John Misenheimer, Andrew
    Cruse, Adam Cruse, Henry Pence, George Ritchey, and
    Michael Sides.
    Sold land on Dutch Buffalo Creek to John Berger, Jr.
    in July 1806.
Meredith, Lewis
    Owned land on Mill Creek, a branch of Coddle Creek
    in the northern part of Cabarrus County in 1784. He
    was of Hertford Co., NC in 1784.
Mewionunk, Anthony
    Owned land on Dutch Buffalo Creek in 1784.
Michael, William
    Owned land on Muddy Creek in 1783.
Miller, Andrew & Margaret Miller
    Married July 28, 1795 in Mecklenburg Co., James
    Maxwell, bondsman.
Miller, Francis & Polly Bigger
    Married in Cabarrus Co., bond dated March 12, 1803,
    bondsman, Robert Bigger.
    1810: Francis and Polly, and wife 26-44, 1 male 10-
    15, and 3 females -10.
    The 1850 Cabarrus Co. census shows Francis as 72 and
    Mary as 68.
    Francis shows up in the 1860 Cabarrus Co. census as
    82 years old.
Miller, George & Regina Plyler
    1800: George 26-44, 1 female 16-25, 1 male 10-15, 1
    female 10-15, 4 males -10, and 2 females -10. Listed
    next to Andrew Sides, Godfred Lype, Philip Barnhart,
    Randle Studevant, Thomas Allin, and Jesse Herrin.

1810: George 45+, 1 female 26-44, 3 males 16-25, 2
males 10-15, 2 females 10-15, 2 males -10, and 2
females -10.
George owned land on Adams Creek
Miller, George
1810: George 26-44, 1 female 45+, 1 female 26-44, 1
female 16-25, and 5 females -10.
Miller, Henry
1810: Henry and wife 26-44, 2 males 10-15, 1 female
10-15, and 2 females -10.
Miller, Jacob
1800: Jacob and wife 45+, 1 male 16-25, 1 female 16-
25, 2 males 10-15, 1 male -10, and 3 females -10.
Listed next to John Melchor, George Misenheimer,
Conrad Litaker, Abram Misenheimer, Peter Quilman,
and Jacob Rinehart.
1810: Jacob and wife 45+, 1 male 16-25, 1 female 16-
25, 1 male 10-15, 1 female 10-15, 1 male -10, and 2
females -10.
Miller, James & Ann Russell
Children: Mary A. (Alexander Gilbert White), John W.
(Ann Stierwalt), Eleanor (Robert B. Miller)
Ann was the daughter of James Russell and Jane
Carson
James bought land on Irish Buffalo Creek in July
1806 from Lewis Townsend and wife Jean Russell. Jean
was the daughter of Ann's uncle, Robert Russell.
1810: James and Ann 26-44, 1 female 10-15, 2 males -
10, and 2 females -10.
1790 - Miller, John
son of Philip and Eleanor Miller
Owned land on Clear Creek and Campbell Creek in
1779.
1790 - Miller, Mathew
Owned land on Clear Creek
Miller, Peter
1800: Peter and wife 45+, 2 males 16-25, and 5
females 16-25. Listed next to James Gailor, James
Sullivan, Robert Martin, Robert Miller, Josiah
Deweast, and Robert Stanford.
1790 - Miller, Philip & Eleanor 201
Died April 1797, children: John, James (Ann
Russell), dau (John Nelson), dau (Adam Ormond)
Philip's will was probated on April 1797 in
Mecklenburg.
Owned land on Clear Creek in 1779.
Miller, Robert
1800: Robert and wife 26-44, 1 male 10-15, 2 females
10-15, 3 males -10, and 1 female -10. Listed next to
Peter Miller, James Gailor, James Sullivan, Josiah
Deweast, Robert Stanford, and Hugh Heare.
1790 - Minster, Frederick & Dorothy 223

Children: Barbara (James Russell), John Michael
(Peggy Misenheimer), David, Washington, Hannah,
Catherine, Polly, Frederick Michael. Children need
to be proven.
1800: Frederick and wife 26-44, 1 male 16-25, 1
female 16-25, 2 males 10-15, and 4 females -10.
Listed next to Jacob Mitchell, Mathias Mitchell,
Jr., Mathias Mitchell, Sr., Jacob Misenheimer, John
Neshler, Sr., and Michael Awalt.
Sold land on Adams Creek and Anderson Creek to
Christian Rinehart in Jan 1807.
1810: Frederick and wife 45+, 2 females 16-25, 1
male 10-15, 2 females 10-15, 1 male -10, and 1
female -10.
Millster, John Michael & Peggy Misenheimer
     Married in Cabarrus Co., bond dated May 20, 1808,
     bondsman, William A. Russell.
     1810: Michael 45+, 1 female 16-25, and 1 female -10.
     John died in March 1850 at the age of 66.
1790 - Misenhimer, Abraham
     1800: Abram 26-44, 1 female 45+, 1 male 10-15, 2
     females 10-15, 3 males -10, and 2 females -10.
     Listed next to Jacob Miller, John Melchor, George
     Misenheimer, Peter Quilman, Jacob Rinehart, and John
     Shoe.
     Bought land on Dutch Buffalo Creek from Michael
     Romer in Jan 1806.
     1810: Abraham and wife 45+, 1 male 16-25, 1 female
     16-25, 2 males 10-15, and 2 females 10-15.
Misenheimer, George & Rosena Long
     1800: George 45+, 1 female 26-44, 1 male 16-25, 1
     male 10-15, 2 females 10-15, 3 males -10, and 2
     females -10. Listed next to Conrad Litaker, Philip
     Litaker, Jonas Lype, John Melchor, Jacob Miller, and
     Abram Misenheimer.
     Married in Cabarrus Co., bond dated July 17, 1806,
     bondsman, John H. Brandon.
     1810: George and wife,and wife 45+, 1 female 26-44,
     3 males 16-25, 1 female 16-25, 1 male 10-15, 1
     female 10-15, 1 male -10, and 2 females -10.
     Rosanah Misenheimer is listed in the 1860 Cabarrus
     Co. census as 74 years old.
Misenheimer, Jacob
     1810: Jacob and wife 16-25, and 1 male -10.
1790 - Misenhimer, Jacob & Elizabeth
     Owned land on Lick Branch, a branch of Dutch Buffalo
     Creek in the Mount Pleasant area, and between Dutch
     Buffalo Creek and Little Coldwater Creek, and wife
     sides of Umberford Branch in 1777.
     1800: Jacob 45+, 1 female 26-44, 2 females 16-25, 2
     males 10-15, 2 males -10, and 3 females -10. Listed
     next to Federick Minster, Jacob Mitchell, Mathias

Mitchell, Jr., John Neshler, Sr., Michael Awalt, and
James Scott.
1810: Jacob and wife 45+, 1 male 16-25, 1 female 16-
25, 2 males 10-15, and 2 females 10-15.
Misenhamer, Jacob
1810: Jacob household consisted of 1 male 10-15, 2
females 10-15, and 2 males -10.
Misenheimer, Jacob
1810: Jacob and wife 16-25, and 2 males -10.
Misenhamer, Jacob
1810: Jacob and wife,and wife 16-25, and 2 males -
10.
1790 - Misenhimer, John
Owned land on Dutch Buffalo Creek and Adam Creek in
the Mount Pleasant area in 1783.
1800: John 45+, 1 female 16-25, 1 male 10-15, 2
females 10-15, 1 male -10, and 2 females -10. Listed
next to Andrew Cruse, Adam Cruse, George Goodman,
Sr., William Mensinger, Henry Pence, and George
Ritchey.
1810: John 45+, 1 female 45+, 2 males 16-25, 3
females 10-15, and 1 female -10.
Misenheimer, John
1800: John and wife 16-25. Listed next to William
Stow, George Smith, Andrew Slough, James Little,
Henry Howell, and James Love.
Misenhamer, John
1810: John and wife 16-25, and 1 male -10.
Misenhamer, John
1810: John and wife 26-44, and 1 male -10.
Misenhamer, John
1810: John and wife 26-44, 1 male -10, and 1 female
-10.
Misenheimer, John
1810: John 16-25, 2 females 16-25, and 1 female -10.
1790 - Misenhimer, Peter
1800: Peter 45+, 1 female 26-44, 2 females 16-25, 1
male 10-15, 1 female 10-15, 2 males -10, and 2
females -10. Listed next to Henry Plylor, David
Fink, Andrew Cariker, George Hartman, Henry Linker,
and William Gordin.
Misenhamer, Peter
1810: Peter and wife 16-25, and 1 male -10.
Misenheimer, Tobias
1810: Tobias 16-25, 2 females 26-44, 1 male -10, and
1 female -10.
Mitchel, David
1810: David household consisted of 1 male and 1
female and wife 45+, 1 male and 1 female, and wife
26-44, 1 male 10-15, and 3 females -10.
Mithcell, Henry
Owned land on Back Creek in 1785.

Died in or before 1790.
1790 - Mitchell, Jacob
    1800: Jacob and wife 26-44, 2 males -10, and 2
    females -10. Listed next to Mathias Mitchell, Jr.,
    Mathias Mitchell, Sr., Jacob Lewis, Frederick
    Minster, Jacob Misenheimer, and John Neshler, Sr.
Mitchell, John & Elizabeth
    Owned land on Rocky River in 1769 that he sold to
    Jonathan Newman and Moses Andrews. He bought land on
    a branch of Coddle Creek in 1769. John was of Rowan
    Co. in 1769.
Mitchell, John & Rebecca Baker
    Married Jan 31, 1797 in Mecklenburg Co., George
    Baker, bondsman.
    dau of George & Rachel Baker
    Owned land on Rocky River near Charles Campbell.
    1810: John household consisted of 1 male 45+, 1 male
    26-44, 1 female 26-44, 1 female 16-25, 1 male 10-15,
    and 3 females -10.
Mitchell, Joseph & Rachel
    Owned land on Rocky River, Rockwide Creek, and
    Stoney Creek in 1779.
    Joseph died in or before 1781.
1790 - Mitchell, Mathias, Jr.
    1800: Mathias and wife 26-44, 2 males -10, and 1
    female -10. Listed next to Mathias Mitchell, Sr.,
    Jacob Lewis, John Long, Jacob Mithcell, Frederick
    Minster, and Jacob Misenheimer.
    1810: Mathias and wife 26-44, 1 female 10-15, 1 male
    -10, and 3 females -10.
1790 - Mitchell, Mathias, Sr.
    Owned land on Little Coldwater Creek and Great
    Coldwater Creek in 1782.
    1800: Mathias and wife 45+, 3 males 16-25, 1 female
    16-25, and 2 females 10-15. Listed next to Jacob
    Lewis, John Long, Daniel Cline, Mathias Mitchell,
    Jr., Jacob Mithcell, and Frederick Minster.
Mitchell, Rabeckah
    1800: Rabeckah 45+, and 1 male -10. Listed next to
    Joshua Cheek, Abigel Griffin, Rabeckah Ford, George
    Garmon, Henry Smith, Jr., and Henry Smith, Sr.
1790 - Mitchell, William
    Owned land on Muddy Creek in 1781.
Mitchler, David
    David sold land on Cold Water Creek in Oct 1811.
Mitchler, Mathias
    Children: David
    Mathias died before 1811.
1790 - Mock, Thomas & Mary 223
    Children: Mathias, Elizabeth, Margaret, John Michael
    (Barbara Beaver), Thomas (Margaret Kertner), Conder.
    In Mecklenburg Co. in 1778.

1800: Thomas and Mary, and wife 45+, 3 males 16-25,
and 1 female 16-25. Listed next to Archibald
McLarty, Charles McNelond, James Means, Thomas
Peneneger, John Patterson, and Hugh Patterson.
Mock, Thomas & Margaret Kertner
Married in Cabarrus Co., bond dated Sept 9, 1807,
bondsman, William A. Russell.
1810: Thomas' and Margaret, and wife 16-25, and 1
male -10.
Thomas owned and sold land on Flat Run branch of
Irish Buffalo Creek in April 1813.
1790 - Moffit, Martha
Owned land on Coddle Creek
Montgomery, Samuel
Owned land on Clear Creek in 1778 and sold a tract
for the Rocky Spring meeting house and burial
ground.
Monteith, Nathaniel
1810: Nathaniel 26-44, 2 females 16-25, 1 male 10-
15, and 1 male -10.
Moose, Jacob
1800: Jacob 45+, 1 female 26-44, 1 male 10-15, 2
males -10, and 2 females -10.
Morgan, Enoch
1800: Enoch and wife 26-44, 1 female over 45, 1 male
16-25, 2 males 10-15, 2 males -10, and 1 female -10.
Listed next to James Morrison, John Morrison,
William Morrison, Charles McGinnis, Walter Farr, and
William Morrison.
1810: Enoch and wife 45+, 1 male 10-15, 1 female 10-
15, 2 males -10, and 2 females -10.
Morgan, James
1810: James and wife 16-25, and 1 female -10.
Morris, Christian
1800: Christian and wife 26-44, 2 females 16-25, 1
male 10-15, and 2 females 10-15. Listed next to
George Moyer, Godred Uery, William Goodwin, Daniel
Blackwelder, Philip Barnhart, and Godfred Lype.
Morris, Griffin & Nancy
1800: Griffin 45+, 1 female 26-44, 1 male 16-25, 3
males 10-15, 2 females 10-15, 1 male -10, 1 female -
10. Listed next to Matthew Campbell, James Stafford,
Thomas Davis, Cunningham Harris, Elisha Spears, and
James Harris.
1810: Nancy 45+, 4 males 16-25, and 1 female 10-15.
Morrison, Andrew & Elizabeth Sloan, Margaret Potts
Owned land on Rocky River in 1782.
Morrison, Carson R.
1810: Carson and wife 16-25, and 1 male -10.
Morrison, Duncan & Susannah Cole
Children: John, Ann

Duncan sold land on the north side of Coddle Creek
to Abel Corzine in July 1806.
Duncan died before April 1799.
Morrison, James & Sarah Carrithers
1810: James and wife 26-44, 1 male 10-15, 3 females
10-15, and 2 females -10.
James moved to Buncombe Co., NC, then TN, then on to
Illinois. Before his death in 1842 he returned to TN
where he died.
Son of Robert & Sarah Morrison
1790 - Morrison, James & Jennet
Children: James, Jenny McLarty (Alexander), Mary
Russel (Robert), William (Catarine Russel), John
(Mary McCurdy), Elizabeth (David Russel), Rachel
(John Gingles), Robert (Margaret McCombs, Mary
Wiley), James M. (Margaret Johnston), Samuel (Sarah
Johnston, Mary McKee Stafford)
Brother of John (Mary) and Robert (Sarah)
Owned land on Caldwell Creek in 1771.
James was born 1726, died Oct 30, 1804
Jennet was born 1735, died Feb 4, 1810
Buried in Spears Cemetery of Rocky River Church
Morrison, James & Margaret Pharr, Mary Johnston
James and Margaret were married July 19, 1789
James and Mary were married Dec 2, 1830
Children: John (died at 3 mo.), Malinda Sarah
(Robert Brice Cochran), Mary (Robert Russel, son of
David & Elizabeth Morrison Russel), Samuel F.
(Rachel Gingles), Penelope (Alexander W. Harris),
Jenny (Joshua Teeter), James Cunningham, Dorcas (Eli
John McGinnis, John Gingles), Margaret Clementine
(Jeremiah G. Stegall), Catherine
James died Sept 4, 1846
Margaret died Nov 24, 1817
Mary died May 25, 1845
James and his wives are buried in Spears Cemetery in
Cabarrus County.
Son of John and Mary Morrison
Morrison, James McEwen & Elizabeth Morrison
Children: William Allison (Mary Eliza Gilmore,
Margaret W. Gillespie), Abigail Lucinda (died at the
age of 13), James Quincey (Melissa Isabella Cox),
infant son died at 5 days old, Catherine Elizabeth
(Jonathan T. Cloud, David Brasell), Robert Hall,
Russell Cicero (died at the age of 6), Jane Erixena
(James Smith), Lucinda Abagail (Peter Johnson), Hugh
McEwen (Mary Narcissus Markert, Margaret Frances
McClure), Margaret Josephine (Peter Johnson), Sarah
Elvira (died at the age of 2)
James and Elizabeth moved to Alabama with many other
family members in 1816, then on to Water Valley,
Miss. about 1835.

James was sheriff of Dallas County, Ala for twelve
years.
Son of William and Catherine Russell Morrison
Morrison, James M. & Margaret Johnston
    Children: Elam Johnston, Matilda (Richard King),
    James McKemie, Nathaniel (Ruth Louise Alexander),
    Columbus (Sarah Sutton Johnston, Jane Young),
    William Stanhope (Helena Kerr), baby girl, died as
    an infant.
    Married Sept 10, 1799 in Mecklenburg Co., William
    Johnston, bondsman.
    James & Margaret home was located 14 miles east of
    Charlotte, but they are buried in Spears Cemetery in
    the Rocky River Church area. He owned land on
    Caldwell Creek in 1779.
    James was a tanner and his homeplace was known as
    Morrison Tanyard.
    Son of James and Jennet Morrison
Morrison, James
    1810: James and wife 16-25, and 1 male -10.
Morrison, John & Jane Bradshaw, Dolly Rogers
    Children: Cynthia (Joel B. Alexander), Silas H.,
    Elias Denson (Jennie Kimmons), Levi Rogers
    Married in Mecklenburg County, bond dated April 5,
    1791, bondsman, John Morrison
    John moved his family to Bedford Co., TN, but when
    is unknown.
    John son Silas was preaching for some years in TN
    before 1827 and moved to Alabama in 1829.
    Son of Robert & Sarah Morrison
Morrison, John & Mary McCurdy
    Children: James (Francis Brown), Archibald, infant
    daughter-born and died same day, Washington (Mary
    Ann Dinkins, Sara Rosana Patton), Margaret Sellars
    (James H. Burns), John Milton (Harriet Amelia
    Newell), William Newton (Sarah Varick Cuzzens), Mary
    Gingles (Charles Harrison Gingles), Jane Jeanette
    Marvin (George Cook Marvin), Cynthia Caroline McKee
    (Samuel), Robert Harvey (Mary Ann Stuart)
    Lived in the Rocky River Church area and known as
    "McCurdy John".
    1800: John and Mary 26-44, and 2 males -10. Listed
    next to William Morrison, Alexander Hughey, Robert
    Harris, James Morrison, Enoch Morgan, and Charles
    McGinnis.
    1810: John and wife 26-44, 1 male 10-15, 4 males -
    10, and 1 female -10.
    Son of James & Jennet Morrison
Morrison, John & Mary
    Children: Daughter (William Driskill), Sarah (?
    Ross), Jane (Samuel Huie), Elizabeth, James

(Margaret Pharr, Mary Johnston), John (Margaret
Pickens), Elias (Mary Stewart), Robert, Mary
Brother of James (Jennet) and Robert (Sarah)
John died as a result of wounds he received in the
Revolutionary War, about 1777, and Mary died 1781.
And wife are buried in Spears Cemetery in Cabarrus
County.
Brother of James (Jennet) and Robert (Sarah)
Morrison, John & Margaret Pickens
    Children: Martha Bonneau, William Pickens (Rosanna
    Gingles), Jane Amanda (John Huie, David White, Col),
    Mary Erixene (James McKemie White), Elizabeth Sarah
    (William Franklin White), Elias Alexander, Margaret
    Lucinda, John Franklin (Elvira McClelland), James
    Leonidas (Elizabeth White)
    John and Margaret are buried at Rocky River
    Presbyterian Church.
    Son of John & Mary Morrison
1790 - Morrison, Robert C. & Sarah
    Children: William (Abigail McEwen), Elizabeth
    (William Andrew), Jean (Daniel Caldwell), John (Jane
    Bradshaw, Dolly Rogers), James (Sarah Carrithers),
    Phoebe (Robert Caldwell), Sarah (James Watson
    Bradshaw), Robert (Susannah Walker), Thomas (never
    married), Mary, Martha (Samuel R. Garrison)
    Brother of John (Mary) and James (Jennet)
    Owned land on Rocky River and McKee & Reedy Creek.
    Robert was born 1728, died Aug 10, 1810.
    Sarah was born 1739, died Oct 6, 1816.
    Buried in Spears Cemetery of Rocky River Church.
    Brother of James (Jenett) and John (Mary).
Morrison, Robert & Susannah Walker
    Children: Ziza (Margaret Melissa Carothers), Rachel,
    Sarah D., James, Robert McAmie (Elizabeth Huggins-no
    children), Jane, Susan Teresia (Samuel Alexander
    Pickens), Addison Walker (Julia Hardy), William
    Andrew (Mary Hardy)
    Robert and Susannah moved to Bedford Co., TN in
    1814. After Robert death, Susannah and most of the
    family moved to Bentonville, Ark. in the fall of
    1852.
    Son of Robert and Sarah Morrison
Morrison, Robert & Margaret McCombs, Mary Wiley
    1810: Robert and wife 26-44, 1 male -10, and 4
    females -10.
    Robert was the son of James and Jennet Morrison.
Morrison, Samuel & Sarah Johnston, Mary McKee Stafford
    Children: Tirza, (Samuel Gingles), Cyrus (Mary
    Moore), James Elijah (Mary Letitia Krider, Julia L.
    Coulter St. John), William Johnston (Mary A.
    Newell), Harvey (Margaret Cochran, Martha Pharr),
    Sarah (Walter Franklin Pharr), Samuel Newton,

Pinkney (Elizabeth Clementine Russell), Elizabeth C.
(Sandy McKinley), George Leroy (Margaret Pharr),
Elam (Mary Emily Moreland), John Dwight (Cynthia
Elizabeth Wilson), Quincy Columbus (Susan E.
Grey) The first six children were by Sarah Johnston, the
rest were by Mary.
Samuel and Sarah were married Oct 9, 1800: and
Samuel and Mary were married April 21, 1812.
1810: Samuel and wife 1 female 10-15, and 4 males -
10.
Samuel lived to the age of 93 and lived in the Rocky
River Church area all his life.
Samuel was the son of James and Jennet Morrison.
Sarah was born 1784, died Dec 14, 1810.
In the 1860 Cabarrus Co. census Samuel is listed as
81 and Mary is listed as 75 years old.
Morrison, Susanna
1800: Susanna 26-44, 1 male -10, and 1 female -10.
Listed next to John Patterson, Thomas Rogers,
Elizabeth Holly, William Glover, John Kesler, and
James Martin.
Morrison, Thomas (never married)
Thomas was born 1784, died July 17, 1815
Buried in Spears Cemetery of Rocky River Church
Son of Robert C. and Sarah Morrison
1790 - Morrison, William & Abigail McEwen
Children: Sarah (Andrew Walker), James McEwen (Eliza
Morrison), Margaret (John Kimmons), Hugh Hall, Jean
Erixene, Erixene (Cyrus A. Alexander, M.D.), Robert
Hall (Mary Graham), three other children who died as
infants
1810: William 45+, Abigail 26-44, 2 females 16-25, 1
female 10-15, and 1 male -10.
Son of Robert & Sarah Morrison
Married Aug 4, 1785
Abigail was born 1760, died Oct 6, 1825
William was born 1753, died Nov 10, 1821
Buried in Old Rocky River Cemetery
William owned land on McKee Creek and was known as
"Miller William".
1790 - Morrison, William & Catharine Russel
Children: Jeanet (David Russel), Robert Carson
(Prudence Alexander), Catharine, Elizabeth (James
McEwen Morrison), James K. (Cynthia King), William
Russell (Nancy McCaully/Maulby), Catharine (Edward
Wood, Benjamin Alexander Glass)
1810: William 26-44, Catherine 45+, 2 males 10-15, 1
female 10-15, and 1 female -10.
Son of James & Jennet Morrison
William and Catherine moved to Dallas County,
Alabama with many other family members in 1816.
Morrow, Thomas

Owned land on the Long Branch of Clear Creek in
1785.
Morton, Robert
Owned land on Coddle Creek in 1777.
1790 - Morton, Samuel & Ann
Children: William, Samuel
Owned land between Coddle Creek and Alton Run in
1775.
Moses, Widow
1810: the widow 26-44, 3 males 16-25, 2 males 10-15,
2 females 10-15, and 1 female -10.
Moyer, George
1800: George and wife 26-44, 3 males -10, and 1
female -10. Listed next to Godfred Uery, William
Goodwin, Daniel Cline, Christian Morris, Daniel
Blackwelder, and Philip Barnhart.
1810: George and wife 26-44, 1 male 16-25, 2 males
10-15, 1 female 10-15, 2 males -10, and 2 females -
10.
Moyer, Harmon
1800: Harmon 26-44, 1 female 45+, 1 male 10-15, 1
female 10-15, and 3 males -10. Listed next to Daniel
Faggot, Henry Fite, Rabeckah Heninger, Daniel Bost,
Dorothy Petry, and Francis Funderburk.
Moyer, John
1810: John and wife 26-44, 1 male 16-25, 2 males 10-
15, 3 males -10, and 1 female -10.
John sold to George Miller on Adam Creek in July
1812.
1790 - Moyer, Mathias
Children: George
Owned land on Meeting House Branch of Dutch Buffalo
Creek in the Mount Pleasant area, and on Adam Creek
in 1783.
1800: Mathias 26-44, 1 female 45+, and 1 male -10.
Listed next to Nicholas Ridenhour, Martin Harkey,
Paul Barringer, Isaac Blackwelder, George Bost, and
Martin Blackwelder.
Moyer, Widow
1810: the widow household consisted of 1 female 26-
44, 1 female 16-25, and 2 males 16-25.
1790 - Murph, Jacob
Children: Margaret, Jacob, Rudolph, Rachel, Dolly,
Daniel
1800: Jacob and wife 26-44, 1 female 16-25, 2 males
10-15, 1 females 10-15, 1 female 10-15, 2 males -10,
and 2 females -10. Listed next to Jacob Krider, Sr.,
Manasah Dresser, Jacob Krider, Jr., Paul Walton,
Sarah Nowls, and John Yoman.
Murrey, James
1810: James and another male 16-25, 2 females 10-15,
and 1 female -10.

Myer, Jacob
    Owned land on Dutch Buffalo Creek, Mount Pleasant
    area in 1774.
Mussgenung, Jacob
    Jacob registered his brand and mark for horses and
    cattle in Oct 1798.
Neil, Edward
    1800: Edward family contained himself and wife 26-
    44, 2 females 10-15, 3 males -10, 2 females -10.
    Listed next to Joseph Welsh, Alexander Scott, Robert
    Davis, William Andrew, Francis Greer, and James
    Snell.
1790 - Neal, James
    Owned land on Coddle Creek in 1777.
    James died in or before 1792.
    1800: James' widow is shown as 45+, with 1 male 16-
    25, 2 females 16-25, 2 males 10-15, and 1 female 10-
    15. Listed next to Samuel Martin, James McCaleb,
    William Douglass, John Neil, Samuel Pickens, George
    Ross, and Joseph Ross, Sr.
Neil, John
    1800: John and wife 26-44, 3 males -10, and 2
    females -10. Listed next to Widow Neil, Samuel
    Martin, James McCaleb, Samuel Pickens, George Ross,
    and Joseph Ross, Sr.
Neill, Richard
    Richard bought 2 tracts on Coddle Creek in Jan 1814.
1790 - Neely, Hugh
    Owned land on Mallard Creek 1778.
Neeley, Isaac
    1800: Isaac family consisted of himself and wife 16-
    25, and 1 male -10. Listed next to Peter Huey,
    William L. Alexander, James Scott, Hector McAharon,
    Valentine Kirkpatrick, and Alexander Allin.
Neely, John
    1810: John 26-44, 1 female 45+, 1 female 26-44, 1
    female 16-25, 1 male -10, and 1 female -10.
Neely, Sarah
    1800: Sarah 45+, 1 male 16-25, 1 female 16-25, 1
    female 10-15, and 1 female -10. Listed next to Isaac
    McClennon, Joseph McNeely, Aaron Wallis, Aaron
    Curry, Valentine Faggot, and John Barringer.
1790 - Neely, Thomas
    Owned land on Back Creek and Reedy Creek in 1777.
    Died in or before 1794.
Neely, Thomas
    1810: Thomas 26-44, and 1 female 16-25.
1790 - Nelson, John & ? Miller
    John's wife was the daughter of Philip and Eleanor
    Miller
    Children: Samuel Nelson who married Margaret Moore
    1790 Mecklenburg

Owned land on Muddy Creek in 1773.
1790 - Neas/Ness/Kneese, Boltes (Bolser)
        Owned land on Dutch Buffalo Creek in 1779.
Ness, Paulser & Franney
        Owned land on Dutch Buffalo Creek and on the north
        side of Rocky River in 1786, near Samuel Black and
        Johanes Jegler.
1790 - Newill, David & Ann
        David died before Oct 1803.
Newel, David
        1810: David age is not shown. His household
        consisted of 1 female 26-44, 2 males 10-15, and 2
        females -10.
1790 - Newill, Francis
        Children: David
        Owned land on and wife sides of Anderson Creek, a
        branch of Rocky River in 1774.
        1800: Francis and wife 45+, 1 female 26-44, 1 male
        16-25, and 1 female 16-25. Listed next to Hannah
        McFaddon, William Johnston, Joseph Bigger, James
        Bradshaw, Jr., John Cromwell, and Archibald
        McCurdey.
        1810: Francis 45+, 1 male 26-44, 2 females 26-44,
        and 2 males -10.
Newell, John
        1800: John and wife 26-44, and 2 males -10. Listed
        next to William Newell, Benjmain Cockran, Thomas
        White, Sr., Joseph Bigger, William Johnston, and
        Hannah McFaddon.
Newel, Johnston
        1810: Johnnston 26-44, and 2 females 26-44.
1790 - Newill, William
        Children: Eli
        In Mecklenburg Co. in 1777.
        1800: William and wife 45+, 1 female 26-44, 1 male
        26-44, and 1 female 16-25. Listed next to Benjamin
        Cockran, Thomas White, Sr., Robert White, John
        Newell, Joseph Bigger, and William Johnston.
        1810: William 26-44, 1 female 16-25, and 2 males -
        10.
Newman, Jonathan & Rebecca
        Owned land on Clarke Creek, a branch of Rocky River
        in 1769.
Nishler, David
        1800: David 26-44, 1 female 16-25, 1 male -10, and 1
        female -10. Listed next to Jacob Overcash, Mathias
        Cook, John Cook, Martin Slough, John Still, and
        Gideon Almon.
        1810: David and wife 26-44, 2 males 10-15, 1 female
        10-15, and 3 females -10.
1790 - Nichler/Neshler, John, Sr.
        Owned land on Coldwater Creek in 1777.

1800: John and wife 45+, 3 females 16-25, 2 males
10-15, and 3 females -10. Listed next to Jacob
Misenheimer, Frederick Minster, Jacob Mitchell,
Michael Awalt, James Scott, and John Conder.
1810: John and wife 45+, 2 males 16-25, 2 females
16-25, and 2 females 10-15.

Nichler, John
1800: John 26-44, 1 female 16-25, and 1 female -10.
Listed next to Benjamin Biggs, William Houston, Sr.,
Thomas McCain, Athen Almore, Robert Martin, and
James Sullivan.

Nicler, Joseph
Joseph is listed in the 1860 Cabarrus Co. census as
being 71 years old.

Neishler, Nicholas & Elizabeth Barberick
Married in Cabarrus Co., bond dated Feb 18, 1804,
bondsman, George Misenheimer.
Children: Mary, Francis, Jackson L.
1810: Nicholas and wife 26-44, 2 males -10, and 2
females -10.
Nicholas is listed in the 1850 Cabarrus Co. census
as 79 and Elizabeth is 63 years old.

Nowls, Sarah
1800: Sarah 45+, 2 males 16-25, 1 female 16-25, and
1 male -10. Listed next to Paul Walton, Jacob Murph,
Jacob Krider, Sr., John Yoman, Peter Overcash, and
Henry Plott.

Nussman, Adolph
Children: Catharine, John, Daniel, Barbara,
Elizabeth
Adolph died before April 1797.

Nuesman, John
1810: John and wife 26-44, 1 male 16-25, 1 male -10,
and 3 females -10.

Nuesman/Nooseman, Paul
1810: Paul 26-44, and 1 female 16-25.

Oliphant, David
Owned land between Horton Branch of Anderson Creek
and Muddy Creek. David moved to Charleston, SC
sometime before 1778. He owned 17,000 acres in the
Welch Tract which he began to sell off in 1778.
Thomas Polk acted as his attorney for these sales.

Osbourne, Christopher
1810: Christopher and wife 16-25, 1 male -10, and 1
female -10.
Christopher bought on land on Anderson Creek in
April 1812.

Osborn, Jonathan
Sold land on Anderson Creek to William Bost in Oct
1805.

1790 - Ovenshine/Abenshine, Christian
Children: Rhinehold, Catharine

Owned land on Adams Creek and Coldwater Creek in
1783.
Christian died April 1800
Ovenshine, Kenatt
Owned land near Adams Creek and Hamby Branch in
1784.
Ovenshine, Mathias
Died in or before 1775.
1790 - Ovenshine/Abenshine, Rinholt
Children: John
1800: Rinholt and wife 45+, 1 male 26-44, 1 male 16-
25, 1 female 16-25, and 1 female 10-15. Listed next
to Jacob Hoover, Charles Clover, John Barger, John
Lippard, Michael Goodman, and Henry Fesperman.
Rinehold owned land near Adams Creek and Dutch
Buffalo Creek in 1784.
Overcash, George
1800: George and wife 26-44, 3 males -10, and 1
female -10. Listed next to Charles Bane, John
Wilson, George Carosine(Corzine), John Rumple,
Josiah Bradly, and David McKinly.
1810: George 45+, 1 female 26-44, 2 males 10-15, 1
female 10-15, 2 males -10, and 4 females -10.
George bought land on Coddle Creek from Henry Corum
in Jan 1812.
Overcast, Henry
1810: Henry and wife 26-44, 1 female 16-25, 1 male -
10, and 3 females -10.
Overcash, Jacob
1800: Jacob and wife 26-44, and 2 males -10. Listed
next to Mathias Cook, Henry Plott, Peter Overcash,
David Nishler, Martin Slough, and John Still.
Overcast, John
1800: John 16-25, 1 male 16-25, and 1 female 16-25.
Listed next to Vachel Holbrooks, John Weddington,
William Correll, Hezekiah Glover, John Means, and
James Means.
1810: John 26-44, 1 female 45+, 1 male -10, and 3
females -10.
Overcast, Michael
Children: Henry
1800: Michael and wife 26-44, 2 males -10, and 1
female -10. Listed next to Daniel Krider(Crider),
Phillip Shive, George Harkman, Jacob Krider(Crider),
Jr., Manasah Dresser, and Jacob Krider(Crider), Sr.
Overcash, Peter
1800: Peter and wife 26-44, 1 female 10-15, 1 male -
10, and 2 females -10. Listed next to John Yoman,
Sarah Nowls, Paul Walton, Henry Plott, John Cook,
and Mathias Cook.
Bought land on Little Cold Water Creek from John
Furr in Jan 1806.

1810: Peter 45+, 1 female 26-44, 1 female 16-25, 1
male 10-15, 2 females 10-15, 1 male -10, and 3
females -10.
Ovestwald, Henry
1800: Henry and wife 26-44, 1 male 16-25, 1 male 10-
15, and 1 male -10. Listed next to John House,
Martin Harky, Jacob Harky, Christian Hurlohor,
Christian Hurlohor, Jr., and Henry Heren.
Parish, David
1810 David and wife 26-44, 1 male -10, and 1 female
-10.
Parish, Tapley
1810: Tapley and wife 26-44, 1 male 16-25, and 2
females -10.
Parker, Charles
1810: Charles 26-44, 1 female 45+, 1 female 16-25, 1
male -10, and 2 females -10.
Parks, Charles & Hannah Irvin/Irwin
Children: John, Polly
Married July 23, 1801 in Cabarrus Co., John Houston,
bondsman.
Charles was bondsman for Samuel L. Erwin and Rachel
Huie in 1802, and he was security for the
administration of Robert Erwin estate in April 1806.
He was bondsman for Catherine Miller and Leonard
Sides in 1803.
1790 - Parks, Hugh & Margaret
Owned land on Coddle Creek
In Mecklenburg Co. in 1754.
Parks, Hugh, Jr
Owned land on Coddle Creek in 1778.
1790 - Patterson, Alexander
Son of Robert Patterson.
1800: Alexander and wife 26-44, 1 male 10-15, and 1
female 10-15. Listed next to John Baker, John Smith,
James Cannon, Hugh Carrithers, Alexander McClary,
and Levi Russell.
1810: Alexander 26-44, 1 female 45+, 1 female 16-25,
and 1 male -10.
Patterson, Hugh
Owned land on Rocky River in 1783.
Hugh was a wheelright.
1800: Hugh and wife 26-44, 1 female 10-15, and 1
female -10. Listed next to John Patterson, Thomas
Penenger, Thomas Mock, Benjamin Patton, Ann Patton,
and Caleb Phifer.
1810: Hugh and wife 26-44, 1 female 16-25, and 1
female 10-15.
1790 - Patterson, John
Children: 4 males born 1790-1800: 1 female -10 1800.
Owned land on Longreen branch of Coldwater Cr. near
Joseph Rogers, Caleb and Martin Phifer in 1777.

1800: John and wife 26-44, 1 female 16-25, 4 males -
10, and 1 female -10. Listed next to Thomas
Penenger, Thomas Mock, Archibald McLarty, Hugh
Patterson, Benjamin Patton, and Ann Patton.
John owned land on Cold Water Creek at the Rowan Co.
line which he sold to Jacob Deal of Rowan Co. in Jan
1812.
Patterson, John
1800: John and wife 26-44, 3 males -10, and 2 -10.
Listed next to Thomas Rogers, Elizabeth Holly, Jean
McLusky, Susanna Morrison, William Glover, and John
Kesler.
Patterson, Joseph & Rebekah
Owned land on Rocky River in 1769.
Son of William Patterson.
1790 - Patterson, Robert
Heirs: Martha, Alexander, Esther, and Charles.
Owned land on Longreen branch of Coldwater Creek in
1784.
1800: Robert 45+, 2 females 26-44, and 1 female 10-
15. Listed next to James Plunket, Jr., Paul Phifer,
Martin Phifer, John Purviance, David Reese, and
Joseph Rogers.
1810: Robert 45+, 2 females 26-44, 1 female 10-15,
and 1 male -10.
1790 - Patterson, William
1800 an Elizabeth Patterson is listed in the census
and William is not. She could be the widow of
William. Her household consisted of just herself
45+.
Son of Joseph Patterson
1790 - Patton, Benjamin
Owned land on Irish Buffalo Creek in 1782
Son of Joseph Patton
1800: Benjamin and wife 45+, and 1 female 26-44.
Listed next to Hugh Patterson, John Patterson,
Thomas Penenger, Ann Patton, Caleb Phifer, and
Martin Phifer.
1790 - Patton, Joseph
Children: William, Samuel, Benjamin B., Dove,
George, Polly
1800: Joseph 45+, 1 female 26-44, 1 male 16-25, 2
males 10-15, 1 male -10, and 2 females -10. Listed
next to Elizabeth Patterson, Joseph Ross, John
Tagert, Isaac Workman, William Fraser, and Morgan
Hall.
1810: Joseph and wife 45+, 2 males 16-25, 1 female
16-25, 1 male 10-15, and 1 female 10-15.
Samuel sold land between Coddle Creek and Irish
Buffalo Creek to his son Benjamin in Jan 1812.
Samuel moved to Jefferson Co., TN., time unknown.
He was the son of Samuel and Ann Patton.

1790 - Patton, Samuel & Ann
        Children: James, John, Joseph, Thomas, William
        Son of Joseph Patton
        Owned land on Wolf Meadow Branch of Coddle Creek and
        Irish Buffalo Creek in 1774. Also owned land on
        Armstrong Branch of Buffalo Creek, on and wife sides
        of Camp Branch of Coddle Creek, and Three Mile
        Branch.
        Samuel died before 1800.
        1800: Ann 45+, and 1 female 26-44.
Peacock, John & Rebecca
        Children: Samuel, Constantine, Betsy
        John died before Jan 1814.
Pealer, Michael
        1800: Michael and wife 26-44, 2 females 10-15, 3
        males -10, and 1 female -10. Listed next to Joseph
        Russell, Celia Russell, Robert Sullivan, Henry
        Propst, Leonard Barberick, and John Gallimore.
Peanix, Gallant
        1800: Gallant and wife 26-44, 1 male -10, and 1
        female -10. Listed next to William McCray, William
        Hamilton, Morgan Hall, Molly Peanix, Martin Gun, and
        Elizabeth Skiliton.
Peanix, Molly
        1800: Molly 26-44, 1 female 16-25, 1 male 10-15, and
        1 male -10. Listed next to Gallant Peanix, William
        McCray, William Hamilton, Martin Gun, Elizabeth
        Skiliton, and Jean McLusky.
        Peck, Frederick
        1800: Frederick and wife 45+, 1 male 16-25, 2
        females 16-25, 3 females 10-15, and 1 female -10.
        Listed next to James McMahon, Jacob Moose, William
        Louder, Joseph Woolever, Peter Troutman, and Drury
        Rogers.
        1810: Frederick and wife 45+, and 1 female 10-15.
        Frederick registered his mark for cattle and horses
        in Oct 1798.
Peck/Pick, John
        1810: John and wife 26-44, 2 males -10, and 2
        females -10.
Pence, Henry
        1800: Henry and wife 16-25, and 1 male -10. Listed
        next to William Mensinger, John Misenheimer, Andrew
        Cruse, George Ritchey, Michael Sides, and george
        Stickleather.
1790 - Pence, Jacob
        Children: Christina, Adam, Valentine, Felty
Penel, Valentine
        1810: Valentine 16-25, 1 female 45+, 1 female 26-44,
        1 female 10-15, and 1 male -10.
Peninger, Asemus

1800: Asemus' and wife 26-44, 2 males 10-15, and 3
females -10. Listed next to George File, Mathias
Beam, Michael Wiser, Charles Seffrid, Tobias Cress,
and Henry Cuthezen.
Penninger/Beninger, Martin
1800: Martin and wife 26-44, 2 males -10, and 3
females -10. Listed next to Michael Gatchey, Henry
Gatchey, Jacob Dewatt, George Seffred, Michael
Wiser, and Mathias Beam.
1810: Martin 45+, 1 female 26-44, 2 males 10-15, 2
females 10-15, 2 males -10, and 1 female -10.
Penenger, Thomas
1800: Thomas' and wife 26-44, 1 female 10-15, and 4
males -10. Listed next to Thomas Mock, Archibald
McLarty, Charles McNelond, John Patterson, Hugh
Patterson, and Benjamin Patton.
Pence/Binse, Catherine
1810: Catherine 45+, 1 male 16-25, 1 female 16-25,
and 1 female -10.
Penee, Catherine
1810: Catherine 26-44, 1 male 16-25, 1 female 16-25,
and 1 female -10.
Penney, Robert
Owned land on and wife sides of Mill Creek, a branch
of Coddle Creek in 1783.
Son of William & Elizabeth Penney.
1790 - Penney, William & Elizabeth
Children: Robert
Owned land on Mill Creek, a branch of Coddle Creek
and on the west side of Buffalo Creek in 1773.
Peter, Jacob
1810: Jacob 26-44, 1 female 16-25, and 2 males -10.
Petry, Dorothy
1800: Dorothy 26-44, 1 male 16-25, 1 female 16-25, 3
males 10-15, and 1 male -10. Listed next to Daniel
Bost, Harmon Moyer, Daniel Faggot, Francis
Funderburk, Andrew Slough, and George Smith.
Petre, John
1810: John and another male, and wife 16-25, and 1
female 45+.
Pharrow, Andrew
1810: Andrew and wife 26-44, 1 female 16-25, 1 male
10-15, 1 male -10, and 1 female -10.
1790 - Phifer, Caleb, Col, & Barbara
Owned land on Longreen branch of Coldwater Creek, at
the branch of Little Coldwater Creek in 1778.
son of Martin Phifer, Sr. and Margaret.
1800: Caleb and wife 45+, 1 female 16-25, 1 male 10-
15, 2 females 10-15, 1 male -10, and 2 females -10.
Listed next to Ann Patton, Benjamin Patton, Hugh
Patterson, Martin Phifer, Paul Phifer, and James
Plunket, Jr.

1810: Caleb and wife 45+, 1 make 16-25, 2 females
16-25, and 1 male 10-15.
1790 - Phifer, George
Died before 1797.
Phifer, George
1810: George 26-44, 1 male 16-25, 1 female 16-25, 1
male 10-15, and 2 males -10.
1790 - Phifer, Jacob
Died before 1802. Father of Sally who married Henry
Young and Anna who married George Dry. George Dry,
by power of attorney, signed for Sally Young share
of estate as well as his wife share in Jan 1802.
Owned land on Coldwater Creek at the branch of
Little Coldwater Creek
Phifer, John & Catherine Barringer
Children: Martin
Owned land on Coldwater Creek at Three Mile Branch
and at the branch of Little Coldwater Creek in 1771.
Catherine was the daughter of Paul Barringer.
John died in 1777.
Phifer, John F.
1810: John 45-or over, 1 male 26-44, 2 females 16-
25, and 3 males -10.
John bought land on and wife sides of Three Mile
Branch in April 1813.
John was born 1785, and died Dec 27, 1828.
1790 - Phifer, Martin, Capt
Children: Martin
died Dec. 1, 1827 Rev. Vet Col.
Bought land of Rice Dulin on Cold Water Creek from
the sheriff in Jan 1806.
Owned land on Adam Creek in 1783.
1800: Martin 26-44, 1 female 16-25, 1 male 16-25,
and 1 female 10-15. Listed next to Caleb Phifer, Ann
Patton, Benjamin Patton, Paul Phifer, James Plunket,
Jr., and Robert Patterson.
Martin died between 1808 and 1813.
He was the son of Martin Phifer, Sr and Margeret.
1790 - Phifer, Martin, Sr. & Margaret
Children: Caleb, Martin, Paul, daughter married to
John Simianer?
Son of John and Catherine Barringer Phifer.
Owned land on Cold Water Creek at the Longreen
branch, Armstorng branch, and at the branch of
Little Coldwater Creek in 1764.
Martin died in or before 1791.
Phifer, Mathias
1800: Mathias and wife 26-44, 1 females 16-25, 1
female 10-15, and 4 males -10. Listed next to James
Hughey, Samuel Hughey, Samuuel Ferguson, James
Carson, John Russell, and David Russle.
Phifer, Paul & Jean Alexander

Children: John N., George Alexander
Married Jan 9, 1792 in Mecklenburg Co., Nathaniel
Alexander, bondsman.
1800: Paul and Jean, and wife 26-44, 1 male 26-44,
and 2 males -10. Listed next to Martin Phifer, Caleb
Phifer, Ann Patton, James Plunket, Jr., Robert
Patterson, and John Purviance.

Phillips, John
1810: John and wife 16-25, and 1 male -10.

Phillips, Nathan
1810: Nathan 26-44, 1 female 45+, 1 female 26-44, 1
male -10, and 4 females -10.
Nathan bought land on Caldwell Creek in April 1813.

Phillips, William
Owned land on Anderson Creek, a branch of Rocky
River in 1782.

Pickens, Alexander
1810: Alexander and wife 16-25, and 1 female -10.

Pickens, Hugh
1800: Hugh and wife 26-44. Listed next to Duncan
Smith, John Jones, Benjamin Alexander, John
Alexander, James Alexander, and William Gray.
Sold land to Joseph Welch on Mulberry Branch in July
1806.
1810: Hugh 26-44, 2 males 10-15, 2 males -10, and 2
females -10.

1790 - Pickens, Samuel, Capt
Children: James
Owned land on Rocky River in 1773.
Samuel filed a suit against Robert Stanford for
slander in April 1798.
1800: Samuel and wife 45+, 1 female 26-44, 2 males
16-25, 3 males 10-15, 1 female 10-15, 2 males -10,
and 1 female -10. Listed next to John Neil, Widow
Neil, Samuel Martin, George Ross, Joseph Ross, Sr.,
and Jean Ross.
1810: Samuel and wife 45+, 2 males 26-44, 3 males
16-25, 2 females 16-25, 1 male 10-15, and 1 female
10-15.
A Samuel Pickens, born NC, age 72, is in Lowndes
dist., Lowndes Co., AL in 1850.

1790 - Pickens, William
Owned land on a head branch of Rocky River in the
Welsh Tract and on Pickens Creek, a branch of Twelve
Mile Creek in 1754.

Pines, Jacob
1800: Jacob and wife 45+, 1 female 16-25, 2 males
10-15, and 2 females 10-15. Listed next to Peter
Cauble, Peter Limeboh, George Clontz, John Edleman,
John File, and Jacob Fisher.

Plaster, Abraham
Abraham owned land on Adam Creek.

Plaster, John
        1800: John and wife 26-44, and 2 males -10. Listed
        next to John Shoe, Jacob Rinehart, Peter Quilman,
        Abraham Plaster, Leonard Sides, and Andrew Slough.
        John owned land on Adam Creek.
Pless, Henry
        1800: Henry 26-44, 1 male 16-22, 1 female 26-44, 1
        male -10, and 3 females -10. Listed next to Jacob
        Boager, Peter Boager, John Cauddle, Martin Uery,
        Jacob Hodgeman, and George Clontz.
        1810: Henry and wife 26-44, 3 females 10-15, and 2
        males -10.
Pless, Henry
        1810: Henry and wife 26-44, 1 male 10-15, 2 females
        10-15, and 3 females -10.
Pletter/Plaster, Abraham & Susannah
        Owned land on Umberford branch of Buffalo Creek in
        1782.
        1800: Abraham and wife 45+. Listed next to John
        Plaster, John Shoe, Jacob Rinehart, Leonard Sides,
        Andrew Slough, and Barnard Sifferd.
Plott, Henry
        1800: Henry and wife 26-44, and 3 males -10. Listed
        next to Peter Overcash, John Yoman, John Cook,
        Mathias Cook, and Jacob Overcash.
Plot, Isaac
        1810: Isaac 26-44, 1 female 10-15, 3 males -10, and
        1 female -10.
Plott, John
        1800: John 26-44, and 1 female 16-25. Listed next to
        Isaac Loftin, Christian Dry, Hannah Voiles, James
        McGraw, William McGraw, and Nicholas Curzine.
        1810: John 26-44, 1 female 45+, 1 male 10-15, 2
        males -10, and 2 females -10.
Plunket, Houston
        1810: Houston 26-44, 2 females 16-25, 2 males -10,
        and 2 females -10.
1790 - Plunket, James, Sr & Fereby (Shinn ?)
        Children: James, Jr
        A James Plunket made deed of gift to his step-
        daughter, Jane Shinn in April 1806.
        Owned land on Rocky River in 1782.
        1800: James 45+, 1 female 26-44, 1 female 16-25, 3
        males -10, and 1 female -10. Listed next to William
        Harris, Elizabeth Harris, David Taylor, James
        Russell, James Scott, and William L. Alexander.
        James may have died 1810.
1790 - Plunket, James, Jr & Agness Houston
        Children: John Houston (Elizabeth Purviance)
        Married in Mecklenburg County, bond date Jan 3,
        1783, bondsman, John McCacharn.
        Sheriff of Cabarrus in 1800.

1800: James and Agness 26-44, 1 male 16-25, 3 males
10-15, 1 male -10, and 2 females -10. Listed next to
Paul Phifer, Martin Phifer, Caleb Phifer, Robert
Patterson, John Purviance, and David Reese.
1800: James and wife 26-44, 3 males 10-15, 2 females
10-15, 1 male -10, and 1 female -10.
1810: James' age is not shown. His household
consisted of 1 female 26-44, 2 males 16-25, 1 female
16-25, 1 male 10-15, and 1 female -10.
Owned a grist mill on Coddle Creek in 1802
Owned land on Rocky River

Plunket, John Houston & Elizabeth Purviance
Married Feb 18, 1804 in Cabarrus Co., Robert Ross &
John Plunket, bondsmen.
Elizabeth was the daughter of John and Nancy
Ferguson Purviance.

Plunket, Joseph & Polly Lee
Bound in or before 1811, guardian was John McCurdy
Married July 5, 1813, Benjamin Shinn, bondsman.

Plylor, Frederick
1800: Frederick 45+, 1 female 26-44, 2 males 16-25,
1 female 16-25, and 1 female -10. Listed next to
George Hartsell, Leonard Hartsell, John Hagler, Sr.,
George M. Redling, Andrew Rinehart, and Frederick
Starnes.

Plylor, Henry
1800: Henry and wife 26-44, 4 females 10-15, 2 males
-10, and 1 female -10. Listed next to David Fink,
Andrew Cariker, Philip Cariker, Jr., Peter
Misenheimer, George Hartman, and Henry Linker.
1810: Henry and wife 45+, 4 females 16-25, 2 males
10-15, and 1 female 10-15.

1790 - Polk, Charles, Capt & Mary Alexander
Owned land on Clear Creek in 1780.
Charles died in or before 1812.
Mary died before 1796, daughter of Hezekiah and Mary
Alexander

1790 - Polk, Charles
Owned land on Clear Creek.
Died in or before 1821.

1790 - Polk, John, Jr & Elinore
Owned land on Clear Creek in 1780.
1800: John 26-44, 1 female 26-44, 1 female 16-25, 1
male 10-15, 1 female 10-15, 1 male -10, and 1 female
-10. Listed next to John Brown, Douglass Winchester,
Charles Freeman, George Tucker, Jr., Cistra Brint,
and Mary Cagle.

1790 - Polk, William
1800: William and wife 45+. Listed next to George
Long, John Reed, Joshua Tucker, William Smith,
George Tucker, Sr., and Joh Wisiner.

1790 - *Porter, James & Ruth

Children: Mary T. (? Orman), Margaret B.J., John
G.(maybe L.), James J., dau (? Lewis)
Granddaughter: Mary K.P. Lewis
James was born 1756, died 1825
Ruth was born 1756, died March 18, 1828
Ruth will was probated in Aug 1829
James & Ruth lived in the Mount Pleasant area, but
their daughter was buried in Steel Creek Cemetery in
1793.
Porter, Peter
Released from prison April 1812.
Posey, Elizabeth
1800: Elizabeth 26-44, 1 male 10-15, and 2 females -
10. Listed next to Ezekiel Wright, Elenor Erwin,
John Robinson, William Wiley, Arthur McCree, and
Robert Allison.
Potts, Henry
1800: Henry and wife 26-44, and 3 males -10. Listed
next to John Wiley, Jean Russle, Joseph White, Mary
White, Roland Voiles, and Robert Lee.
Powell, Able
1800: Able and wife 45+, 1 male 10-15, 2 males -10,
and 2 females -10. Listed next to John Ford, Dennis
Clay, James Clay, John Powell, John Carruthers, and
Michael Garmon.
Powell, John
1800: John and wife 45+, and 1 male 10-15. Listed
next to Able Powell, John Ford, Dennis Clay, John
Carruthers, Michael Garmon, and Travis Gullino.
Pressley, David
Not in the 1800 census. Moved to Buncombe Co., NC
before 1807.
1790 - Props/Propst, Henry
Children: (unproven) Henry (Katey Cress), John
(Polly Cress), Elizabeth (Mathias Barnhart)
Fined for swearing unlawfully in Oct 1806 court in
Cabarrus County.
Henry was a doctor.
1800: Henry and wife 26-44, 3 males 10-15, 3 males -
10, and 1 female -10. Listed next to Michael Pealer,
Joseph Russell, Celia Russell, Leonard Barberick,
John Gallimore, and John Skilhouse.
Propst, Henry & Katey Cress
Married in Cabarrus Co., bond dated April 6, 1808,
bondsman, Tobias Cress.
1810: Henry household consisted of 3 males 16-25, 1
female 16-25, 1 male -10, and 2 females -10.
Propes, Michael
1810: Michael household consisted of 2 males 16-25,
1 female 26-44, 1 female 16-25, 2 males 10-15, and 1
male -10.
Purviance, Alexander

Alexander estate settlement took place in 1798.
Letter of Admin. To David Purviance, James Harris
and Francis Ross, security.

1790 - Purviance, David
Owned land on Coddle Creek and on the north side of
Rocky River opposite James Love in 1775.

Purviance, David & Ebby McKinly
Married in Cabarrus Co., Aug 14, 1806, John Black,
bondsman.
1810: David 26-44, 1 female 16-25, 2 females 10-15,
1 male -10, and 1 female -10.
David died Oct 2, 1839, buried in Rocky Springs
Presbyterian Church Cemetery.
An Isabella Pervins died in Cabarrus Co. in April
1860 at the age of 75 from asthma.
David bought land on Clear Creek and Muddy Creek at
a tax sale in Jan 1812.

1790 - Purviance, James
Children: Patsy, Linney, Even, Dolly, James
1800: James and wife 26-44, 2 males 10-15, 1 male -
10, and 3 females -10. Listed next to John Caragin,
James Caragin, Sr., Hugh Heare, Thomas Voiles, John
McGraw, and William Atkinson.
James was the coroner for Cabarrus County.
He died before 1812 and Moses Rogers was appointed
guardian of these named children.

1790 - Purviance, John & Nancy Ferguson
Children: Elizabeth (John Houston Plunket), David
Simpson, Matilda, Margaret J., Alexander Caldwell,
John Graham, James, Samuel, Nancy, Eliza Sellars
1800: John and Nancy, and wife 26-44, 1 male 10-15,
2 females 10-15, 3 males -10, and 1 female -10.
Listed next to Robert Patterson, James Plunket, Jr.,
Paul Phifer, David Reese, Joseph Rogers, and Seth
Rogers.
1810: John 45+, 1 female 26-44, 2 males 10-15, 1
female 10-15, 2 males -10, and 3 females -10.
Nancy died in 1833.

Purviance, John & Elizabeth Lisenbay
Married in Cabarrus Co., Dec 27, 1798, Robert
Purviance, bondsman.

Purviance, Robert & Sally Miller ?
Married in Rowan Co., April 28, 1793, James Miller,
bondsman
1810: Robert and wife 26-44, 2 females 10-15, and 3
females -10.

Purviance, Robert
1800: Robert 16-25, 1 female 45+, 2 females 10-15,
and 1 female -10. Listed next to John Shaver, John
Culpepper, Joseph Shinn, Joshua Hadley, Samuel
Corzine, and Martha Ferguson.

1790 - Query, Alexander

1800: Alexander and wife 45+, 1 male 26-44, 1 male
16-25, 2 females 16-25, and 1 female 10-15. Listed
next to Samuel Meek, John Edmonton, Widow McClain,
John Scoles, James Smith, and Robert Smith.
Query, James & Matilda Alexander
      Married Jan 28, 1807 in Cabarrus Co., Benjamin
      Alexander, bondsman.
      1810: James and wife 26-44, 1 male 16-25, 2 females
      16-25, 1 male -10, and 1 female -10. Listed next to
      Benjamin Alexander.
Query, Lawrance & Ann
      Lawrance died before April 1806.
Query, Robert & Sidney Alexander
      Married Dec 7, 1799 in Cabarrus Co., Moses
      Alexander, bondsman.
      Sidney was the daughter of Lavinia Alexander, who
      died 1810.
Quilman, George
      1810: George and wife 16-25, 1 male -10, and 1·
      female -10.
1790 - Quilman, Peter
      Children: Aaron, Molly, Peter, Jr, Mary (Solomon
      Fisher), George ? (Catherine Barringer)
      1800: Peter and wife 45+, and 1 male 16-25. Listed
      next to Joseph Starns, Robert Williams, Charles
      Starns, Christopher Leigh, Jonathan Hartzell, and
      John Soseman.
Quilman, Peter, Jr
      1800: Peter and wife 16-25, and 1 male -10. Listed
      next to Abram Misenheimer, Jacob Miller, John
      Melchor, George Misenheimer, Jacob Rinehart, John
      Shoe, and John Plaster.
Ray, William
      1810: William 16-25, 1 female 26-44, and 1 female
      10-15.
Reamer, Jacob
      1810: Jacob and wife 26-44, 1 male 10-15, 1 female
      10-15, 3 males -10, and 1 female -10.
1790 - Redland/Redling, George M.
      1800: George and wife 45+, 2 females 16-25, 2 female
      10-15, 1 male -10, and 3 females -10. Listed next to
      Frederick Plylor, George Hartsell, Leonard Hartsell,
      Andrew Rinehart, Frederick Starnes, and Peter Teame.
Reed, Conrad
      1810: Conrad 26-44, 1 female 16-25, 1 male -10, and
      1 female -10.
Reed, Demsy
      Owned a grist mill on Reedy Creek and bought land on
      Anderson Creek and Muddy Creek in Jan 1813.
Reed, Henry
      1810: Henry and wife 16-25.
1790 - Reed, John

Owned land on Crooked Creek in 1783.
Bought land on Meadow Creek from William Cratton in
Oct 1805.
1800: John 45+, 1 female 26-44, 3 males 16-25, 1
male 10-15, 2 females 10-15, 2 males -10, and 2
females -10. Listed next to Josiah Wallace, Ludwick
Wallace, William Wallace, Moses Alexander (Big),
Moses Alexander, and Hezekiah Alexander.
1810: John 45+, 1 female 26-44, 2 males 16-25, 2
females 16-25, 1 female 10-15, and 1 female -10.

1790 - Reed, John
1800: John and wife 26-44, 2 males 10-15, 1 female
10-15, 2 males -10, and 2 females -10. Listed next
to Joshua Tucker, Isaac Brandon, Mary Cagle, George
Long, William Polk, and William Smith.
1810: John and wife 45+, 1 male 16-25, 4 females 10-
15, and 2 females -10.
John bought 355 acres from William Fincher on
Scaffold Branch of Crooked Creek in April 1812.

Reid, Joseph & Margaret Farr
Married in Cabarrus Co., bond dated April 21, 1803,
bondsman, Thomas Spain.
In the 1850 Cabarrus Co. census, Joseph is listed as
72 and Margaret is listed as 66 years old.

Reese/Rees, David
Owned land on Coddle Creek in 1769.
1800: David 45+, 1 female 26-44, 2 females 10-15,
and 3 females -10. Listed next to John Purviance,
Robert Patterson, James Plunket, Jr., Joseph Rogers,
Seth Rogers, and Francis Ross.

Reese/Rees, James
Owned land on Coddle Creek in 1769.

Reeves, John
1810: John 26-44, 1 female 16-25, and 1 male -10.

Reynolds, Catherine
Children: Ann

Ritchey, Abraham
1810: Abraham ana his wife, and wife 16-25.

Richey, Daniel
1810: Daniel and wife 16-25, and 1 female -10.

1790 - Richey, Henry
Children: John
1810: Henry and wife 45+, 1 male 16-25, 1 female 16-
25, 1 male 10-15, and 1 female -10.
Henry died in 1812. His son, John, gave an oath in
open court that the LWT of his father was destroyed
by his mother.

Richey, Henry
1810: Henry 45+, 1 female 45+, 1 male 16-25, 1 male
10-15, 1 female 10-15, and 1 female -10.

1790 - Richey, Jacob
Owned land on Dutch Buffalo Creek in 1774.

Richey, Michael
    1810: Michael and wife 16-25, and 1 male -10.
Redimour/Ridenaur, Jacob
    1810: Jacob and wife 16-25.
Redimour/Ridenaur, Henry
    1810: Henry and wife 16-25, and 1 male -10.
1790 - Ridenaur, Nicholas
    Owned land on Meeting House Branch in 1783.
    1800: Nicholas and wife 45+, 2 females 16-25, 2
    males 10-15, 1 female 10-15, 3 males -10, and 1
    female -10. Listed next to Martin Harkey, Paul
    Barringer, Jacob Bost, Mathias Moyer, Isaac
    Blackwelder, and George Bost.
Ridley, John
    1800: John 26-44, 1 female 16-25, and 2 males -10.
    Listed next to George Fink, John Furor, Jr., Arthur
    Underwood, Caleb Douss, Tobius Clutz, and Rabeckah
    Heninger.
1790 - Rigey/Ritchey, George
    1800: George 26-44, 1 female 16-25, and 3 males -10.
    Listed next to Henry Pence, William Mensinger, John
    Misenheimer, Michael Sides, George Stickleather, and
    Peter Simmons.
    1810: George 45+, 1 female 26-44, 2 males 16-25, 2
    males 10-15, 1 female 10-15, and 1 female -10.
Ritchey, John
    1800: John and wife 16-25, and 1 female -10. Listed
    next to Peter Boiles, Henry Ludwick, Henry Walker,
    Michael Walker, Leonard Cluttz, and John Cluttz.
    1810: John and wife 26-44, 1 male 10-15, 1 female
    10-15, 1 male -10, and 3 females -10.
Ridley, John
Rimer/Rymer, George
    1810: George 45+, 1 female 26-44, 1 male 16-25, 1
    male 10-15, 3 males -10, and 1 female -10.
Rimer, Jacob
    1800: Jacob and wife 26-44, 1 male 16-25, and 2
    males -10. Listed next to John Duke, Micheal
    Goodman(Big), Peter Weaver, Tobias Stirewalt,
    William Ryal, and Henry Lineboh.
Rimer, Michael
    1810: Michael and wife 16-25, 1 male -10, and 1
    female -10.
Rinehart, Andrew
    Died in or before 1789.
Rinehart, Andrew & Lediah Almon
    Married Dec 19, 1799 in Cabarrus Co., Gideon Almon
    bondsman. 1800 Andrew household consisted of just
    himself, 26-44, and Lediah 16-25. Listed next to
    George M. Redling, Frederick Plylor, George
    Hartsell, Frederick Starnes, Peter Teames, and
    Martin Wedinhouse.

Rinehart, Christian
        Bought land on Adams Creek and Anderson Creek from
        Frederick Milster in Jan 1807.
Rinehart, Jacob
        1800: Jacob consisted of himself 16-25, 1 female
        45+, 1 female 16-25, and 1 male 10-15. Listed next
        to Peter Quilman, Abram Misenheimer, Jacob Miller,
        John Shoe, John Plaster, and Abraham Plaster.
Reinhart, Phillip
        1810: Phillip and wife 26-44, and 2 females -10.
Riss, David
        1810: David 45+, 1 female 26-44, 2 females 16-25, 1
        female 10-15, 3 males -10, and 3 females -10.
Robb, John
        Owned land on Clear Creek in 1783.
Robb, Robert
        Robert was born 1756-1774 with a wife and 2 sons -
        10, and 2 daughters -10 1800.
Robb, William & Elizabeth
        Owned land on Clear Creek in 1779.
        Elizabeth died April 30, 1792, age 40, buried in
        Philadelphia Presbyterian Church Cemetery.
1790 - Robison/Robinson, John
        Owned land on Reedy Creek in 1783.
        Son of Robert Robison.
Robinson, John
        1800: John and wife 26-44, and 2 males -10. Listed
        next to William Gray, James Alexander, John
        Alexander, Elenor Erwin, Ezekiel Wright, and
        Elizabeth Posey.
Robison, John
        1810: John 45+, 1 female 26-44, 1 male 26-44, 1 male
        16-25, 3 males 10-15, 2 males -10, and 2 females -
        10.
Roche, Joachim
        Joachim died before July 1797.
Rodare, Jacob
        1810: Jacob 26-44, 1 female 16-25, and 1 male -10.
Rogers, Carson & Ibby McKinley
        Married in Cabarrus Co., bond dated 1809, bondsman,
        1810: Carson and Ibby, and wife 16-25, and 2 males -
        10.
        Ibby was the daughter of David McKinley.
Rogers, Drury & Ritte Bankston
        Married Feb 26, 1800 in Rowan Co., Benjamin Rogers,
        bondsman.
        1800: Drury 26-44, and Ritte 16-25. Listed next to
        Peter Troutman, Joseph Woolever, Frederick Peck,
        Charles Carter, Henry Melchor, John Cauble, and
        Nicholas Rough.
Rodgers, George

1810: George and wife 45+, 1 male 16-25, and 1
female 16-25.
1790 - Rogers, Hugh & Elizabeth
Owned land on Coldwater Creek and English Buffalo
Creek near John and Martha Rogers in 1778.
Hugh is shown in the 1850 Union Co. census as 80,
and Elizabeth as 65.
Rogers, John & Peggy James
Married in Cabarrus Co., bond dated Feb 2, 1805,
bondsman, Solomon Casey.
In the 1850 Cabarrus Co. census John is listed as 73
and Margaret is listed as 67 years old.
1790 - Rogers, John & Margaret Russel 111
Married in Mecklenburg County, bond dated May 12,
1789, bondsman, David Russel
Owned land on Coldwater Creek.
1790 - Rogers, John & Martha   132
Married before 1764.
Owned land on English Buffalo Creek in 1764 and
1778, near William Balch and James Black.
near Hugh, Mathew and William Rogers
1800: John and Martha, and wife 26-44, 1 male 16-25,
2 males 10-15, 1 female 10-15, and 1 male -10.
Listed next to Levi Russell, Alexander McClary, Hugh
Carrithers, William Means, Moses Rogers, and Thomas
Caruthers.
Rogers, John
1810: John and wife 26-44, and 1 female 10-15.
Son of George.
1790 - Rogers, Joseph
Owned land near Longreen Branch of Coldwater Creek,
and Three Mile Creek in 1764.
1800: Joseph and wife 45+, 1 female 26-44, 3 males
16-25, and 1 female 16-25. Listed next to David
Reese, John Purviance, Robert Patterson, Seth
Rogers, Francis Ross, and John Simeoner.
Rodgers, Joseph
1810: Joseph 26-44, and 1 female 16-25.
Son of George Rodgers.
1790 - Rogers, Moses
1800: Moses and wife 26-44, 1 male 10-15, 1 female
10-15, 2 males -10, and 2 females -10. Listed next
to William Means, John Rogers, Levi Russell, Thomas
Caruthers, Richard Marlin, and William Corell.
1810: Moses 45+, 1 female 26-44, 1 male 16-25, 1
female 16-25, 1 male 10-15, 1 female 10-15, 2 males
-10, and 2 females -10.
1790 - Rogers, Seth
on Wolf Meadow Branch and Irish Buffalo Creek. A
Seth Rogers died in Hanover, Lancaster Co., PA in
June 1758 who had brothers Hugh and George, and wife
Katharine. No children named.

Seth owned land on Irish Buffalo Creek in 1785. He
was near Frederick Carlock (Clary) and witnessed a
couple of deeds for him. Also close by was William
White.
1800: Seth and wife 26-44, 2 males 10-15, 3 males -
10, and 2 females -10. Listed next to Joseph Rogers,
David Reese, John Purviance, Francis Ross, John
Simeoner, and Martin Shive.
1810: Seth and wife 45+, 4 males 16-25, 4 males -10,
and 2 females -10.

1790 - Rogers, Thomas
Owned land in the Welsh Tract on Rocky River between
Anderson Creek and Muddy Creek in 1779.

Rogers, Thomas & Winifred
1800: Thomas' and wife 26-44, 2 males 10-15, 2 males
-10, and 1 female -10. Listed next to Elizabeth
Holly, Jean McLusky, Elizabeth Skiliton, John
Patterson, Susanna Morrison, and William Glover.
1810: Thomas' and wife 26-44, 2 males 16-25, 1
female 16-25, 1 male 10-15, and 2 males -10.
Thomas is shown in the 1850 Union Co. census as 81
and Winiford is 71.

Ross, Adam
Owned land on Wolf Meadow Branch of Coddle Creek in
1785.

1790 - Ross, Francis & Esther Carruthers
Owned land on Sugar Creek in 1779.
1800: Francis 45+, 1 male 45+, 1 female 45+, 1 male
26-44, 1 male 26-44, 3 males 16-25, 2 females 16-25,
1 male 10-15, and 1 female -10. Listed next to Seth
Rogers, Joseph Rogers, David Reese, John Simeoner,
Martin Shive, and Daniel Doherty.
1810: Francis and wife 45+, 3 males 26-44, 2 males
16-25, and 3 females -10.
Francis died in or before 1822.
Esther was the daughter of Hugh and Sarah Purviance
Carruthers.

1790 - Ross, George
1800: George and wife 45+, 1 male 16-25, 1 male 10-
15, and 1 female -10. Listed next to Samuel Pickens,
John Neil, Widow Neil, Samuel Martin, Joseph Ross,
Sr., Jean Ross, and John Ross.

Ross, Isaac & M.
Isaac was born March 1, 1708, died Feb 13, 1760
M was born June 30, 1722, died May 20, 1766
Buried in Spears Cemetery of Rocky River Church.

Ross, James
1810: James and wife 45+, 2 males 16-25, 2 females
16-25, 2 males 10-15, and 1 female 10-15.

Ross, John & Elizabeth
1800: John 26-44, 1 female 16-25, and 1 female -10.
Listed next to Jean Ross, Joseph Ross, Sr., George

Ross, James Stevenson, David Templeton, and James
Tanner.
    1810: John and Elizabeth, and wife 26-44, 1 female
    16-25, 1 male -10, and 4 females -10.
1790 - Ross, Joseph Anthony, Sr
    Children: Joseph, Jr
    1800: Joseph and wife 45+, 1 male 10-15, 1 female
    10-15, 3 males -10, and 2 females -10. Listed next
    to George Ross, Samuel Pickens, John Neil, Jean
    Ross, John Ross, and James Stevenson.
Ross, Joseph, Jr
    1800: Joseph 26-44, 1 female 16-25, 1 male 10-15, 1
    male -10, and 1 female -10. Listed next to John
    Tagert, John Smith, Thomas Dobson, Elizabeth
    Patterson, Jospeh Patton, and Isaac Workman.
Ross, Joseph
    1810: Joseph and wife 26-44, 1 male 10-15, and 5
    females -10.
Ross, Nicholson
    Estate sale held in Cabarrus Co. in 1774.
Ross, Peter
    Owned land on Hamby Branch, a branch of Rocky River
    in 1784.
Ross, Samuel
    1810: Samuel 16-25, 1 male 16-25, 1 female 45+, 2
    females 16-25, and 1 female 10-15.
1790 - Ross, William & Jean 225
    Died April 1800
    Owned land on Clear Creek in 1783.
    1800: Jean 45+, 2 males 16-25, 2 males 10-15, and 3
    females -10. Listed next to Joseph Ross, Sr., George
    Ross, Samuel Pickens, John Ross, James Stevenson,
    and David Templeton.
1790 - Ross, William & Elizabeth
    Owned land on Wolf Meadow Branch of Coddle Creek and
    Coldwater Creek in 1783.
Ross, William, Jr.
    William sold land to Daniel Boger on Rocky River and
    Hamby Run in July 1813.
Rough, Nicholas
    1800: Nicholas 45+, 1 female 26-44, 2 males 10-15, 2
    males -10, and 2 females -10. Listed next to John
    Cauble, Henry Melchor, Charles Carter, John Barger,
    Charles Clover, and Jacob Hoover.
Rumple, John
    Children: Peter, Jacob, Caty, John ?
    John's estate settlement appears in the Cabarrus Co.
    court records in July 1806.
    1800: John and wife 26-44, 1 male 10-15, 2 females
    10-15, 1 male -10, and 1 female -10. Listed next to
    George Overcash, Charles Bane, John Wilson, Josiah
    Bradly, David McKinly, and Frances Linse.

Rumple, John & Polly Winecoff
Married in Cabarrus Co., May 11, 1807, Thomas Mock,
bondsman.
John Rumple bought land on Third Branch from John
Houston in July 1806.
Rusle, Allison W.
1810: Allison and wife 45+, 1 female 26-44, 1 male
16-25, and 1 female 10-15.
Russel, Celia
Celia is believed to be a daughter of James and
Susanna Russell. Listed next to Joseph Russell,
known son of James and Susanna Russell.
1800: Celia 16-25, 1 male -10, and 1 female -10.
Listed next to Robert Sullivan, James Martin, John
Kesler, Joseph Russell, Michael Pealer, and Henry
Propst.
1810: Cele 26-44, and 1 female -10.
1790 - Russel, David & Jane
Children: David (Margaret Neely?), Matthew, Margaret
(John Rogers), Jinsey, Martha, Mary (George
Campbell), Isabell (Robert Mitchell), Elizabeth.
David owned land between Clark Creek, a branch of
Mallard Creek and Long Creek in 1767, and at the
head Branch of Mallard Cr & Long Cr 1783.
Zaccheus Wilson is named as son-in-law in David
will. David was born March 27, 1733, died March 28,
1802 and is buried in Hopewell Presbyterian Church
Cemetery.
Sons David and Matthew are not in Mecklenburg or
Cabarrus counties in 1800, but a David and Matthew
are in Buncombe Co., NC in 1800.
Russell, David
A David Russell was left a tract of land jointly
with Joseph Rodgers, by virtue of the will of Moses
White in 1766. Moses and Margaret White owned land
on Irish Buffalo Creek. It is unclear whether this
David is the same one who was married to Jane, or if
this was another David. David and Joseph sold this
tract of land to Michael Shaver in 1775.
1790 - Russel, David & Elizabeth Morrison
Children: James Semianes (Margaret Gingles), Robert
(Mary Morrison), Jenny (Noah Corzine), Jane (James
Tucker), Elizabeth (Samuel Holbrook), Catharine
(Samuel G. White), David Morrison (Elizabeth
Purvians), Mary Ann (George Corzine), William
Gingles (Margaret Teresa Davis), Rachel (William Lee
Gingles).
1800: David and Elizabeth 26-44, 2 males 10-15, and
2 females -10. He listed next to John Russell, James
Carson, Mathias Phifer, Mary Russle, Hardin Chitley,
and John Martin.
Fined on April 20, 1803 for contempt of court.

1810: David and Elizabeth, and wife 26-44, 1 male
16-25, 1 female 16-25, 1 female 10-15, 2 males -10,
and 3 females -10.
Owned land on Clear Creek
Deed from Thomas Love to David, a tract of 131 acres
on the south side of Clear Creek and on and wife
sides of Goose Creek.
Deed of Gift to son James, a tract of 66 acres on
the south side of Rocky River beginning at Clear
Creek next to Thomas Love and Jeremiah Clontz.
(1810)
David was the son of James and Jane Carson Russell.
Elizabeth was the daughter of James and Jeanett Hall
Morrison.
David and wife are buried in Old Rocky River
Cemetery
Russell, David Morrison & Elizabeth Purvians
    Children: David R., Robert Washington (Sarah Flow),
    Sarah (Samuel Pinckney Caldwell)
    Buried in Poplar Tent Church Cemetery
    Son of David and Elizabeth Morrison Russell
Russle, Hamilton
    1810: Hamilton 26-44, 1 female 16-25, and 1 male -
    10.
1790 - Russel, James & Susannah
    Children: Levi (Sarah Fibbs), Joseph (Hannah Fibbs),
    Ellen (Thomas Littleton), and possibly Polly (Isaac
    Davis). Isacc Davis was bondsman for Ellen Russell
    and Thomas Littleton, a known daughter of James &
    Susannah, and he was also bondsman for John Russell
    and Ruth Davis.
    James owned land on Half Meadow Branch of Coddle
    Creek and at a draft of the three mill branches. He
    was next to Alexander Robison. He died about 1791.
    1800: Susannah 45+, 3 females 10-15.
1790 - Russel, James & Jane/Jean Carson
    Children: Robert (Mary Morrison), John (Mary
    Ferguson), Rachel (Patrick Hays), Catharine (William
    Morrison), David (Elizabeth Morrison), Jean (John
    G.L. Huie), William (Sarah McRee), Mary Russell
    (Matthew Russel), Eleanor (John Taggart), Ann (James
    Miller)
    James owned lots in Charlotte that the
    administrators of his estate were empowered to sell
    in Jan 1802. He owned land on the west side of
    Buffalo Creek and was deeded 306 acres on Buffalo
    Creek from his father Robert in 1775. He also owned
    land on Coddle Creek. James died suddenly in Feb
    1799, leaving a noncupative will. His death was just
    one week after his son William's death. Yellow fever
    could have been the cause of their deaths as there
    was an epidemic to the north and south of the state

at about that time. North Carolina surely had cases
of yellow fever as well, but is not reported as
being of epidemic proportions.
1800: Jean (Jane) 45+, 1 male 16-25, 1 female 16-25,
and 1 female 10-15. Listed next to Joseph White,
John McKinley, Murdoch Campbell, John Wiley, Henry
Potts and Mary White.
1810: Jean 45+ and 1 female 16-25.
James was born 1733, died Feb 21, 1799.
Jane was born 1741, died July 29, 1823
Buried in Old Rocky River Cemetery
Jane was the daughter of Robert & Rachel Carson of
Uklwain township, Chester Co., PA.
1790 - Russel, James & Nancy ?
In 1790 James' household consisted of just himself
and wife.
1800: James 45+, 1 female 26-44, 1 female 10-15, 1
male -10, and 3 females -10. Listed next to James
Plunkett, Sr., Elizabeth Harris, James Scott,
William Alexander, and Peter Huey.
1810: James 45+, 1 female 26-44, 3 females 16-25,
and 1 male 10-15.
A James Russell was bondsman for Joseph Russell and
Hannah Fibbs in 1801, but it is not clear whether it
was this James or the James married to Barbara
Milnster.
Russel, James & Barbara Milnster
Married In Cabarrus Co., bond dated April 24, 1803,
bondsman, Lewis Townsend.
Son of Robert & Mary Morrison Russel.
Moved to Buncombe Co., NC.
Russel, James & Eleanor Russell
1810: James 16-25, Eleanor 26-44, 1 male 10-15, 1
male -10, and 1 female -10.
James was the son of John and Mary Ferguson Russell,
and Eleanor was his cousin, the daughter of William
and Jeanette Roberson Russell.
About 1816, James and Eleanor moved to Dallas Co.,
AL with Eleanor parents, who lived in Abbeville Co.,
SC at the time.
Russel, James Semianes & Margaret Gingles
Children: Rachel Lucinda (Moses Wilson Cuthbertson),
Elizabeth Matilda (Charles Hinson), Jane Malinda
(John W. Long), David Green (died at the age of 3),
Mary (John H. Hood), David Green (Cynthia Crowell),
John Gingles (Rebecca Murphy, Cynthia), Robert Lee
(Margaret S. McEachern), James A. (died at the age
of 2), Margaret A., James A. (Cananizer Crowell,
Samantha Crowell), Rosannah Catherine (James
Crowell), Hannah M. (died at the age of 1)
Married Feb 8, 1809 in Mecklenburg Co., John
Gingles, bondsman.

Son of David and Elizabeth Morrison Russel.
James and Margaret are buried in Union Cemetery in
Union Co., NC. James was killed by Mark Kiser at the
home of Allen Bost in Cabarrus Co. on Aug 5, 1842.
Deed of Gift from James' father David, a tract of 66
acres on the south side of Rocky River at the
beginning of Clear Creek next to Thomas Love and
Jeremiah Clontz. (1810)
Deed from Samuel Gingles (James' brother-in-law) to
James for $500.00, 250 acres on Duck Creek (1834)
1790 - Russel, John & Mary Ferguson
    Children: James Edward (Eleanor Russel), Polly
    (Josiah Shinn), female died before 1800, male,
    Alexander Ferguson (Jane Herron), Jane (Morvil
    Suggs), female (may have died before 1800),
    Zachariah (Sarah Cooke).
    This family has been difficult to put together. The
    proven children are James Edward, Polly, Alexander
    and Jane. Zachariah is not a PROVEN child of John &
    Mary, but the bondsman for his marriage was Morvil
    Suggs who married Jane, possible sister of
    Zachariah. The unidentified male could have been
    Samuel who married Elizabeth Russell, who could have
    been the daughter of Robert & Mary Morrison Russell,
    which would have made them first cousins.
    John was appointed guardian of Hannah Irvin (Irwin)
    in Jan 1800.
    Owned land on the west side of Buffalo Creek and
    Coddle Creek next to James Russel.
    Son of James and Jane Carson Russel
    1800: John and Mary, and wife 26-44, 1 male 16-25, 1
    female 16-25, 2 males 10-15, and 2 females -10.
    Listed next to James Carson, Mathias Phifer, James
    Hughey, David Russle, Mary Russle, and Hardin
    Chitley.
    1810: John and Mary, and wife 45+, 1 male 16-25, 1
    female 16-25, 1 male 10-15, and 1 female 10-15.
Russell, John & Ruth Davis
    Children: male, James Burton (Mary Erwin), John D.,
    McCamie W., Williamson M., Daniel L., Robert B.,
    William D., Jane C., Josephine M.
    Married Aug 12, 1818 in Cabarrus Co., Isaac Davis,
    bondsman.
Russel, Joseph & Hannah Fibbs
    Married Sept 14, 1801 in Cabarrus County, bondsman,
    James Plunket.
    Children: James M., Joseph
    Son of James and Susannah Russel
    1800: Joseph 26-44, Hannah 16-25, 1 male -10, and 2
    females -10. Listed next to Celia Russell, robert
    Sullivan, James Martin, Michael Pealer, Henry
    Propst, and Leonard Barberick.

1810: Joseph 26-44, 1 female 16-25, 1 male 10-15, 2
females 10-15, 2 males -10, and 1 female -10.

Russel, Levi & Sarah Fibbs
Married Nov 25, 1797 in Cabarrus County, bondsman
George Campbell. George Campbell married Mary
Russel, daughter of David and Jane Russel, in 1791
(George Campbell was also a witness to David Russel
will)
Son of James and Susannah Russel.
1800: Levi and Sarah, and wife 16-25, 1 male -10,
and 1 female -10. Listed next to Alexander McClary,
Hugh Carrithers, Alexander Patterson, John Rogers,
William Means, and Moses Rogers.
Levi sold land on the south side of Coddle Creek to
James Callens in Jan 1807 near George Campbell and
Charles Campbell.
By 1810 Levi had moved from the Cabarrus/Mecklenburg
area. He may have gone to Franklin Co., TN. IN 1820
a Levi Russell is there with the following in his
household, 130110-10000.

Russell, Nancy
Nancy appears in the 1850 census for Cabarrus Co.
listed as 87 years old. She is also shown as being
born in Cabarrus Co., but who she was married to is
not known. She appears in the same census that a
James Russell disappears from.

1790 - Russel, Robert & Mary Morrison
Children: Jean, James, William Allison, Elizabeth,
John, Mary
Robert died in 1791, and is buried in Old Rocky
River Cemetery.
1800: Mary 26-44, 1 male 16-25, 1 male 10-15, 1
female 10-15, 2 males -10, 1 female -10. Mary also
had a daughter named Ruth, by John Clontz, and two
sons by Archibald McCurdy named Stewart and
Zaccheus.
Robert was the son of James and Jane Carson Russell,
and Mary was the daughter of James and Jeanette
Morrison.
1810: Mary 26-44, and 2 males 10-15.
Robert and Mary's son John appears to have died
before 1800. He is mentioned in court records prior
to 1800 but not after 1800. Mary's household is also
missing a male child in 1800.

Russel, Robert & Mary Morrison
Children: Margaret Elizabeth (Charles E. Sehorn),
David Morrison (Nancy J. Hunter), Elizabeth Matilda
(Charles S. Huison/Hinson?), Mary
Robert posted an ad in The Charlotte Journal, along
with his brother David Green Russell, offering a
$250.00 reward for the apprehension of Mark Kiser in

Aug 1842. Mark Kiser killed Robert and David father,
James Semianes Russell.
Russel, Robert
    Children: James (Jane Carson), Eleanor (Robert
    Black), William (Jeanette Roberson)
    Owned land on Coddle Creek and Buffalo Creek that he
    deeded to his son James in 1775 before reportedly
    moving to Abbeville County, SC with his son William.
    When this move took place is not known.
    Robert was a withness to the will of John
    Cuzzens(Corzine ?) in 1776.
Russel, Robert & Mary Willson
    Married March 17, 1762 in Rowan Co., bondsman, John
    Corzine and Henry Horrah.
Russel, William Allison & Mary "Polly" McEachern/McAhron
    Married in Cabarrus County, bond dated July 13,
    1808, bondsman, Isaac Shinn
    Son of Robert & Mary Morrison Russel
    Owned land on Three Mile Branch
Russel, William & Sarah McRee
    Married Aug 16, 1797 in Cabarrus County, bondsman,
    David Templeton.
    Children: William James, born one or two months
    after his father death.
    William was born Sept 19, 1772, died Feb 13, 1799
    Buried in Old Rocky River Cemetery
    Son of James and Jane Carson Russel
    Sarah remarried in 1808 to John Alexander of SC.
Ryal, William
    1800: William and wife 26-44, 1 female 16-25, 1
    female 10-15, and 2 females -10. Listed next to
    Tobias Stirewalt, Jacob Rimer, John Duke, Henry
    Lineboh, George Speake, and David Speck.
Sandiford, Noah
    1800: Noah and wife 26-44, 1 male -10, and 2 females
    -10. Listed next to Delphie Lewis, Elizabeth Young,
    Gideon Almon, William McAnulty, John Crumwell, Sr.,
    and Robert McEchron.
1790 - Scales/Scoles, John
    1800: John and wife 26-44 and 1 male -10. Listed
    next to Alexander Query, Samuel Meek, John Edmonton,
    James Smith, Robert Smith, and William Young.
Scartauk, Frederick
    Owned land on Irish Buffalo Creek in 1782.
1790 - Scott, Alexander
    Lived in the Rocky River Church area.
    1800: Alexander and wife 26-44, 1 female 16-25, 1
    male 10-15, 1 female 10-15, 2 males -10, and 3
    females -10. Listed next Robert Davis, George Davis,
    Agness Listenbay, Joseph Welsh, Edward Neil, William
    Andrew.
Scott, Alexander

        1810: Alexander 16-25, and 2 males 10-15.
1790 - Scott, James & Margaret
        James born Dec 3, 1753, died 1817
        Margaret born 1770, died 1801
        Buried in Old Rocky River Cemetery
        Guardian of William James Russell, orphan of William
        Russell.
        Owned land on Back Creek
        1800: James 45+, Margaret 26-44, 2 males 16-25, 1
        female 16-25, 1 male 10-15, 2 females 10-15, and 3
        males -10. Listed next to Michael Awalt, John
        Neshler, Sr., Jacob Misenheimer, John Conder,
        Michael Young, and William Wagoner.
        In 1804, James boarded orphaned 19 year old
        Frederick Barberick.
        1810: James 45+, 1 female 26-44, 2 males 16-25, 3
        males 10-15, and 2 females 10-15.
Scott, James
        1800: James 26-44, 2 females 16-25, 1 male -10, and
        1 female -10. Listed next to James Russell, James
        Plunkett, Sr., William L. Alexander, and Peter Huey.
*Scott, John & Eliza
        Eliza was born 1799, died Dec 27, 1825
Scott, John & Leah Carlock
        Children: Eli, Peggy, John, James, William,
        Alexander C.
        1800: John and wife 16-25, and 2 males -10. Leah
        must have been John second wife.
        Married April 26, 1806 in Cabarrus Co., John McGraw,
        bondsman.
        1810: John 26-44, 1 female 16-25, 1 male 10-15, 3
        males -10, and 1 female -10.
Scott, Robert
        Bought land on Rocky River from John Mitchell, near
        Charles Campbell.
1790 - Scott, William & Dorothea
        Son, John.
        Owned land on Buffalo Creek in 1776.
        1800: Dorothy 45+, and 1 male 45+. Listed next to
        Charles McKinley, Archibald McCurdey, John Cromwell,
        John Scott, John White, James Walker.
Scott, William
        1810: William 26-44, 1 female 16-25, 1 female 10-15,
        1 male -10, and 4 females -10.
Seah, Jacob
        Owned land between Dutch Buffalo Creek and Little
        Coldwater Creek in 1780.
Seales, Signe
        1800: Signe household consisted of 1 female 26-44, 1
        male 16-25, 1 female 16-25, and 2 males 10-15.
        Listed next to George Voiles, Martha Campbell,

Thomas White, Stephen Mayfield, Daniel Little, and
Elias House.
1810: 2 males 26-44, and 1 female 45+.
1790 - Seferit, Barnhart (Sifferd, Barnard)
1800: Barnard and wife 26-44, 1 male 10-15, 2 males
-10, and 4 females -10. Listed next to Andrew
Slough, Leonard Sides, Abraham Plaster, Charles
Sifferd, George Sifferd, and George Uery.
1790 - Seferit, Charles
1800: Charles and wife 45+, 1 female 26-44, 1 male
16-25, and 1 female -10. Listed next to Barnard
Sifferd, Andrew Slough, Leonard Sides, George
Sifferd, George Uery, and Jacob Weaver.
Seffrid, Charles
1800: Charles and wife 45+, 2 males 16-25, and 1
female 16-25. Listed next to Asemus Peninger, George
File, Mathias Beam, Tobias Cress, Henry Cuthezen,
and Conrad Hise.
Seffird, Charles & Susan Dawalt
Married March 17, 1816 in Cabarrus Co., George
Sefrit, bondsman
Seffird, George
1800: George and wife, borh 26-44, 1 male -10, and 4
females -10. Listed next to Charles Sifferd, Barnard
Sifferd, Andrew Slough, George Uery, Jacob Weaver,
and Charles Starns.
Seffird, George
1800: George and wife 16-25, 1 male -10, and 5
females -10. Listed next to Martin Penninger,
Michael Gatchey, Henry Gatchey, Michael Wiser,
Mathias Beam, and George File.
Sefert, George
1810: George and wife 26-44, 1 male 10-15, 1 female
10-15, 1 male -10, and 5 females -10.
Seferate, George
1810: George 26-44, 1 female 26-44, 1 male 10-15, 2
females 10-15, 2 males -10, and 4 females -10.
Seffird, Michael & Rosinah Cress
Married June 9, 1808 in Cabarrus Co., Erasmus
Bening, bondsman.
1810: Michael 26-44, 1 female 45+, 1 female 26-44, 2
males -10, and 1 female -10.
Michael Safret is listed is listed in the 1860
Cabarrus Co. census as 83 years old.
Seffird, William
1800: William and wife 26-44, 2 males -10, and 2
females -10. Listed next to Michael Fesperman, Henry
Fesperman, Michael Goodman, Jacob Dewatt, Henry
Gatchey, and Michael Gatchey.
1810: William 45+, 1 female 26-44, 1 male 16-25, 1
female 16-25, 1 male 10-15, and 1 female 10-15.
Self, Aaron & Peggy Davis

Married Oct 19, 1807 in Cabarrus Co., Archibald
McCurdy, bondsman.
Self, David
    1800: David 26-44, his wife 16-25, 3 males -10, and
    1 female -10. Listed next to Jacob Self, Jr., Jacob
    Self, Sr., John Carlock, Stephen Self, Rabeckah
    Ford, and Abigel Griffin.
1790 - Self, Jacob, Sr
    Owned land on Clear Creek in the 1780.
    1800: Jacob and wife 45+, and 2 males 16-25. Listed
    next to John Carlock, John Vossel, Michael Watters,
    Jacob Self, Jr., David Self, and Stephen Self.
Self, Jacob, Jr
    1800: Jacob 26-44, 1 female 16-25, and 2 males -10.
    Listed next to Jacob Self, Sr., John Carlock, John
    Vossel, David Self, Stephen Self, and Rabeckah Ford.
Self, Stephen
    1800: Stephen and wife 16-25, 1 male -10, and 1
    female -10. Listed next to David Self, Jacob Self,
    Jr., Jacob Self, Sr., Rabeckah Ford, Abigel Griffin,
    and Joshua Cheek.
1790 - Sell, Peter
    Owned land on the headwaters of Little Coldwater
    Creek.
Sellars, Isaac & Rebecca
    Owned land on Rocky River in the 1770
Sensill, Samuel
    Owned land on Cuflon Creek, a branch of English
    Buffalo Creek in 1782.
Sessions, Rue
    1810: Rue and wife 26-44, 1 male -10, and 1 female -
    10.
Sewell, Samuel
    Owned land on Buffalo Creek in 1784.
Sexton, James
    Owned land on Crooked Creek before 1783.
Shandel, John
    1810: John and wife 26-44, and 2 females -10.
Shandy, John
    1810: John 26-44, 1 female 16-25, and 1 male -10.
Shank, Moses
    1810: Moses 45+, 2 males 16-25, and 2 females 10-15.
1790 - Sharpe, Edward, Sr
    Owned land between Coddle Creek and Rocky River in
    1784.
1790 - Sharpe, Ezekel
    1800: Ezekiel and wife 45+, 1 male 26-44, 4 females
    16-25, 2 females 10-15, 1 male -10, and 1 female -
    10. Listed next to Robert McMurray, Jr., William
    Vietch, James Creatton, William Callon, Sr., William
    Callon, Jr., and George Alexander.
1790 - Shaver, John

Owned land on Cold Water and Buffalo Creek in 1783.
1800: John and wife 45+, 1 male 16-25, 1 female 16-
25, 2 females 10-15, 4 males -10, and 1 female -10.
Listed next to John Culpepper, Joseph Shinn, Henry
Brines, Robert Purviance, Joshua Hadley, and Samuel
Corzine.

Shaver, Joseph & Mary Corzine
       Married Sept 7, 1808 in Cabarrus Co., George
       Letsinger, bondsman.

Shaver, Michael
       Owned land on Irish Buffalo Creek in 1775 near John
       Phifer, Samuel Patton, Thomas Mann.

1790 - Shelby, Evan & Susannah
       In Mecklenburg county in 1779.
       Owned land on Beaver Dam branch of Caldwell Creek,
       and Back Creek, branches of Rocky River.

1790 - Shelley/Shelby, Thomas, Capt & Sarah
       Children: Moses, Polly, Sarah, Ebby, Betsy
       Owned land on Clear Creek.
       Thomas died before 1800.
       1800: Sarah at 26-44, 1 male 10-15, 2 females 10-15,
       and 2 females -10. Listed next to John and Andrew
       Davis, David Taylor, William Harris, and Elizabeth
       Harris.

Shepperd, George
       1810: George and wife 26-44, 1 male 10-15, 1 female
       10-15, 1 male -10, and 5 females -10.

Shepherd, Thomas
       1810: Thomas' 26-44, 1 female 16-25, 2 males -10,
       and 1 female -10.

1790 - Shinn, Benjamin & Rebecca Carlock 155
       Children: Silas (Elizabeth Little), Benjamin, Samuel
       (Catherine Barberick), Solomon, Josiah (Polly
       Russel), Moses, Catherine, Sarah (Eli P. Dennis),
       Joseph, Abigail (? Graham), Mary.
       Benjamin died between April and July 1799. Son
       Solomon, minor (born Jan 1784), John Wylie guardian.
       Benjamin, Moses & Josiah orphans, sons Samuel and
       Silas named in the Pleas & Quarter Sessions, Oct
       18,1802 and April 16,1805.
       Benjamin was the son of Samuel and Abigail Urie.

Shinn, Benjamin & Nancy McEachern/McAhron
       Married in Cabarrus County, bond dated July 12,
       1809, bondsman, William Allison Russel
       1810: Benjamin and Nancy, and wife 16-25.
       Son of Benjamin & Rebecca Carlock Shinn

Shinn, Bruthy (Bartholomew ? & Mary Sawyer)
       Bruthy Shinn died before 1798. His estate settlement
       admin. was assigned to Martin Phifer, John Weylie
       and William Scott in Cabarrus County court in Jan
       1798.

Shinn, Catherine

1810: Catherine 26-44, 1 male 16-25, 1 male 10-15, 4
males -10, and 1 female -10.
Shinn, Isaac R. & Ann McEachern/McAhron
    Married in Cabarrus County, bond dated April 24,
    1806, bondsman, James Plunket.
    1810: Isaac 26-44, Ann 16-25, and 3 males -10.
Shinn, John
    Sold land on Coddle Creek to Abel Corzine in 1806.
Shinn, Joseph & Eleanor
    Children: Isaac R. (Ann McAhron), Joseph (Peggy
    Carrothers), John, Benjamin, Jane (? Anderson),
    Sarah (William Houston), Eleanor (Jacob Hudson),
    Leah (Henry Allemong)
Shinn, Joseph & Peggy Carrothers
    Married Sept 6, 1806 in Cabarrus Co., Elias
    Currothers, bondsman
    Son of Joseph & Eleanor
    1810: Joseph and Peggy, and wife 16-25, and 1 female
    -10.
    Moved to Iredell County before 1813
1790 - Shinn, Joseph, Capt & Jane Ross
    Children: Isaac, Elinor, Abigail (John Still), Jean
    (Richard), Sarah, Leah
    Joseph lived next to James and John Russell and
    owned land on Cold Water Creek, and Three Mile
    Branch near Umberford branch in 1780.
    1800: Joseph 45+, 1 male 45+, 1 female 45+, 3
    females 16-25, 3 males 10-15, 1 male -10, and 1
    female -10. Listed next to Henry Brines, James
    Bridges, Aaron Houston, John Culpepper, John Shaver,
    and Robert Purviance.
    Joseph died before April 1806.
    1810: Jean 45+, 1 male 26-44, 1 male 16-25, 1 female
    16-25, 1 male 10-15, 1 female 10-15, and 2 females -
    10.
Shinn, Josiah & Polly Russell
    Children: 1 child, gender unknown.
    Polly was granted a divorce in 1821 on the grounds
    of abandonment.
    Polly was the daughter of John and Mary Ferguson
    Russell.
    Josiah was the son of Benjamin and Rebecca Carlock
    Shinn.
Shinn, Samuel & Catherine Barberick
    Married March 25, 1793 in Cabarrus Co., Leonard
    Barberick, bondsman.
    Samuel died before 1800.
    A Catherine Shinn appears in the 1800 census of
    Cabarrus Co., but the ages and number of children
    indicate that she, and or Samuel, had been
    previously married.

1800: Catherine household consisted of 1 female 45+,
2 males 16-25, 1 female 16-25, 1 male 10-15, 3
females 10-15, 3 males -10, and 3 females -10.
Listed next to Jacob Hutson, Philip Pless/Bless,
George Smith, Lewis Townsend, Murdoch Campbell, and
John McKinley.

Shinn, Samuel & Polly
Samuel's will was probated in Jan 1808 in Cabarrus
County.

Shinn, Samuel
1810: Samuel and wife 26-44, 1 male 16-25, and 4
females -10.

Shinn, Silas & Elizabeth Little
Married in Cabarrus County, bond dated April 28,
1801, bondsman, Daniel Little.
1810: Silas' and wife 26-44, 2 females 16-25, 1 male
16-25, 3 males -10, and 2 females -10.

Shinpock/Shoopink, Andrew
1810: Andrew and wife 26-44, 1 female 10-15, 3 males
-10, and 3 females -10.

Shive, Clarissa
In the 1850 Cabarrus Co. Clarissa is listed as 73
years old and is probably the widow of Martin.

Shive, Martin
1800: Martin 26-44, 1 female 26-44, 1 female 16-25,
and 2 males -10. Listed next to John Simeoner,
Francis Ross, Seth Rogers, Daniel Doherty, Thomas
Dobson, and John Smith. Martin moved his family to
Lafayette Co., MS about 1841. Listed as 82 years old
in 1850 and born in PA.
1810: Martin 26-44, 1 female 16-25, 1 male 10-15,
and 4 males -10.

1790 - Shive, Philip
1800: Phillip and wife 26-44, 1 male 16-25, 1 female
16-25, 2 females 10-15, 3 males -10, and 1 female -
10. Listed next to George Harkman, Henry Simmons,
John Skilhouse, Daniel Krider(Crider), Michael
Overcash, and Jacob Krider(Crider), Jr.
1810: Philip 45+, 1 female 26-44, 1 male 16-25, 1
female 16-25, 1 male 10-15, 1 male -10, and 1 female
-10.

Shoe, Henry & Catherine Herger ˋ
Married Dec 7, 1801 in Cabarrus Co., Martin Herger,
bondsman.
Children: Martin (Barbara ?)
1810: Henry 26-44, 1 female 45+, 1 female 26-44, 2
males -10, and 2 females -10.
Henry died in Cabarrus Co. in 1860 at the age of 79
from chronic diarrhea. Henry and Catherine are
listed in the 1860 Cabarrus Co. census and Catherine
is shown as 81 years old. Henry was born in
Pennsylvania.

Shoe, John & Elizabeth Herger
    Married Nov 23, 1794 in Cabarrus Co., Martin Herger,
    bondsman.
    1800: John and Elizabeth, and wife 26-44, and 2
    males -10. Listed next to Jacob Rinehart, Peter
    Quilman, Abram Misenheimer, John Plaster, Abraham
    Plaster, and Leonard Sides.
    1810: John and wife 26-44, 2 males 10-15, 2 males -
    10, and 3 females -10.
Shurton, Sophia
    1810: Sophia 45+, 1 male 16-25, 1 female 16-25, 1
    male 10-15, 1 female 10-15, and 3 females -10.
Shute, Henry & Mary
    Owned land on the north side of Rocky River in 1779.
Shue, Susannah
    1810: Susannah household consisted of 1 female 45+,
    and 1 female 26-44.
Sides, John & Elizabeth Lytaker
    Children: Elizabeth, Rachel
1790 - Sides, Andrew
    1800: Andrew and wife 45+, and 1 female 16-25.
    Listed next to Godfred Lype, Philip Barnhart, Daniel
    Blackwelder, George Miller, Randle Studevant, and
    Thomas Allin.
    Andrew died before July 1805.
Sides, Leonard
    1800: Leonard 45+, 1 female 45+, 1 male 26-44, and 1
    male 10-15. Listed next to Abraham Plaster, John
    Plaster, John Shoe, Andrew Slough, Barnard Sifferd,
    and Charles Sifferd.
Sides, Leonard & Catherine Miller
    Married Oct 20, 1803 in Cabarrus Co., Charles Parks,
    bondsman.
    1810: Leonard 26-44, Catherine 16-25, 1 male -10,
    and 2 females -10.
1790 - Sides, Michael
    1800: Michael and wife 45+, 1 male 26-44, 1 male 16-
    25, 2 females 16-25, 1 male -10, and 2 females -10.
    (The numbers were very hard to read) Listed next to
    George Ritchey, Henry Pence, William Mensinger,
    George Stickleather, Peter Simmons, and John
    Biggers.
    Michael was given Let. Test. of Andrew Sides in July
    1805 court.
    1810: Michael 45+, 1 female 45+, and 1 male 16-25.
Sides, Nicholas
    1810: Nicholas and wife 45+, 1 male 16-25, and 1
    female 16-25.
Sides, William
    1810: William and wife 26-44, 2 males -10, and 1
    female -10.
1790 - Siminer, John & (?) Phifer ?

1800: John and wife 26-44, and 1 female -10. Listed
next to Francis Ross, Seth Rogers, Joseph Rogers,
Martin Shive, Daniel Doherty, and Thomas Dobson.
John was the clerk of court for Cabarrus County in
the 1790 and died·in or before 1806.
Simmons, Henry
1800: Henry and wife 26-44, 2 males -10, and 1
female -10. Listed next to John Skilhouse, John
Gallimore, Leonard Barberick, George Harkman,
Phillip Shive, and Daniel Krider(Crider).
1810: Henry last name appears to be Symond. His 45+,
1 female 26-44, 1 male 16-25, 1 male 10-15, 1 female
10-15, 2 males -10, and 2 females -10.
Simmons, Peter
No enumeration for Peter Simmons.
1790 - Simmons, Thomas S. & Margaret
Thomas was born 1755, died 1806
Margaret was born 1759, died 1826
Buried in Spears Cemetery of Rocky River Church.
Simmons, William
1810: William and wife 26-44, 1 male 10-15, 1 female
10-15, and 3 females -10.
Sims, Anderson
1810: Anderson 26-44, 1 female 45+, 1 male 16-25, 2
females 10-15, 1 male -10, and 1 female -10.
Sizemore/Sysmore, Peter
1810: Peter and wife 26-44, 1 female 10-15, 1 male -
10, and 3 females -10.
Skilhouse, John
1800: John and wife 26-44, 1 female 10-15, and 3
males -10. Listed next to John Gallimore, Leonard
Barberick, Henry Propst, Henry Simmons, George
Harkman, and Phillip Shive.
Skiliton, Elizabeth
1800: Elizabeth 45+, and 1 female 16-25. Listed next
to Martin Gun, Molly Peanix, Gallant Peanix, Jean
McLusky, Elizabeth Holly, and Thomas Rogers.
Elizabeth died in or before 1804.
Skilinton, John Brown & Martha (Matty) Caldwell
Married June 27, 1791 in Mecklenburg Co., John
Hamilton, bondsman.
1800: John and Martha, and wife 26-44, 1 male -10,
and 2 females -10. Listed next to Stephen Alexander,
William Houston, Robert Allison, Joseph Alexander,
Robert Andrews, and Moses Andrews.
1810 John and Martha, and wife 26-44, 1 female 26-
44, 1 male 10-15, and 2 females 10-15.
Skilliton, Joseph
1810: Joseph 26-44, 1 female 16-25, 1 male -10, and
1 female -10.
Sledge, John

1810: John and wife 26-44, 2 males 10-15, 1 female
10-15, 3 males -10, and 2 females -10.
Slough, Andrew
1800: Andrew 45+, 1 female 26-44, and 1 female -10.
Listed next to Leonard Sides, Abraham Plaster, John
Plaster, Barnard Sifferd, Charles Sifferd, and
George Sifferd.
Slough, Andrew
1800: Andrew 26-44, 1 female 45+, and 1 female -10.
Listed next to Francis Funderburk, Dorothy Petry,
Daniel Bost, George Smith, William Stow, and John
Misenheimer.
Son of Jacob Slough
Slough, Daniel & Margaret Misenhimer
Married Dec 28, 1803 in Cabarrus Co., David Suther,
bondsman.
1810: Daniel 16-25, 1 female 26-44, 1 female 16-25,
3 males -10, and 1 female -10.
Daniel bought land on Flat Run Branch of Irish
Buffalo Creek in April 1813.
Slough, George
1810: George and wife 16-25, and 2 males -10.
1790 - Slaugh/Stough, Jacob & Margaret
Children: Jacob (Esther Suther), Martin, Andrew
1800: Jacob 45+, 1 male 16-25, 2 females 16-25, and
3 females -10. Listed next to Thomas Goodman, Jacob
Lingle, John Cluttz, Philip File, and Joseph Gray.
1790 - Slowgh/Slough, Martin
Son of Jacob Slough
1800: Martin and wife 45+, 1 male 16-25, 2 males 10-
15, 1 female 10-15, and 2 females -10. Listed next
to David Nishler, Jacob Overcash, Mathias Cook, John
Still, Gideon Almon, and Elizabeth Young.
1810: Martin and wife 45+, 1 female 26-44, 1 male
16-25, and 2 females 10-15.
Slough, Michael
1810: Michael 26-44, 1 female 45+, 1 female 16-25, 1
male 10-15, and 1 male -10.
1790 - Smith, David & Mary
In Mecklenburg county in 1784.
Owned land on Rocky River and Clark Creek
Smith, Duncan
1800: Duncan household consisted of just himself 26-
44. Listed next to John Jones, Benjamin Alexander,
James Caragin, Hugh Pickens, John Alexander, and
James Alexander.
Duncan was delared a lunatic in July 1813. His
guardian was Hugh Smith.
1810: Duncan household consisted of just himself 26-
44.
Smith, George

1800: George 45+, 1 male 26-44, 1 female 26-44, 1 male 16-25, and 2 males -10. Listed as a resident of Concord along with Lawrence Snapp, John Master, Philip Bless, Jacob Hudson, and Samuel Hughey. 1810: George and wife 26-44, 1 male 16-25, 1 male 10-15, and 1 female -10.

Smith, George
1800: George household consisted of 1 male 45+, 1 male 26-44, 1 female 26-44, and 2 males -10. Listed next to Lawrence Snapp, William Townsend, Cevilia Campbell, Philip Pless, Jacob Hutson, and Catherine Shinn.
Bought land on Cold Water Creek in 1805 from James Bridgers.

1790 - Smith, George
In 1790 the only George Smith in Mecklenburg Co. was listed as having 2 females as well as himself in his household. He was also located in the area between Mount Pleasant and Rocky River.
1800: George household consisted of 1 male 45+, 1 male 26-44, 1 female 26-44, 1 female 10-15, 2 males -10, and 3 females -10. Listed next to Andrew Slough, Francis Funderburk, Dorothy Petry, William Stow, John Misenhimer, and James Little.
1810: George 45+, 1 female 26-44, 2 females 16-25, 2 males 10-15, 2 females 10-15, 1 male -10, and 3 females -10.

1790 - Smith, Henry, Jr.
1800: Henry 26-44, and wife 16-25. Listed next to George Garmon, Rabeckah Mitchell, Joshua Cheek, Henry Smith, Sr., Andrew Freeman, and Charles Freeman.

1790 - Smith, Henry, Sr.
Owned land on Rocky River in 1784.
1800: Henry and wife 45+, 2 males 16-25, and 1 female 16-25. Listed next to Henry Smith, Jr., George Garmon, Rabeckah Mithcell, Andrew Freeman, Charles Freeman, and Douglass Winchester.

Smith, Hugh
1810: Hugh and wife 45+, 1 male 26-44, 2 females 16-25, 1 male 10-15, and 1 male -10.

Smith, Jacob
1800: Jacob and wife 26-44, 1 male 16-25, and 4 females -10. Listed next to Caleb Woolfe, John White, Jr., James Walker, John McClennon, Aaron Wallis, and Joseph McNeely.
1810: Jacob and wife 26-44, 2 females 16-25, 3 males -10, and 3 females -10.

1790 - Smith, James & Leah
Owned land at a ford in Coddle Creek 1800.
1810: James 45+, 1 female 26-44, 1 female 16-25, 2 males 10-15, 1 male -10, and 1 female -10.

Smith, James Patton & Elizabeth Frasor
    Married Sept 4, 1805 in Cabarrus Co., Israel Frezer,
    bondsman.
    1810: James and wife 26-44, 1 female 26-44, and 2
    females -10.
1790 - Smith, James
    Owned land between Rocky River and Coddle Creek next
    to Dr. Nathaniel Alexander in 1784.
1790 - Smith, John & Barbara
    Children: Jacob (Leah Haulton), Margaret
    1800: John 45+, 1 female 16-25, 1 male 10-15, and 1
    male -10. Listed next to James Canror, David Suther,
    Dudly Tounsend, John Baket, Alexander Tatterson, and
    Hugh Carrithers. (The decision that this John Smith
    is the one listed next to these neignbors is based
    solely on the location of the named neighbors and
    land records. As is indicated above, John Blair
    Smith could have been the same John Smith who
    married Barbara, though there were two John Smith's
    in Cabarrus County 1800.
1790 - Smith, John Blair
    Owned land on Coddle Creek (could have been John and
    Barbara, see above.)
    1800: John 45+, 1 female 26-44, 1 male 16-25, and 1
    male -10. Listed next to Thomas Dobson, Daniel
    Doherty, Martin Shive, John Tagert, Joseph Ross, and
    Elizabeth Patterson.
    1810: John 26-44, 1 female 45+, 1 female 26-44, and
    1 female 10-15.
1790 - Smith, Robert, Col & Sarah
    Robert died before Oct 1805 in Cabarrus County.
Smith, Robert Washington
    1800: Robert and wife 45+, 1 female 26-44, and 2
    males 16-25. Listed next to James Smith, John
    Scoles, Alexander Query, William Young, Catherine
    Flemmon, and Mary Fulham.
    Sold land on Rocky River to Charles Harris in Oct
    1805.
    Bought land on Rocky River from James Creaton in Oct
    1805.
    Bought land on Rocky River from Adam Meek in April
    1807.
Smith, Robert W.
    1810: Robert 26-44, 1 female 45+, 1 male 26-44, 1
    female 26-44, 1 male 16-25, and 2 females 16-25.
1790 - Smith, William & Catherine Miller
    Married Aug 12, 1790 in Mecklenburg Co., Samuel
    Montieth, bondsman.
    1800: William and wife 16-25, and 2 males -10.
    Listed next to William Polk, George Long, John Reed,
    George Tucker, Sr., John Wisiner, and George
    Barnhart.

1810: William and wife 26-44, 2 males 10-15, and 2
males -10.
Snapp, Lawrence
1800: Lawrence 16-25, and 1 male 16-25. Listed next
to William Townsend, Cevilia Campbell, James Hadley,
George Smith, Philip Pless, and Jacob Hutson.
Snapp, Lawrence
1800: Lawrence in listed as a resident of Concord.
His 16-25, and 1 male 16-25. Listed with John
Master, George Smith, Philip Bless, Jacob Hudson,
and Samuel Hughey.
Snell, James & Jeanne McKinly
Married July 5, 1796 in Cabarrus Co., Charles
McKinly, bondsman.
1800: James and Jeanne 26-44, and 2 males -10.
Listed next to Francis Greer, William Andrew, Edward
Neil, Mark Evans, Isaac McLennon, and Robert Curry.
Snider/Snyder, John
1810: John and wife 16-25, and 1 male -10.
Snoddy, Andrew
Owned land on the east side of Coddle Creek in 1783.
Sauceman, Daniel
1810: Daniel and wife 26-44, 1 male 16-25, 1 male
10-15, 2 females 10-15, 3 males -10, and 1 female -
10.
Sosseman, Henry
Owned land on Dutch Buffalo Creek in 1784.
Sauceman, Jacob
1810: Jacob 26-44.
Sossaman, John
Children: Henry (Peggy McClellan), Elizabeth,
Martin, Amelia, Daniel ? (Elizabeth McClellan),
Jacob ?
1800: John and wife 26-44, 1 male -10, and 2 females
-10. Listed next to Jonathan Hartzell, Christopher
Leigh, Peter Quilman, Daniel Cline, William Goodwin,
and Godfred Uery.
Spears, Elisha & Margaret Alexander
Married Dec 27, 1797 in Cabarrus County, Patrick C.
Hays, bondsman.
1800: Elisha and Margaret 16-25, and 2 males -10.
Listed next to Cunningham Harris, Griffin Morris,
Matthew Campbell, James Harris, Jeremiah Johnston,
and George Campbell.
1810: Elisha and wife 26-44, and 4 males -10.
Spears, Isaiah
1810: Isaiah and wife 26-44, 1 male 16-25, 1 female
16-25, 1 male 10-15, 3 females 10-15, 1 male -10,
and 3 females -10.
Isaiah sold land on East Meadow Creek to John Reed
in Oct 1812.
Spears, Joseph

1810: Joseph 26-44, 1 female 45+, 2 females 16-25, 1
male -10, and 2 females -10.
Joseph and Elisha Spears sold land on Caldwell Creek
in Jan 1814.

Spears, Josiah
1800: Josiah 26-44, 1 female 16-25, and 3 females -
10. Listed next to Samuel McCurdy, John Black, Jr.,
Robert McEchron, James Bradshaw, Sr., Martha Watson,
and Archibald White.

Spears, Solomon
1800: Solomon and wife 26-44, and 4 females -10.
Listed next to Aaron Townsend, William Morrison,
Walter Farr, David White, William W. Spears, and
Agness Listenbay.
1810. Solomon and wife 26-44, 3 females 10-15, 3
males -10, and 2 females -10.

Spears, William W.
1800: William 26-44, and wife 16-25. Listed next to
David White, Solomon Spears, Aaron Townsend, Agness
Listenbay, George Davis, and Robert Davis.
1810: William and wife 26-44, and 4 males -10.

1790 - Spears, William & Agness
William was born 1731, died March 2, 1803
Owned land on Reedy Creek in 1774.
Buried in Spears Cemetery of Rocky River Church

Speck, David/Devolt? & Barbara Berger
Married May 13, 1794 in Cabarrus Co., Michel Evalt,
bondsman.
1800: David 26-44, 1 male 16-44, 1 female 26-44, and
1 female -10. Listed next to George Speake, Henry
Lineboh, William Ryal, Jacob Cassock, Henry Cress,
and John Cauddle.

Speek, David
1810: David 26-44, 1 female 26-44, 1 male 10-15, 3
females 10-15, and 3 females -10.

Speck/Speake, George
1800: George 26-44, 1 female 16-25, and 2 males -10.
Listed next to Henry Lineboh, William Ryal, Tobias
Stirewalt, David Speck, Jacob Cassock, and Henry
Cress.

1790 - Stafford, James, Sr
1790 - Stafford, James, Jr
Children: James Biggers, Samuel McKee, Elihu
1800: James 26-44, 2 males 16-25, 1 male 10-15, 2
females 10-15, 3 males -10, and 1 female -10. Listed
next to Thomas Davis, Robert Harris, Jr., George
Harris, Matthew Campbell, Griffin Morris, and
Cunningham Harris.

Stafford, James
1810: James and another male 16-25, 1 female 16-25,
and 2 males 10-15.

Stafford, Moses

1810: Moses 26-44, 1 female 16-25, and 1 female -10.
Stafford, William
        1810: William 26-44.
Stallons, William
        1810: William and wife 16-25.
1790 - Stanford, Robert
        Children: Solomon, Darcus, Polly, Samuel, Hannah
        1800: Robert and wife 26-44, 2 males -10, and 2
        females -10. Listed next to Josiah Deweast, Robert
        Miller, Peter Miller, Hugh Heare, James Caragin,
        Sr., and John Caragin.
        Robert died before the April session of court in
        1812. His orphans were to be brought to court.
1790 - Starns, Charles
        1800: Charles 26-44, 1 female 16-25, 1 male 10-15, 2
        males -10, and 1 female -10. Listed next to Jacob
        Weaver, George Uery, George Sifferd, Robert
        Williams, Joseph Starns, and Peter Quilman.
1790 - Starns, Fredrick & Mary Fisher
Starns, Frederick & Madlene Kline
        Married July 3, 1794 in Cabarrus Co., Joseph Starns
        & Herman Myer, bondsmen.
        1800: Frederick and Madlene, and wife 26-44, 3 males
        -10, and 1 female -10. Listed next to Andrew
        Rinehart, George M. Redling, Frederick Plylor, Peter
        Teame, Martin Wedinhouse, and Arthur Underwood.
Starns, John & Mary Hise
        Married July 20, 1802 in Cabarrus Co., David Suther,
        bondsman.
Starns, Joseph & Rachel Rice
        Married Aug 16, 1796 in Mecklenburg Co., Frankline
        Wance, bondsman.
        1800: Joseph household consisted of himeself 26-44,
        Rachel 16-25, 1 male -10 and 1 female -10. Listed
        next to Robert Williams, Charles Starns, Jacob
        Weaver, Peter Quilman, Christopher Leigh, and
        Jonathan Hartzell.
        1810: Joseph household consisted of 1 male 45+, 1
        female 26-44, 1 male 26-44, 1 male 10-15, 1 female
        10-15, 3 males -10, and 1 female -10.
1790 - Stevenson, James
        Children: Daniel ? (Christina Barringer)
        Owned land on Dutch Buffalo Creek in 1784, though
        1800 he is near others who owned land on Coddle
        Creek.
        1800: James and wife, both 45+, 1 male 16-25, 2
        females 16-25, 1 male 10-15, 1 female 10-15, and 3
        females -10. Listed next to John Ross, Jean Ross,
        Joseph Ross, Sr., David Templeton, James Tanner, and
        William Wallis.
Stickleather, George

1800: George 26-44, 1 female 16-25, 1 female 10-15,
and 2 females -10. (Numbers very hard to read)
Listed next to Michael Sides, George Ritchey, Henry
Pence, Peter Simmons, John Biggers, and Henry
Walker.
Stierwalt, Jacob
    Jacob sold land to George Goodman on Dutch Buffalo
    Creek in July 1813. He also sold to John Stierwalt
    in Jan 1814.
Stierwalt, John & Mary
    Owned land on Dutch Buffalo Creek.
Stierwalt, Tobias
    1800: Tobias and wife 16-25. Listed next to Jacob
    Rimer, John Duke, Michael Goodman(Big), William
    Ryal, Henry Lineboh, and George Speake.
    1810: Tobias' and wife 26-44, 3 males -10, and 1
    female -10.
Steirwalt, Tobias
    1810: Tobias' and wife 26-44, 3 males -10, and 1
    female -10.
Stighler, George
    1810: George 26-44, 1 female 45+, 1 female 26-44, 2
    males 10-15, and 3 males -10.
Still, John & Abigail Shinn, Mary Murph
    John and Abigail were married Jan 10, 1796 in
    Cabarrus Co.
    1800: John and Abigail, and wife 26-44, 1 male -10,
    and 1 female -10. Listed next to Martin Slough,
    David Nishler, Jacob Overcash, Gideon Almon,
    Elizabeth Young, and Delphie Lewis.
    John and Mary were married Jan 14, 1808, in Cabarrus
    Co.
    John bought land previously owned by Joseph Shinn,
    dec'd, lying on Great Cold Water Creek in April
    1807.
    1810: John 26-44, 1 male 16-25, 1 female 16-25, 1
    male 10-15, 1 female 10-15, 1 male -10, and 2
    females -10.
Stinson, James
    1810: James and wife 45+, 1 female 26-44, 1 male 16-
    25, 3 females 16-25, and 1 female 10-15.
Stewart, Matthew
    Matthew owned land on or near Coddle Creek.
Stewart, William & Jean
1790 - Stough, Andrew
    Owned land on Buffalo Creek in 1784.
Stough/Stow, Archibald
    In the 1860 census, Archibald is listed as 72 years
    old.
Stough, George & Barbara Goodman
    Married March 24, 1806 in Cabarrus Co., Martin
    Blackwelder, bondsman.

Stough/Stought, Martin
        Owned land near Lick Branch of Cold Water Creek in
        1784.
Stough, Michael & Katy House
        Married Oct 27, 1807 in Cabarrus Co., Phillip
        Bearnhart, bondsman
Stough/Stow, William
        1800: William 26-44, 1 female 26-44, 1 female 16-25,
        2 males 10-15, 1 male -10, and 3 females -10. Listed
        next to George Smith, Andrew Slough, Francis
        Funderburk, John Misenheimer, James Little, and
        Henry Howell.
        1810: William and wife 45+, 2 males 16-25, 2 females
        16-25, 1 male 10-15, 2 females 10-15, and 3 females
        -10.
Stricker, Daniel
        1810: Daniel 45+, 1 female 26-44, 1 male 16-25, 3
        females 16-25, 1 male 10-15, 1 female 10-15, 2 males
        -10, and 2 females -10.
Strube, John
        1810: John 26-44, 1 female 16-25, and 1 female -10.
1790 - Stuart, John
        1800: John and wife 45+, 2 males 16-25, 1 female 16-
        25, 1 male 10-15, and 2 females -10. Listed next to
        James Love, Henry Howell, James Little, George
        Teater, Isham Clay, and George Kizer.
1790 - Sturdivant, Randall
        Children: James, Creasy, Susannah, Rebecca
        1800: Randall and wife 26-44, 1 female 16-25, 1
        female 10-15, 2 males -10, and 1 female -10. Listed
        next to George Miller, Andrew Sides, Godfred Lype,
        Thomas Allin, Jesse Herrin, and Jacob Buzzard.
Suggs, Morvil & Jane Russel
        Married in Cabarrus County, bond dated Jan 8, 1816,
        bondsman Jacob Bost
        Jane was the daughter of John & Mary Ferguson Russel
        Morvil ordered to pay child support to Catharine
        "Caty" Nisler in Jan 1815 court. A court case was
        heard in April 1816.
Sullivan, James
        1800: James 26-44, 1 female 45+, 2 males -10, and 2
        females -10. Listed next to Robert Martin, Athen
        Almore, John Niehler, James Gailor, Peter Miller,
        and Robert Miller.
Sullivan, Robert
        1800: Robert 26-44, 1 male 16-25, 1 female 16-25,
        and 3 males -10. Listed next to James Martin, John
        Kesler, William Glover, Celia Russell, Joseph
        Russell, and Michael Pealer.
Suther, Daniel & Peggy Cress
        Married in Cabarrus Co., bond dated Nov 19, 1814,
        bondsman, John Suther.

In 1850, Daniel is listed in the Cabarrus Co. census
as 59 and Margaret is 57 years old.

1790 - Suther, David
Children: David, Rhineholt - children not proven.
Son of Samuel, who died before 1797. Cabarrus County
Court of Pleas and Quarters Sessions, 1797-1805.
Samuel widow moved to SC by July 1800. David
appointed deputy sheriff of Cabarrus Jan 1801.

Suther, David & Catherine Hise
Married April 21, 1795 in Cabarrus Co., Conrad Hise,
bondsman.
1800: David and Catherine, 26-44, and 2 females -10.
Listed next to Dudly Tounsend, John Winecough,
William Wagoner, James Cannon, John Smith, and John
Baker.
1810: David and wife 26-44, 2 females 10-15, 2 males
-10, and 2 females -10.

1790 - Suther, John
John bought land from Jacob Boger on Dewalt Branch
in Jan 1812.
He was the son of Samuel.

Suther, Rhineholt & Margaret Walter, Barbara Winecoff
Rhineholt and Margaret were married July 18, 1808 in
Cabarrus Co., David Suther, bondsman.
Rhineholt and Barbara were married Sept 17, 1818 in
Cabarrus Co., David Minster, bondsman.
Rhinehold is listed in the 1860 Cabarrus Co. census
as being 77 years old.

1790 - Suther, Samuel
Children: John, David
The widow Suther moved to SC after Samuel death.
Owned land on Dutch Buffalo Creek, and also owned
land or lived in Orange County at some time.

Suther, Samuel
1810: Samuel household consisted of 2 males 16-25,
and 2 females 16-25.

Swink, Jacob
Owned land on Shenawolf branch of Rocky River in
1773.

Tagert, John & Eleanor Russel
Children: Elizabeth, Catherine M. (William Morrison
Russell), dau, dau, Mary, John Newton (Sarah, Nancy
Caroline Morgan)
Married Sept 5, 1797 in Cabarrus Co., Willam
Russell(Eleanor brother), bondsman.
John & Eleanor lived near Joseph Rogers, Daniel
Dougherty, Joseph Patton and William Fraser.
1800: John 26-44, Eleanor, 16-25, and 1 female -10.
Listed next to John Smith, Thomas Dobson, Daniel
Doherty, Joseph Ross, Elizabeth Patterson, and
Joseph Patton.
1810: John and Eleanor, and wife 26-44, and 4

females -10.
Eleanor was the daughter of James and Jane Carson
Russel.
John and Eleanor moved to Dallas Co., Alabama about
1816 or after with many other members of the family.
1790 - Tanner, James & Margaret
        Children: John, Margaret, Daniel, Esther (Andrew
        Houston), Ann, Joseph, Mary (John Potts), James
        1800: James and wife 26-44, 1 male 16-25, 1 male 10-
        15, 3 females 10-15, 1 male -10, and 1 female -10.
        Listed next to David Templeton, James Stevenson,
        John Ross, William Wallis, Thomas McCain, and
        William Houston, Sr.
        James died before 1810.
        1810: Margaret 26-44, 2 males 16-25, 2 females 16-
        25, 1 female 10-15.
Tanner, John
        Owned land on Coddle Creek in 1773.
Tanner, John
        1810: John and wife 16-25.
        John moved to Iredell Co. before 1814.
1790 - Tasey, Alexander
        Children: David Rogers-born Jan 1785
        Bondsman for Robert Campbell and Jane Turner, widow
        of John Turner, Mecklenburg County, bond dated March
        30, 1791. Alexander died 1800: or before, in
        Cabarrus County.
1790 - Taylor, David
        Children: James (Nancy Dotson), John (Elizabeth
        Hall) - Not proven.
        1800: David and wife 26-44, 2 males -10, and 2
        females -10. Listed next to Sarah Shelby, John and
        Andrew Davis, William Harris, Elizabeth Harris, and
        James Plunkett, Sr.
        1810: David 45+, 1 female 26-44, 1 male 26-44, 1
        male 10-15, 2 females 10-15, 1 male -10, and 2
        females -10.
Taylor, Joseph S.
        1810: Joseph and wife 16-25.
Taler, Peter
        1810: Peter 16-25, 1 female 45+, 2 females 16-25,
        and 1 male -10.
Taylor, William
        1810: William 16-25, 1 female 26-44, and 2 males -
        10.
1790 - Teem, Jacob
        A daughter of Jacob married Andrew Dry.
        He owned land on and wife sides of Hamby Run in
        1784.
Teame, Peter
        1800: Peter and wife 45+, 1 male 26-44, 1 female 26-
        44, 1 male -10, and 3 females -10. Listed next to

Frederick Starnes, Andrew Rinehart, George M.
Redling, Martin Wedinhouse, Arthur Underwood, and
John Furor, Jr.
1810: Peter 45+, 1 female 26-44, 1 female 16-25, 1
male 10-15, 2 females 10-15, 2 males -10, and 4
females -10.
Teater, George
    1800: George and wife 45+, 1 male 16-25, 1 male 10-
    15, and 3 females -10. Listed next to John Stuart,
    James Love, Henry Howell, Isham Clay, George Kizer,
    and Andrew Watts.
Tater, Jacob
    1810: Jacob and wife 16-25, and 1 male -10.
Teeter/Tator, John
    1810: John 26-44, 1 female 45+, 1 female 26-44, 3
    males 10-15, 1 female 10-15, and 2 females -10.
Templeton, Archibald
    Owned land on Coddle Creek in 1784.
    Son of David Templeton, Sr.
Templeton, David, Sr.
    Children: David, Archibald, James, Samuel
    Owned land on Coddle Creek near Mills Creek in 1761.
    David died before 1784.
1790 - Templeton, David
    Owned land on Coddle Creek.
    Son of David Templeton, Sr.
    1800: David and wife 45+, 2 males 16-25, 1 female
    16-25, 2 males 10-15, and 1 female 10-15. Listed
    next to James Stevenson, John Ross, Jean Ross, James
    Tanner, William Wallis, and Thomas McCain.
    Moved to Burke County before 1813.
Templeton, James
    Owned land on Coddle Creek in 1781.
Templeton, Samuel
    Owned land on east side of Coddle Creek in 1778.
1790 - Tetter, George
Thomas, Isaac J.
    1810: Isaac and wife 26-44, 2 males 16-25, and 2
    males -10.
Thomas, James
    1810: James 26-44, 1 female 45+, 1 female 26-44, 1
    male 10-15, 1 female 10-15, 3 males -10, and 3
    females -10.
Torrence, Albert
*Torrence, James
    Son of Albert Torrence
    James was born 1795, died Jan 22, 1827
Townsend, Aaron & Martha Neely
    Married Feb 27, 1797 in Cabarrus Co., Thomas Neely,
    bondsman
    1800: Aaron family consisted of himself and Martha,
    and wife 16-25, and 1 male -10. Listed next to

William Morrison, Walter Farr, Charles McGinnis,
Solomon Spears, David White, and William W. Spears.
1810: Aaron and Martha 26-44, 1 male 10-15, 2 males
-10, and 1 female -10.
Townsend, Aaron
    1810: Aaron and wife 26-44, 1 male 10-15, 1 female
    10-15, 3 males -10, and 1 female -10.
Townsend, Charles & Isabella Clay
    Married March 12, 1818 in Cabarrus Co., Moses Clay,
    bondsman.
 Townsend, Charles
    Owned land on Buffalo Creek in and before 1783.
    1800: Charles and wife 45+. Listed next to George
    Carlock, Levi Curzine, Thomas Clark, Even Jones,
    Thomas White, and Martha Campbell.
1790 - Townsand, Dudley
    1800: Dudly and wife 26-44, 1 male 10-15, 1 female
    10-15, and 2 males -10. Listed next to John
    Winecough, William Wagoner, Michael Young, David
    Suther, James Cannon, and John Smith.
Townsend, James & Fanny Chamberlain
    Married March 15, 1805 in Cabarrus Co., Lewis
    Townsend, bondsman
    James bought land on Cold Water Creek in Oct 1805
    from James Bridgers.
Townsend, Lewis & Jean Russel
    Children: Robert Russell (Carolyn Jenkins), James,
    William, dau, dau, dau, son, dau
    Jean was the daughter of Robert and Mary Morrison
    Russell.
    Married March 20, 1798 in Cabarrus Co., David Russel
    (Jean's uncle), bondsman.
    1800: Lewis 26-44, 2 females 16-25, and 1 male -10.
    Listed next to Catherine Shinn, Jacob Hutson, Philip
    Pless/Bless, Murdoch Campbell, John McKinley, and
    Joseph White.
    Lewis and Jean sold land on Irish Buffalo Creek in
    July 1806 to James Miller and moved to Buncombe
    County sometime before 1810 along with Jean brother
    James Russell (Barbara Milnster)
    Lewis died before 1820.
1790 - Townsand, William
    1800: William and wife 26-44, 2 females 16-25, 2
    males 10-15, 2 males -10, and 2 females -10. Listed
    next to Cevilia Campbell, James Hadley, John Martin,
    Lawrence Snapp, and George Smith.
    1810: William 45+, 1 female 26-44, 1 male 16-25, 1
    male 10-15, 3 females 10-15, and 1 female -10.
Treas, Daniel
    1810: Daniel and wife 26-44, and 1 female -10.
Treece, Peter

1810: Peter and wife 26-44, 2 males -10, and 2
females -10.
Owned land on Bear Creek
1790 - Troutman, Peter & Catharine
Children: Jacob, Peter (Catherine Peck), Henry,
Lawrence, Peggy, Betsy, Sophia
1800: Peter and wife 26-44, 1 male 16-25, 1 male 10-
15, 1 female 10-15, 2 males -10, and 2 females -10.
Listed next to Joseph Woolever, Frederick Peck,
James McMahon, Drury Rogers, Charles Carter, and
Henry Melchor.
1810: Catherine 26-44, 2 males 16-25, 1 female 16-
25, 1 male 10-15, 2 females 10-15, 1 male -10, and 1
female -10.
Troutman, Peter & Catherine Peck
Married in Cabarrus Co., bond dated Sept 26, 1801,
bondsman, John Peck.
1810: Peter and Catherine, and wife 26-44, 1 male -
10, and 3 females -10.
In the 1860 Cabarrus Co. census, Peter is listed as
81 years old.
1790 - Tucker, George, Jr
1800: George and wife 26-44, 1 male 10-15, 2 females
10-15, 1 male -10, and 4 females -10. Listed next to
John Polk, John Brown, Douglass Winchester, Cistra
Brint, Mary Cagle, and Issac Brandon.
1790 - Tucker, George, Sr
Children: Peter, John, Barbara, Leonard, daughther
married to Leonard Cagle ?
George owned land on Dutch Buffalo Creek and Rocky
River in 1775.
1800: George and wife 45+, 2 males 16-25, 1 female
16-25, 1 male 10-15, 2 females 10-15, and 1 male -
10. Listed next to William Smith, William Polk,
George Long, John Wisiner, George Barnhart, and John
Suther.
Tucker, John
1800: John 26-44, 1 female 16-25, 1 male -10, and 2
females -10. Listed next to Henry Coledg, Peter
Tucker, Peter Long, Thomas Ingram, David Cowell, and
Abraham Leftenburg.
1810: John and wife 26-44, 1 female 45+, 1 male 10-
15, 2 females 10-15, and 3 females -10.
Tucker, Joseph
1810: Joseph 26-44, 1 female 45+, and 1 female 26-
44.
Tucker, Joshua
1800: Joshua and wife 16-25, and 2 males -10. Listed
next to Isaac Brandon, Mary Cagle, Cistra Brint,
John Reed, George Long, and William Polk.
Tucker, Lewis
1810: Lewis and wife 16-25.

Tucker, Peter
    1800: Peter and wife 16-25, 1 male -10, and 1 female
    -10. Listed next to Peter Long, Valentine Watts,
    John Walls, Henry Coledg, John Tucker, and Thomas
    Ingram.
Turner, Elijah
    Elijah, born April 1784, lost his eyesight while
    apprenticed to David Purviance in April 1798.
Udy, Bernhard
    Children: Barbara, Dorothea, Maudalene, Daniel
    (Catherine Light)
    Bernhard died before Oct 1797. His orphan children
    were put in the care of Robert Williams.
Uery, George
    1800: George and wife 45+, 1 male 16-25, 1 female
    16-25, 2 males 10-15, and 1 female -10. Listed next
    to George Sifferd, Charles Sifferd, Barnard Sifferd,
    Jacob Weaver, Charles Starns, and Robert Williams.
    1810: George and wife 45+, 2 males 16-25, 1 female
    10-15, and 1 male -10.
Urey, George
    1810: George household consisted of just himself 26-
    44.
Uery, Godfred
    1800: Godfred and wife 45+. Listed next to William
    Goodwin, Daniel Cline, John Soseman, George Moyer,
    Christian Morris, and Daniel Blackwelder.
Uery, Martin
    1800: Martin and wife 45+, 1 male 16-25, 1 male 10-
    15, and 2 females -10. Listed next to Henry Pless,
    Jacob Boager, Peter Boager, Jacob Hodgeman, Geoge
    Clontz, and Peter Limeboh.
Underwood, Arthur
    1800: Arthur and wife 45+, and 1 female 16-25.
    Listed next to Martin Wedinhouse, Peter Teame,
    Frederick Starnes, John Furor, Jr., George Fink, and
    John Ridley.
Urey, George & Elizabeth Best
    Married in Cabarrus Co., bond dated March 13, 1830,
    bondsman, William H. Archibald.
    Children: Jacob, Nancy
    George is listed in the 1850 Cabarrus Co. census as
    62 and Elizabeth is listed as 61.
Vanderburg, Frances
    Frances bought land on Hamby Run in Oct 1811.
Vietch, William
    1800: William 45+, and 1 male -10. Listed next to
    James Creatton, Charles Campbell, John Callon,
    Robert McMurray, Ezekiel Sharpe, and William Callon,
    Sr.
Voyls, Abel

Abel sold land with Rolin and Thomas Voyls to Conrad
Lyteker on Cold Water Creek in July 1805.

Voils, David
1810: David 16-25.

Voiles, George
1800: George and 1 female 16-25. Listed next to
Martha Campbell, Thomas White, Even Jones, Signe
Seales, Stephen Mayfield, and Daniel Little.

Voiles, Hannah
1800: Hannah 45+, 1 male 16-25, 1 female 16-25, 3
males 10-15, 1 male -10, and 2 females -10. Listed
next to Robert Lee, Roland Voiles, Mary White,
Christian Dry, Isaac Lofton, and John Plott.

Voils, Jesse ?
Children: Daniel, Thomas (Easter Hadley), Abel.
Thomas and Abel moved to Washington Co., Indiana
Territory before 1816.
Jesse Voils died in Cabarrus County before July
1805.

Vossel, John
1800: John and wife 16-25, and 1 female -10. Listed
next to Michael Watters, John Gray, Beverly Gray,
John Carlock, Jacob Self, Sr., and Jacob Self, Jr.

Voials, Rachel
1810: Rachel 26-44, 1 male 26-44, and 1 male 10-15.

Voyls, Rolin/Roland
1800: Roland 16-25, 1 female 16-25, and 1 male -10.
Listed next to Mary White, Henry Potts, John Wiley,
Robert Lee, Hannah Voiles, and Christian Dry.
Sold land on Cold Water Creek with Thomas and Abel
Voyls in 1805.
1810: (Rayley Viles) Roland and wife 26-44, 1 male
10-15, 3 males -10, and 1 female -10.

1790 - Voyls, Thomas
Executor of William Voyls.
Moved to Washington Co., Indiana Territory with his
brother Abel sometime before 1816.
1800: Thomas and wife 45+, 1 female 16-25, 1 male
10-15, 1 female 10-15, and 3 males -10. Listed next
to James Purviance, John Caragin, James Caragin,
Sr., John McGraw, William Atkinson, and George
Carosine(Corzine).

Voils, Thomas
1810: Thomas 26-44, 1 female 16-25, 1 male -10, and
1 female -10.

1790 - Voyls, William
William owned land on Voil Branch of Cold Water
Creek in 1784 and his LWT was proven in Jan 1798.

Waggoner, Phillip & Katy Lyerly
Married in Cabarras Co., bond dated July 3, 1809,
bondsman, Paul Carriker.
1810: Phillip 26-44, Katy 16-25, and 1 femaled -10.

Phillip died in Cabarrus Co. in March 1860 at the
age of 77 from paralysis. He was a blacksmith.
1790 - Wagginor, William
        Owned land on Coldwater Creek in 1784.
        1800: William 45+, his wife, 26 - 44, 3 males 10-15,
        1 female 10-15, 2 males -10, and 2 females -10.
        Listed next to Michael Young, John Conder, James
        Scott, John Winecough, Dudly Tounsend, and David
        Suther.
Wagoner, William
        1810: William and wife 26-44, 1 male 16-25, 2 males
        -10, and 2 females -10.
Walbert, Christopher
        Owned land on Coldwater Creek
Walcher, Adam & Christina
        Children: Henry, Martin (Polly Culp), Frederick
        (Delilah Blackwelder)
Woliver, Jacob
        1810: Jacob and wife 16-25, 1 male -10, and 1 female
        -10.
Walker, Andrew & Sarah Morrison
        Children: Isaac Stanhope (Jane), Caroline (David
        White, Col), Susan, Abigail, James Hall
        Andrew was a soldier in the War of 1812-1814
        Andrew and Sarah are buried at Rocky River
        Presbyterian Church in Cabarrus County.
        Sarah was the daughter of William and Abigail McEwen
        Morrison.
Walker, Archibald
        1810: Archibald and wife 16-25, and 3 males -10.
Walker, Frederick
        1810: Frederick and wife 45+, 2 males 16-25, 1
        female 16-25, 2 females 10-15, 2 males -10, and 1
        female -10.
Walker, Henry
        1800: Henry and wife 26-44, and 3 males -10. Listed
        next to John Biggers, Peter Simmons, George
        Stickleather, Henry Ludwick, Peter Boiles, and John
        Ritchey.
Walker, Henry
        1810: Henry 45+, 1 female 26-44, 3 females 10-15, 2
        males -10, and 2 females -10.
Walker, James & Esther Black
        Married May 26, 1796 in Cabarrus Co., John Walker,
        bondsman
        Owned land on Irish Buffalo Creek.
Walker, James
        Owned land on a ridge between English Buffalo Creek
        and Coddle Creek in 1779.
        1800: James 45+, 1 female 26-44, 1 male 16-25, 1
        male 10-15, 2 females 10-15, 1 male -10, and 2
        females -10. Listed next to John White, John Scott,

Dorothy Scott, John White, Jr., Caleb Woolfe, and
Jacob Smith.
1810: James and wife 45+, 1 male 16-25, 2 females
16-25, 1 male 10-15, and 1 female 10-15.
Walker, Michael
1800: Michael 26-44, 2 females 16-25, 2 females 10-
15, 2 males -10, and 2 females -10. Listed next to
John Ritchey, Peter Boiles, Henry Ludwick, Leonard
Cluttz, John Cluttz, and Jacob Lingle.
1810: Michael 45+, 1 female 26-44, 3 females 16-25,
2 males 10-15, and 1 female 10-15.
Walker, Michael
1810: Michael 26-44, 1 female 26-44, 2 males 16-25,
5 females 16-25, and 1 female 10-15.
1790 - Wallace, Aron
1800: Aaron and wife 26-44, 1 female 10-15, 2 males
-10, and 1 female -10. Listed next to John
McClennon, Jacob Smith, Caleb Woolfe, Joseph
McNeely, Isaac McClennon, and Sarah McNeely.
1810: Aaron and wife 26-44, 1 male 10-15, 1 female
10-15, and 1 female -10.
1790 - Wallace, James & Jean
Owned land on Coddle Creek in 1780
Wallace, James
Owned land on Rocky River in 1769.
1790 - Wallace, Jediah & Patsey Canon
Married Feb 25, 1803 in Cabarrus Co., John Canon,
bondsman.
1810: Jediah 45+, 1 female 26-44, 1 male 16-25, 2
females 16-25, 1 male 10-15, 1 female 10-15, 2 males
-10, and 2 females -10.
1790 - Wallace, John
Legatees: Ludwick, William, Esther, Jediah (Patsy
Canon)
Owned land on and wife sides of Wolf Meadow Branch
in 1778.
Wallace, Joseph & Margaret
Owned land on Rocky River at the county line and
made his living as a carpenter.
Wallace, Josiah
1800: Josiah 26-44, 1 female 45+, and 1 male 10-15.
Listed next to Ludwick Wallace, William Wallace,
David Crawford, John Reed, Moses Alexander (Big),
and Moses Alexander.
1790 - Wallace, Ludwick
Owned land between Coddle Creek and Wolf Meadow
Branch in 1783.
Son of John Wallace
1800: Ludwick and another male 45+, 1 female 26-44,
2 females 16-25, 1 male 10-15, and 2 females 10-15.
Listed next to William Wallace, David Crawford,

Joseph Young, Josiah Wallace, John Reed, and Moses
Alexander (Big).
Wallace, William
        1810: William and wife 26-44, 1 male 10-15, 2
        females 10-15, 3 males -10, and 3 females -10.
Wallace, William
        1800: William and wife 26-44, and 3 males -10.
        Listed next to David Crawford, Joseph Young, Andrew
        Alexander, Ludwick Wallace, Josiah Wallace, and John
        Reed.
Wallis, William
        1800: Williams 45+, 1 female 26-44, 1 male 10-15, 3
        females 10-15, 1 male -10, and 2 females -10. Listed
        next to James Tanner, David Templeton, James
        Stevenson, Thomas McCain, William Houston, Sr., and
        Benjamin Biggs.
        1810: William 45+, 1 female 26-44, 2 males 16-25, 4
        females 16-25, 1 male 10-15, and 3 females 10-15.
Walls, John
        1800: John and wife 16-25, 2 males -10, and 1 female
        -10. Listed next to Andrew Watts, George Kizer,
        Isham Clay, Valentine Watts, Peter Long, and Peter
        Tucker.
1790 - Walter, Nicholas
        Owned land on Cold Water Creek in 1783.
Walter, Nicholas
        Nicholas died in 1775.
Walter, Nicholas
        1810: Nicholas and wife 16-25, 2 males -10, and 1
        female -10.
1790 - Walter, Paul
        Owned land on Cold Water Creek in 1783.
Walter, Paul
        1810: Paul and wife 45+, 1 female 26-44, 2 males 10-
        15, 1 male -10, and 2 females -10.
Walten, Nicholas
        Owned land on Cold Water Creek in 1783.
Walton, Paul
        1800: Paul and wife 26-44, 1 male 16-25, 1 female
        16-25, 1 male 10-15, 1 female 10-15, 1 male -10, and
        2 females -10. Listed next to Jacob Murph, Jacob
        Krider, Sr., Manasah Dresser, Sarah Nowls, John
        Yoman, and Peter Overcash.
Warden, John
        Owned land on Duck Creek in 1779.
Warner, Hardin
        Owned land on Muddy Creek in 1779.
Watson, Thomas & Martha
        1800: Martha 45+, 1 male 16-25, and 1 female -10.
        Listed next to James Bradshaw, Sr., Josiah Spears,
        Samuel McCurdy, Archibald White, Samuel White, and
        John White, Jr.

Thomas' LWT was proven by James Watson Bradshaw in
Oct 1798. Letter of test. To William Watson.
Watson, William
    1810: William 26-44.
Watters, Michael
    1800: Michael 16-25, 2 females 16-25, and 3 females
    -10. Listed next to John Gray, Beverly Gray, John
    Garmon, John Vossel, John Carlock, and Jacob Self,
    Sr.
1790 - Watts, Andrew
    1800: Andrew and wife 45+, and 1 female -10. Listed
    next to George Kizer, Isham Clay, George Teater,
    John Walls, Valentine Watts, and Peter Long.
Watts, James & Peggy Morrison
    Married April 10, 1811 in Cabarrus Co., John
    Niblack, bondsman
Watts, Peter & Charity Hamilton
    Married June 7, 1813 in Cabarrus Co., Jeremiah
    Right, bondsman
Watts, Valentine
    1800: Valentine 26-44, 1 female 16-25, 1 male -10,
    and 1 female -10. Listed next to John Walls, Andrew
    Watts, George Kizer, Peter Long, Peter Tucker, and
    Henry Coledg.
Watters, Michael
Weaver, Henry
    Henry was overseer of a road from Fayetteville Road
    to Buffalo Creek in April 1798.
Weaver, Jacob
    1800: Jacob 26-44. Listed next to George Uery,
    George Sifferd, Charles Sifferd, Charles Starns,
    Robert Williams, and Joseph Starns.
    Jacob bought land on Shaney Wolf Creek in Oct 1812.
Weaver, Peter
    1800: Peter and wife 26-44, 1 male 10-15, and 2
    females -10. Listed next to George Goodman, Jr.,
    Henry Cline, Conrod Hise, Michael Goodman(Big), John
    Duke, and Jacob Rimer.
Weddington, John & Polly Frasor
    Children: Cyrus, Peggy, Mellison, Matty, Ruth,
    Caroline, Addison
    John and Polly were married Aug 22, 1805 in Cabarrus
    Co., William Fresor, bondsman.
    1800: John and wife 26-44, 1 male 10-15, 1 male -10,
    and 3 females -10. Listed next to William Corell,
    Richard Marlin, Thomas Caruthers, Vachel Holbrooks,
    John Overcast, and Hezekiah Glover.
    1810: John 45+, 1 male 26-44, 1 female 26-44, 1 male
    16-25, 1 female 16-25, 1 male 10-15, 1 male -10, and
    3 females -10.
    John died 1812.

There was only one John Weddington in Cabarrus
County 1800: so Polly was probably John second wife,
but that needs to be proven. He was accused of a
shooting disturbance in court in April 1812, along
with Thomas Benson and John Cress.
Weddington, Josiah Watson
        Josiah was given 2 deeds for land on Rocky River and
        Coddle Creek, from his father, Samuel in Oct 1813.
Weddington, Samuel & Elizabeth Bradshaw
        Married Nov 23, 1787 in Mecklenburg Co., Robert
        Weddington, bondsman.
        Children: Josiah Watson
        1800: Samuel and Elizabeth, and wife 26-44, 1 female
        10-15, 4 males -10, and 1 female -10. Listed next to
        Charles Dorton, Samuel Blair, Thomas Black, Jean
        White, Robert White, and Thomas White, Sr.
        1810: Samuel and Elizabeth 26-44, 3 males 16-25, 1
        female 10-15, 1 male 10-15, 1 male -10, and 3
        females -10.
        Samuel owned a plantation on Rocky River.
Wadington, William
        1810: William 26-44, 1 female 45+, 1 female 16-25, 1
        male -10, and 1 female -10.
Weddington, William & Polly McLarty
        Married Jan 7, 1806 in Cabarrus Co., James Russell,
        bondsman.
        William bought land on the east side of Rocky River
        at a tax sale in April 1812.
        1810: William 26-44, Polly 16-25, 1 male -10, and 1
        female -10.
Wedinhouse, Martin
        1800: Martin household consisted of just himself,
        45+. Listed next to Peter Teame, Frederick Starnes,
        Andrew Rinehart, Arthur Underwood, John Furor, Jr.,
        and George Fink.
Weir, James
        1810: James 26-44, 1 female 16-25, and 3 females -
        10.
1790 - Welch, Joseph
        1800: Joseph and wife 26-44, 1 female 16-25, 1 male
        10-15, 1 female 10-15, 1 male -10, and 1 female -10.
        Listed next to Alexander Scott, Robert Davis, George
        Davis, Edward Neil, William Andrew, and Francis
        Greer.
        1810: Joseph 45+, 1 female 26-44, 2 females 16-25,
        and 1 male 10-15.
        Joseph owned a mill on or near Fuda Creek.
West, John
        Spent 176 days in jail, ending in Jan 1816.
Whitacre/Whitecur, Jesse
        1810: Jesse and another male 26-44, and 1 female 16-
        25.

1790 - White, Archabeld
        Children: Archibald, Jr. (Esabal Edgar), John,
        Joseph, Samuel, Mary, John, Thomas, daughter married
        to James Walker, daughter married to Hugh Edgar.
        Archibald owned land on Anderson Creek near Hugh
        Edgar in 1778.
        1800: Archibald and wife 45+, 1 male 26-44, 1 female
        16-25, and 1 female -10. Listed next to Martha
        Watson, James Bradshaw, Sr., Josiah Spears, Samuel
        White, John White, Jr., and James Black.
White, Archibald
        1810: Archibald 26-44, 1 female 16-25, 2 males -10,
        and 3 females -10.
White, Archibald
        1810: Archibald 26-44, 1 female 26-44, 1 male 10-15,
        and 3 females -10.
White, Archibald
        1810: Archibald 26-44, 1 female 26-44, 3 males -10,
        and 1 female -10.
White, Archibald
        1810: Archibald 26-44, 1 female 26-44, 1 male 16-25,
        and 3 females -10.
1790 - White, David
        1800: David family consisted of himself and wife 26-
        44, 2 males 10-15, 1 female 10-15, 1 male -10, and 3
        females -10. Listed next to Solomon Spears, Aaron
        Townsend, William Morrison, William W. Spears,
        Agness Listenbay, George Davis, and Robert Davis.
        1810: David and wife 45+, 2 males 16-25, 1 female
        16-25, and 2 females 10-15.
White, George
        Appointed overseer of the streets of Concord in
        April 1806.
1790 - White, James & Mary
        James died before 1800.
        Owned land on Dutch Buffalo Creek and the south side
        of Rocky River in 1784.
        1800: Mary 26-44, 1 female 10-15, and 1 male -10.
        Listed next to Henry Potts, John Wiley, Jean Russle,
        Roland Voiles, Robert Lee, and Hannah Voiles.
White, John, Jr & Sally
        1800: John and Sally, and wife 16-25, and 1 male -
        10. Listed next to James Walker, John White, John
        Scott, Caleb Woolfe, Jacob Smith, and John
        McClennon.
        1810: John and Sally 26-44, 1 male 10-15, 3 males -
        10, and 1 female -10.
        John died in 1841, Sally died in 1852.
White, John, Jr
        Son of Archibald White
        1800: John and wife 26-44, and 1 female -10. Listed
        next to Samuel White, Archibald White, Martha

Watson, James Black, John Black, Jr., and Thomas
Black.
1810: John and wife 26-44, 4 males -10, and 1 female
-10.
1790 - White/Wite, John
Children: Thomas
Owned land on Poplar Ridge between English Buffalo
and Coddle Creek in 1771.
1800: John and wife 45+, 1 female 26-44, 1 male 16-
25, and 1 male 10-15. Listed next to John Scott,
Dorothy Scott, Charles McKinley, James Walker, John
White, Jr., and Caleb Woolfe.
1810: John 45+, 1 female 26-44, 1 male 10-15, 2
males -10, and 1 female -10.
1790 - White, Joseph W. & Frances
1800: Joseph 45+, 1 female 26-44, 3 males -10, and 2
females -10. Listed next to John McKinley, Murdoch
Campbell, Lewis Tounsend, Jean Russle, John Wiley,
and Henry Potts.
1810: Joseph 45+, 1 female 26-44, 2 females 16-25, 3
males 10-15, 3 males -10, and 2 females -10.
Joseph was born 1762, died Oct 6, 1842
Frances was born 1765, died Sept 7, 1823
Buried in Old Rocky River Cemetery
Son of Archibald White.
White, Moses & Margaret Givens
Children: Givens
Moses died in 1766.
David Russell and Joseph Rogers inherited 144 acres
from the will of Margaret White dated 1773. They
sold the land to Micheal Shaver in 1775.
White, Robert
1800: Robert and wife 16-25. Listed next to Jean
White, Samuel Weddington, Charles Dorton, Thomas
White, Sr., Benjamin Cockran, and William Newel.
White, Samuel
Owned land on the middle fork of Anderson Creek in
1782.
Son of Archibald White
1800: Samuel and wife 45+, 1 female 26-44, 1 male
16-25, 1 male 10-15, 2 females 10-15, 2 males -10,
and 2 females -10. Listed next to Archibald White,
Martha Watson, James Bradshaw, Sr., John White, Jr.,
James Black, and John Black, Jr.
1810: Samuel and wife 45+, 1 male 26-44, 1 male 16-
25, 2 females 16-25, 2 males 10-15, and 1 female -
10.
1790 - White, Thomas, Sr.
1800: Thomas and wife 26-44, 1 female 16-25, 2 males
10-15, and 3 males -10. Listed next to Robert White,
Jean White, Samuel Weddington, Benjamin Cockran,
William Newell, and John Newell.

Son of Archibald White
White, Thomas
        1810: Thomas 45+, 1 female 45+, 2 males 16-25, 1
        female 16-25, and 2 males 10-15.
White, Thomas
        1810: Thomas 26-44, 1 male 10-15, 2 males -10, and 2
        females -10.
1790 - White, Thomas
White, Thomas W. & Margaret
        1800: Thomas and Margaret, and wife 16-25, 1 male -
        10, and 2 females -10. Listed next to Even Jones,
        Charles Tounsend, George Carlock, Martha Campbell,
        George Voiles, and Signe Seales.
        A Thomas White, Jr. bought land on Cold Water Creek
        from James Bridgers in Oct 1805.
        Margaret was born 1778, died July 18, 1809 and is
        buried in Old Rocky River Cemetery.
        1810: Thomas 26-44, 1 female 26-44, 1 male 10-15, 2
        females 10-15, 2 males -10, and 3 females -10. There
        was another Thomas White in Cabarrus Co. 1810: with
        only 2 females -10. This could be the Thomas who was
        married to Margaret, but the rest of the children
        didn't seem right.
        Thomas was the son of John White.
White, William S.
        1810: William and wife 16-25, 2 males -10, and 1
        female -10.
1790 - White, William
        Children: Thomas, Robert
        In Mecklenburg in 1785. Owned land on Wolf Meadow
        Branch of Coddle Creek.
        Died before Jan 1800.
White, William W., Sr & Jean
        Children: Jean, Sarah, William
        William was born March 12, 1751, died July 10, 1794
        Jean was born 1754, died May 18, 1837
        Buried in Old Rocky River Cemetery
        1800: Jean 45+, 1 female 16-25, 3 females 10-15, and
        1 male -10. Listed next to Samuel Weddington,
        Charles Dorton, Samuel Blair, Robert White, Thomas
        White, Sr., and Benjamin Cockran.
Wiggins, Hardin
        1800: Hardin and wife 45+, 1 female 16-25, 1 male
        10-15, and 4 males -10. Listed next to William
        Gordin, Henry Linker, George Hartman, Eve Wilhelm,
        George Wilhelm, and Daniel Boger.
Wiley, Evan Shelby & Polly McCaleb
        Married Nov 26, 1804 in Cabarrus Co., James McCaleb,
        bondsman.
        1810: Evan and Polly, and wife 16-25, and 2 males -
        10.
        Son of Oliver and Mary Wiley

Wyley, James
        Owned land on Rocky River in 1768.
        James was mentioned in the estate settlement of
        William Sample in 1769.
        James died in 1772.
1790 - Wylie, James & Sarah Shanks
        Married July 20, 1790 in Mecklenburg Co., James
        Shanks, bondsman.
        Owned land on Neal branch of Reedy Creek, a branch
        of Rocky River.
Wylie, John
        Oldest brother of James Wiley of New River, VA.
        John owned land on Neal branch of Reedy Creek, a
        branch of Rocky River in 1772.
        John died before 1779.
1790 - Wiley, John
        1800: John 45+, 1 male 16-25, 1 female 16-25, and 1
        male -10. Listed next to Jean Russle, Joseph White,
        John McKinley, Henry Potts, Mary White, and Roland
        Voiles.
Wylie, Joseph & Margaret Smith
        Married Jan 21, 1792 in Mecklenburg Co., James
        Wilson, bondsman.
Wyley, Moses
        Died in 1767.
Wiley, Moses & Mary
        Mary died June 7, 1818
        Buried in Spears Cemetery of Rocky River Church
        Cyrus Campbell was orphaned at the age of 14 yrs, 6
        months in April 1804. April 14, 1804 court he was
        apprenticed to Moses Wiley.
        1810: Moses and wife 26-44, 1 male 10-15, 1 female
        10-15, 2 males -10, and 2 females -10.
Wiley, Oliver
        1810: Oliver 16-25, 1 female 45+, and 1 female 16-
        25.
Wiley, Oliver & Peggy Morrison
        Children: Isaac, Mary, Hannah, James, Oliver H.
        Married Oct 27, 1801 in Mecklenburg Co., Samuel
        McCurdy, bondsman.
        1810: Oliver and Peggy, and wife 16-25, and 2 males
        -10.
        Son of Oliver & Mary Wiley
1790 - Wiley, Oliver & Mary
        Children: Mary (Robert Morrison), Oliver (Peggy
        Morrison), Elinor (Samuel McCurdy), William
        (Margaret Cromwell), Evan Shelby (Polly McCaleb),
        Margaret (Robert Kirkpatrick), Hannah (Cyrus
        Campbell), Leah (Matthew Phifer), Esther (John
        Robison), Agnes (Alick McKibben), Mary (Elijah
        Baker)

Oliver owned land on the south side of Clear Creek
in 1772.
1800: Oliver and Mary 45+, 2 males 16-25, 1 male 10-
15, 1 female 10-15, and 2 females -10. He was listed
next to Moses Wiley, Robert Bain, Robert Robb,
Elenor and James McMurray.
Oliver was born 1741, died Dec 1802
Mary was born 1744, died Aug 21, 1822
Buried in Spears Cemetery of Rocky River Church
Wiley, William & Margaret Cromwell
Married March 13, 1798 in Cabarrus Co., John
Cromwell, bondsman.
1800: William household consisted of William 16-25,
Margaret 26-44, and 1 female -10. Listed next to
Elizabeth Posey, Ezekiel Wright, Elenor Erwin,
Arthur McCree, Robert Allison, and William Houston.
1790 - Wilie, William & Martha
Owned land on the north side of McKee Creek in 1785.
1790 - Wilhelm, George & Eve
Children: George, John ? (Elizabeth Bost) - John not
proven.
George died before 1800.
1800: Eve 45+, 2 females 16-25, 2 males 10-15, and 2
females -10. Listed next to Hardin Wiggins, William
Gordin, Henry Linker, George Wilhelm, Daniel Boger,
and Chares Barnhart.
George's LWT was proven in July 1797.
Eve sold land on Hamby Run to Francis Vanderburg in
Oct 1811.
Wilhelm, George
1800: George and wife 16-25, 1 male -10, and 1
female -10. Listed next to Eve Wilhelm, Hardin
Wiggins, William Gordin, Daniel Boger, Charles
Barnhart, and John Barnhart.
1810: George 26-44, 1 female 45+, 1 female 26-44, 1
male 10-15, 1 female 10-15, 2 males -10, and 2
females -10.
Williams, John George
Owned land on the north side of English Buffalo
Creek in 1784.
Williams, Robert
1800: Robert and wife 26-44, 1 male 10-15, 2 females
10-15, 2 males -10, and 2 females -10. Listed next
to Charles Starns, Jacob Weaver, George Uery, Joseph
Starns, Peter Quilman, and Christopher Leigh.
1790 - Williamson, James
Owned land on the branches of Rocky River in 1784.
1790 - Wilson, David
Owned land on the Tinker branch of Coddle Creek in
1776.
David may have died in 1820.
1790 - Wilson, Isaac

Owned land near Coddle Creek in 1785.
1790 - Wilson, John
         1800: John and wife 45+, 3 males 10-15, 1 male -10,
         and 1 female -10. Listed next to George
         Carosine(Corzine), William Atkinson, John McGraw,
         Charles Bane, George Overcash, and John Rumple.
1790 - Wilson, John
         Moved to TN before 1800: with Zachias Wilson
1790 - Wilson, Thomas, Sr & Margaret
         Owned land on the south side of Rocky River in 1771.
1790 - Winchester, Dugles
         1800: Douglass' and wife 45+, 1 male 26-44, 1 male
         16-25, 1 male 10-15, and 1 female -10. Listed next
         to Charles Freeman, Andrew Freeman, Henry Smith,
         Sr., John Brown, John Polk, and George Tucker, Jr.
1790 - Winchester, William
         Owned land near the head of Meadow Spring on Rocky
         River in 1782.
Winecoff, Daniel & Barbara Walcher
         Married in Cabarrus Co., bond dated Sept 10, 1804,
         Michael Winecoff, bondsman.
         1810: Daniel and Barbara, and wife 26-44, 1 male -
         10, and 2 females -10.
Winecoff, David & Elizabeth Walker
         Married in Cabarrus Co., bond dated July 7, 1800:
         bondsman, John Cline.
         1810: David and Elizabeth, and wife 26-44, 2 females
         16-25, 1 male -10, and 1 female -10.
Winecoff, Godrey & Sarah Misenheimer
         Married in Cabarrus Co., bond dated Nov 15, 1814,
         bondsman, Michael Winecoff.
         Godfrey is listed in the 1850 Cabarrus Co. census as
         57 and Sarah is 56 years old.
Winecough, John
         1800: John and wife 45+, 4 males 16-25, 1 female 16-
         25, 1 female 10-15, 1 male -10, and 1 female -10.
         Listed next to William Wagoner, Michael Young, John
         Conder, Dudly Tounsend, David Suther, and James
         Cannon.
         1810: John and wife 45+, 1 male 10-15, and 1 female
         10-15.
Winecoff, Mathias & Mary Sloop
         Married in Cabarrus Co., bond dated Feb 20, 1804,
         bondsman, David Winecoff. The marriage bond actually
         shows Mathias' name as Mathew, but no Mathew appears
         in the census of 1810 or 1820, only a Mathias who
         appears to have been married about the time of this
         marriage bond.
         1810: Mathias 26-44, 1 female 16-25, 2 males -10,
         and 1 female -10.
         Mathias is listed in the 1850 Cabarrus Co. census as
         75 years old.

1790 - Winesaugh (Winecoff), Michael
        Children: Daniel (Barbara Walcher), Michael
        (Margaret Goodnight), David (Elizabeth Walker)
        Owned land on Three Mile Branch of Cold Water Creek
        in 1782.
1790 - Winesaugh, Michael, Jr. & Margaret Goodnight
        Children: John Michael
        Married Aug 2, 1802 in Cabarrus Co., Mathias Mock,
        bondsman.
        1810: Michael and wife 26-44, 1 male 10-15, 4 males
        -10, and 1 female -10.
Wise, John
        1810: John 26-44, 1 female 16-25, and 1 male 16-25.
Wise, Philip
        Owned land near Voil branch of Cold Water Creek in
        1784.
Wiser, John & Nancy
        Owned land near Robert Farr in Jan 1807.
Wiser, Philip
        Philip's LWT was proven by Henry Townsend and
        William Hunter in Oct 1798.
1790 - Wisel/Wiser, Michael
        1800: Michael and wife 45+. Listed next to George
        Seffred, Martin Penninger, Michael Gatchey, Mathias
        Beam, George File, and Asemus Peninger.
        Michael's will is recorded in Will Book "A", pg 91,
        Cabarrus County. He died before July 1805.
Wisner, David & ???, Ruth Chamberlin
        1800: David 26-44, 1 female 16-25, and 1 male -10.
        Listed next to Henry Howell, John Howell, Joseph
        Howell, Sr., William Bugg, Henry Cagle, and James
        Clay.
        Married March 17, 1803 in Cabarrus Co.
Wisiner, John & Margaret Cook
        Married July 17, 1797 in Cabarrus Co., Philip Wiser,
        bondsman
        1800: John and Margaret, and wife 16-25. Listed next
        to George Tucker, Sr., William Smith, William Polk,
        George Barnhart, John Suther, and Christian
        Barnhart.
Witenhouse, Malcolm
        1810: Maclcom and wife 45+, 1 female 16-25, 1 male -
        10, and 1 female -10.
1790 - Witenhouse, Martin & Sally Koon
        Married May 11, 1801 in Cabarrus Co., Philip Jordon,
        bondsman.
Woodside, Jean
        1810: Jean 45+, 1 male 16-25, and 1 female 16-25.
Woolfe, Caleb
        1800: Caleb and wife 26-44, 1 male 16-25, 1 male 10-
        15, 3 females 10-15, 1 male -10, and 1 female -10.
        Listed next to John White, Jr., James Walker, John

White, Jacob Smith, John McClennon, and Aaron
Wallis.
Woolever, Joseph
    1800: Joseph and wife 26-44, 1 male 10-15, 2 males -
    10, and 3 females -10. Listed next to Frederick
    Peck, James McMahon, Jacob Moose, Peter Troutman,
    Drury Rogers, and Charles Carter.
Workman, Isaac
    1800: Isaac and wife 16-25, and 1 male -10. Listed
    next to Joseph Patton, Elizabeth Patterson, Joseph
    Ross, William Fraser, Morgan Hall, and William
    Hamilton.
Workman, John
    1810: John 26-25, 1 female 45+, 1 female 26-44, and
    1 female 16-25.
Wright, Ezekiel
    1800: Ezekiel and wife 26-44, 1 male 10-15, 1 male -
    10, and 3 females -10. Listed next to Elenor Erwin,
    John Robinson, William Gray, Elizabeth Posey,
    William Wiley, and Arthur McCree.
    1810 Ezekiel and wife 26-44, 1 female 16-25, 1 male
    10-15, 1 female 10-15, 2 males -10, and 2 females -
    10.
Wright, William
    1810: William and wife 16-25, 1 male -10, and 1
    female -10.
Yerts, Joseph
    1810: Joseph 45+, 1 female 26-44, 1 male 10-15, 1
    male -10, and 1 female -10.
Yeoman, John
    1800: John and wife 26-44, 1 male -10, and 2 females
    -10. Listed next to Sarah Nowls, Paul Walton, Jacob
    Murph, Peter Overcash, Henry Plott, and John Cook.
    1810: John and wife 45+, 1 female 26-44, and 1
    female 10-15.
1790 - Yewman, John & Catherine
    Children: Catharine, Esther, Elizabeth Young
    John died before April 1799.
Yordon/Yorton, Philip
    Children: Jacob, David
    1810: Philip and wife 26-44, 1 male 16-25, 2 females
    10-15, 1 male -10, and 1 female -10.
Yost, Phillip
    1810: Phillip and wife 26-44, 1 male -10, and 1
    female -10.
    Philip bought 270 acres on Coddle Creek from David
    Templeton of Burke Co. in April 1813.
Young, John & Elizabeth
    1800: Elizabeth 26-44, and 1 female 10-15. Listed
    next to Gideon Almon, John Still, Martin Slough,
    Delphie Lewis, Noah Sandiford, and William McAnulty.
Young, Henry & Sarah Phifer

                  Sarah was the daughter of Jacob Phifer
Young, James & Polly Allison
          Married Feb 20, 1805 in Cabarrus Co., William
          Allison, bondsman.
          1810: James 26-44, Polly 16-25, 2 males -10, and 1
          female -10.
Young, John
          Children: Elizabeth
          Owned land on Little Cold Water Creek in 1777.
Young, Joseph
          Owned land on Coddle Creek in 1763.
Young, Joseph
          1800: Joseph 45+, 3 females 45+, 1 male 16-25, 2
          females 16-25, and 1 female 10-15. Listed next to
          Andrew Alexander, Nelson Gray, Thomas Gray, David
          Crawford, William Wallace, and Ludwich Wallace.
          1810 Joseph and wife 45+, 1 male 16-25, and 2
          females 16-25.
          Joseph was sheriff of Cabarrus County in 1805.
Young, Michael & Catherine Friesland
          Married May 30, 1805 in Cabarrus Co., Mathias Cook,
          bondsman.
          1800: Michael 26-44, 1 male 16-25, 1 female 16-25, 1
          male -10, and 2 females -10. Listed next to John
          Conder, James Scott, Michael Awalt, William Wagoner,
          John Winecough, and Dudly Tounsend.
Young, William
          1800: William 45+, 1 female 26-44, 3 males 16-25, 1
          female 16-25, 5 females 10-15, and 3 females -10.
          Listed next to Robert Smith, James Smith, John
          Scoles, Catherine Flemmon, Mary Fulham, and Susanna
          Russel.
          Owned land on Rocky River and Coddle Creek in 1778.
          1810: William 45+, 1 female 26-44, 1 male 26-44, 1
          male 16-25, 2 females 16-25, 3 males 10-15, 2
          females 10-15, 1 male -10, and 1 female -10.
Young, William & Mary Berry
          Married Feb 4, 1795 in Cabarrus Co., Nathaniel
          Rogers, bondsman
Young, William
          1810 William and wife 26-44, 2 males -10, and 1
          female -10. Listed next to Joseph Young.

www.ingramcontent.com/pod-product-compliance
Lightning Source LLC
Chambersburg PA
CBHW050714280326
41926CB00088B/3028